Mission in Christ's Way

Mission in Christ's Way

AN ORTHODOX UNDERSTANDING
OF MISSION

ARCHBISHOP ANASTASIOS (YANNOULATOS)

Archbishop of Tirana, Durrës and All Albania
Professor Emeritus,
National and Kapodistrian University of Athens
Honorary Member of the Academy of Athens

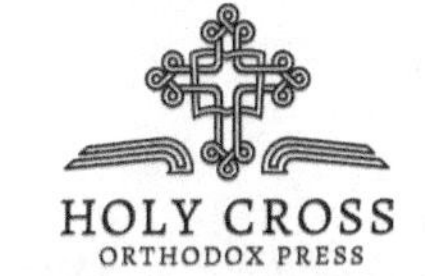

HOLY CROSS
ORTHODOX PRESS

BROOKLINE, MASSACHUSETTS

WORLD COUNCIL OF CHURCHES PUBLICATIONS
Geneva, Switzerland

© 2010 Holy Cross Orthodox Press
Published by
Holy Cross Orthodox Press
50 Goddard Avenue
Brookline, MA 02445
USA

ISBN-13: 978-1-935317-07-4
ISBN-10: 1-935317-07-5

World Council of Churches Publications
Rte de Ferney 150
P.O. BOX 2100
CH-1211 Geneva 2

ISBN-13: 978-2-8254-1541-2

Library of Congress Cataloging-in-Publication Data

Anastasios, Archbishop of Tirana and all Albania, 1929-
    Mission in Christ's way : an Orthodox understanding of mission / Archbishop Anastasios (Yannoulatos).
        p. cm.
    ISBN 1-935317-07-5 (alk. paper)
    1. Orthodox Eastern Church--Missions. 2. Missions--Theory. I. Title.
    BV2123.A48 2010
    266'.19--dc22

                                                            2010008324

CONTENTS

1
"THY WILL BE DONE"
MISSION IN CHRIST'S WAY
(1989)

2
ORTHODOXY AND MISSION
(1964)

3
THE PURPOSE AND MOTIVE OF MISSION
(FROM A THEOLOGICAL POINT OF VIEW)
(1967)

4
THEOLOGY, MISSION AND PASTORAL CARE
(1976)

5

"THY KINGDOM COME"
ORTHODOX WITNESS TO THE MODERN WORLD
(1977)

6
DISCOVERING THE ORTHODOX MISSIONARY ETHOS
(1978)

7
THE ASCENT OF HUMAN NATURE
(1980)

8
EUCHARIST—SERVICE—WITNESS
IN MUTUAL RECIPROCITY
(1983)

9
THE DOXOLOGICAL UNDERSTANDING
OF LIFE AND MISSION
(1984)

10
"YOUR WILL BE DONE"
MISSION IN CHRIST'S WAY
(A Theological Reflection on Mission)
(1987)

11
ORTHODOX MISSION:
PAST, PRESENT AND FUTURE
(1989)

12
DIALOGUES AND MISSION
(1991)

13
THE GLOBAL VISION
OF PROCLAIMING THE GOSPEL
(1995)

14
REDISCOVERING OUR APOSTOLIC
IDENTITY IN THE 21st CENTURY
(2003)

15
INSTEAD OF AN EPILOGUE
«Καί ἰδού ἐγώ μεθ' ὑμῶν εἰμί . . .»
"And lo I am with you . . ."
(Matthew 28:20)
(2002)

INTRODUCTORY LETTER OF
HIS ALL-HOLINESS
ECUMENICAL PATRIARCH
BARTHOLOMEW

Your Beatitude Archbishop of Tirana and All Albania, Anastasios, beloved and endeared brother in Christ and co-celebrant of our Modesty; I extend brotherly greetings in the Lord and address you with great joy.

The contribution of your charismatic and beloved Beatitude to the Orthodox Church is undoubtedly multifaceted and abundantly fruitful, particularly after you were endowed with the priestly and archpriestly office which you accepted and lived from the very beginning as Christ-like work and sacrificial service.

Therefore, we would not be unrealistic in emphasizing the primary and most important role which you played in regenerating and reactivating in our times the missionary practice and service, as a most essential act and obligatory expression of the self-consciousness of the Church toward those God-created brothers and sisters outside the Faith, living throughout all the continents of our planet. From the very beginning various tempting reactions and difficulties raised their prideful head, nevertheless, the abundant Grace of the Lord so empowered you and the other dedicated pioneer servants of the Gospel then, that today Orthodox Christianity is becoming known and accepted as a personal faith by people who before lived in the darkness and the shadow of death. Moreover, holy sanctuaries of the Lord are now being established in places, where before stood the desolating sacrilege of idolatry or the soul-destroying darkness of atheism.

The priceless experience acquired by you in this pioneering endeavor, honorable Beatitude, served also as the basis for the courses of study which you taught in the School of Theology of the University of Athens, as well as the motivation to create a whole series of related lectures and theological studies which you have, most excellently, gathered in the present volume bearing the appropriate title: *Mission in Christ's Way: An Orthodox Understanding of Mission.*

We congratulate, with brotherly love, your Beatitude, blessed by God, for this present most valuable work, we pray fervently that the Triune God, glorified in three Persons and proclaimed by you to the nations—Africa and Albania and throughout the world during your leadership of *Apostoliki Diaconia*—may bless your Beatitude again and again with His mystical graces, in the power of the Holy Spirit, and with unshakable health to continue the work of restoration of the beloved sister Church in Albania; which you have taken upon yourself in obedience to the call of the Mother Church, which has been absolutely justified in expecting so much from you and at times of severe hardships and total absence of any hopeful light.

For these many reasons, I again congratulate you from the heart and extend to your most revered Beatitude a holy kiss in Christ Jesus and remain with profound love that is in Him, and with great honor.

November 4, 2006
Your very reverent Beatitude's
beloved brother in Christ,
Bartholomew of Constantinople

PREFACE

The fact that the Orthodox world often overlooks one of the basic commandments of Christ—"Go therefore and make disciples of all nations"—(Matt 28:19), came to the forefront of theological discussions among the Orthodox at the end of the decade of the 1950's. A spark appeared in 1958 at a Conference of Syndesmos, the Organization of Orthodox Youth, in Thessalonica. After that, with the initiative of the periodical *"Porefthendes—Go Ye,"* the spark became a flame that lit paschal candles in many young souls, and not only the young. Later, this flame was passed on to various local Orthodox Churches and became hearths of steadfast missionary activity. Here is to be found historically the great difference from any previous occasional and rather simple reference to the obligation of Orthodox foreign mission.

A danger which appeared from the very beginning was the creation of the impression that this was a simplistic enthusiasm of the young, seeking some adventure in faraway places, which will soon be abandoned. At the same time, a rather cold current, appealing to the internal needs, sought to extinguish the newly kindled missionary flame.

From the outset, therefore, it became necessary to exert effort to articulate the theological foundation of the Orthodox obligation to witness to "the nations," to those beyond the walls of the Christian world. And this in order to indicate that mission is inseparable from the very nature of the Church. The lectures and studies included in this volume are related primarily with this theological effort. Of these, some were prepared for a primarily Orthodox audience, others served as an Orthodox contribution to the inter-Christian theological thinking related to mission.

The study, "Thy Will Be Done—Mission in Christ's Way," is placed first in this publication in order to emphasize from the beginning that the theme of missions is of interest to all and not merely to a few specialists. Mission is connected with the basic prayer: "Thy will be done on earth as it is in heaven," which Christ himself placed into the mouth of every believer. At the same time, this first study condenses our theological quest and is directed not only to the Orthodox, but also to the Christian ecumene.

The other texts in this book are arrayed in chronological order, thus indicating the unfolding and the undulations of our theological problematics during the last decades.

In the decade of the 70's we had proposed, as inter-changeable words for the terms "mission" (ἱεραποστολή), the biblical term "witness" (μαρτυρία). Emphasizing first its biblical basis: "And you shall be my witnesses . . . to the end of the earth" (Acts 1:8, cf. the words μάρτυς, μαρτυρῶ, μαρτύριον); and secondly, the connection that exists in its meaning to the eye witness, who presents what he knows and experiences, and to the witness (μάρτυς), who is ready to present his evidence (μαρτυρία) with a personal sacrifice (μαρτύριον)—a disposition for martyrdom. Since then, this proposal was adopted by many and it has influenced the inter-Christian terminology by reminding one that in exercising our obligation for sacred mission we are not "judges" or public prosecutors in the world, but witnesses of truth and of love.

In reference to one other proposal I have made in inter-Christian circles, the code phrase: "liturgy after the Liturgy," see the end of Chapter Four in this volume.

The studies, lectures and sermons included in this present collection constitute the "testimony" of a personal theological problematic, sometimes of a secret spiritual agony, which begins with a series of questions only to be then developed, often in pain, with appeals, weeping before the inertia, the confusion and the indifference of those various "authorities," with and without responsibility. They have been prepared for a variety of audiences: youth, theological or broader international settings. This fact has determined the style, the emphasis, and the alternating tones. Most of the texts in this present volume were published for the first time in English. Indicated at the beginning of each text is the occasion for the writing, the year of its first publication, as well as other subsequent publications.

Certain repetitions were omitted and this was so indicated by the symbols [. . .]. We did not, however, omit all the points that were repeatedly covered, thus indicating clearly which points were more critical and had to be emphasized again and again during the years which have passed. Some basic ideas (for example, Mission, Resurrection, Orthodox Spirituality), even when repeated are presented in different contexts and tones. The place of an epilogue is taken by a lecture given on the occasion of an ecumenical Christian anniversary. By grouping these studies and lectures together in this volume, they are a reminder of the familiar musical phrase: "variations on a theme"—the basic motive of mission. Or, more metaphorically, they remind us somehow of the self-contained nature of the Aegean Sea, the variety and unity of the Cycladic Islands.

There was a time when many of the ideas and proposals expressed for the first time in these texts sounded strange or were met with doubt. The attempt to face new problems theologically usually demands daring and the acceptance of some risk. Now, for the most part, they have become accepted into the Orthodox consciousness and are being emphasized by official personalities. At the same time they have contributed to significant decisions made by many in the past decades. Ideas and phrases included in this present collection are being repeated by various people, without reference to their source, or they have become self-evident and are being used like the verses of a popular folk song. Nor are the incidents absent, whereby these same ideas, unassimilated and out of proper context are distorted and utilized as a pretense for preconceived and prejudicial criticism. "Only that in every way, whether in pretense or in truth" the duty to preach Christ to all the world "is proclaimed and in that I rejoice. Yes, and I shall rejoice" (Phil 1:18–19). In any case, in order to have a correct understanding of the proposals and ideas of the author, it is necessary to keep in mind the whole theological thought, stance and activity of the writer.

Included in another volume, entitled *To the End of the Earth*, are the historical missionary studies, which were published during the last decades parallel with the theological ones, and which shed light and determine the various theoretical aspects of Orthodox mission. It is hoped that in subsequent volumes publication may be made of various articles, chronicles, reports, programs, notes and a variety of texts related to the first phase of Orthodox foreign mission in the 20th century.

The introductory Letter of All-Holiness Bartholomew, the Ecumenical Patriarch, is a very significant blessing for the writer. I thank him from the depths of my heart.

I feel a sense of warm gratitude to many volunteer co-workers, who in various ways contributed in the preparation of the present volume. But first of all, I must thank from the heart the precious "co-worker in the Lord," Argyro Kontogeorge, for the tremendous amount of secretarial and translation support given, as well as Anastasia Barksdale, for the excellent contribution to editing these texts for publication; Fr. Panagiotis Chamberas for contributing to the translation generally, particularly chapters 9, 12 and others portions; and Dr. Anton Vrame for all the dedication and details involved with publishing. To the many co-workers in the Lord, with whom we have journeyed together all these many years, and who in many ways have supported me with their precious critiques and sacrificial offerings, I express again and again my gratitude. Our long journey of many years can be summed up in the words of the Psalmist:

"May those who sow in tears reap with shouts of joy! He that goes forth weeping, bearing the seed for sowing, shall come home with shouts of joy, bringing his sheaves with him" (Ps 126:5–6).

The recent missionary endeavor, which began like a soft breeze in the Holy Spirit at the end of the decade of the 1950's, had a clear theological and ecclesiological dimension and contribution; it emphasized and strengthened the awareness of Orthodoxy's ecumenical nature and the obligation to make it active. One witness of this is the texts which follow in this volume.

It will certainly require constant theological reflection, personal experience and participation in the work of mission, in order to make firm and develop seriously the Orthodox witness under the contemporary conditions "to the end of the earth," "until the Lord comes."

Tirana, August 7, 2010
+ Anastasios
Archbishop of Tirana, Durrës and All Albania

1

"THY WILL BE DONE"
MISSION IN CHRIST'S WAY

(1989)

• The basic report to the World Missionary Conference of the World Council of Churches in San Antonio, Texas, 1989. • "Address by the Conference Moderator," (Conference on World Mission and Evangelism, San Antonio, TX, 1989) *International Review of Mission* 78 (1989), pp. 316–328. • *The San Antonio Report, Your Will Be Done. Mission in Christ's Way*, ed., Fr. R. Wilson, Geneva: WCC, 1990, pp. 100–114. Address of the Moderator, Conference on World "Mission and Evangelism," San Antonio, 1989. • German: "Dein Wille geschehe—Mission in der Nachfolge Christi," *Dein Wille geschelhe—Mission in der Nachfolge Jesu Christi*. Welt-missionskonferenz in San Antonio, 1989, Hrsg. J. Wietzke, Otto Lembeck, Frankfurt a. M., 1989, pp. 217–235. • German: *Jahrbuch 6 des Evangeleischen Missionswerkes in Sudwestdeutchland*. Mission bei uns gemeinsam mit den Partnern, Stuttgart, 1989, pp. 82–88. • «Γενηθήτω τό θέλημά Σου - Ἱεραποστολή στά ἴχνη τοῦ Χριστοῦ,» Σάν Ἀντόνιο, Η.Π.Α., *Πάντα τά Ἔθνη* 9 (1990) 33, pp. 3–7, 34, pp. 35–38. • French: "Que ta volontee soit faite—Une mission conforme au Christ," *Supplement a SOP*, Courbevoie, France, 1990, No. 140b. • Swedish: "Ske Din vilja—Mission pa Kristi satt", *Till Hela Varlden—pa Kristii satt*, Uppsala, Svenska Mission radet, (1990), pp. 7–17. • *The Ecumenical Movement, An Anthology of Key Texts and Voices*, eds. M. Kinnamon and B.E. Cope, Geneva: WCC, 1997, pp. 388–392. This report was characterized as "the most solid theological contribution" to the aforementioned World Missionary Conference (Dr. Wietzke, Director of the Evangelisches Missionswerke in Hamburg). "It was Anastasios' presentation that provided the theological framework for the conference theme. Its overall thrust was truly ecumenical in the best sense of the word." (Prof. Dr. D. J. Bosch, Director of the International Academic Journal, *Missionalia*, "Your Will Be Done? Critical Reflection on San Antonio," *Missionalia* 17:2 (1989), p. 127.) • *Ἱεραποστολή στά ἴχνη τοῦ Χριστοῦ. Θεολογικές μελέτες καί ὁμιλίες*, Ἀθήνα 2007.

Human pride, in its individual, social or racial expression, poisons and destroys life in the world at large or in the small communities in which we live. Human will obstinately exalts its autonomy. Loneliness is on the increase, nightmares multiply, and fears mount up. Old and new idols are being erected in the human consciousness. They dance around them. They offer them adulation and worship them ecstatically. And yet at the same time, every so often, new, sensitive voices speak out for a just and peaceful age. New initiatives are being undertaken; a new awareness of worldwide community is growing.

All of these facts come to light in our ecumenical gatherings, sometimes alarmingly, sometimes hopefully. Our problems overwhelm us. We describe them and try to solve them, but when we think we have solved one, three new ones spring up. Our mood keeps swinging, like a pendulum, between hope and despair.

In this world the faithful continue to pray: "Thy will be done, on earth as it is in heaven," proclaiming quietly, but resolutely, that above all human wills there is one will that is redemptive, life-giving, full of wisdom and power, that in the end will prevail. The choice of the theme for our meeting is essentially, I think, a protest and a refusal to accept that which militates against God's loving design, and, at the same time, is an expression of hope and optimism for the future of the world.

A
REALITY AND EXPECTATION

In the petition, "Thy will be done, on earth as it is in heaven," the firm certainty prevails that the Father's will is *already a reality.* Myriads of other beings, the angels and saints, are already in harmony with it. The realization of God's will is not simply a desire; it is *an event* that illuminates everything else. The center of reality is God and His Kingdom. On this, the realism of faith is grounded. On this ontology is based every Christian effort on earth.

To some, to mention "heaven" might seem anachronistic. We usually look for immediate answers, down to earth and realistic—according to our own fixed ideas. We forget, however, that contemporary science and technology have made important leaps forward with regard to a material heaven. A few decades ago, we sought to solve humankind's communication problems by using wires stretched out over the earth's surface. Later on, we used wireless waves, still following the surface of our planet. With the new technology, however, we have discovered that we can communicate better above the earth, by sending wireless waves heavenwards. So in our theological, ecclesial and missionary thinking, if we turn our sight once more to the reality of "heaven," about which Scripture speaks constantly, we shall certainly find new answers to the world's problems and difficulties.

Our Church has not ceased to look in that direction, with prayer and celebration, affirming the supremacy of God's will. In order for this faith to shed light on the mass of problems that oppress us, a theological reference to the significance of the two proposals that form our theme is needed. I shall first attempt a synoptic approach, drawing on the Orthodox tradition of twenty centuries.

Permit me a parenthesis. In 1964, when for the first time the Orthodox were invited to a similar gathering of the Committee on World Mission and Evangelism in Mexico, I remember we were only three representatives. In San Antonio (Texas), we have altogether nearly one hundred participants. Already there has taken place a serious common theological search and an exchange of experience, which we hope will be continued creatively here as well.

1. *"Thy will be done."* In the prayer our Lord taught us that this petition follows two others, with which it forms a group: "Hallowed be Thy name, Thy kingdom come, Thy will be done." The chief characteristic of the three is the eschatological perspective. They all begin to be realized here below, in order to be perfected in the glory of the Kingdom that is to come.

The verb of the petition is in the passive voice. Who exactly is the subject of the action? A preliminary answer says, God. In this petition, God's intervention is sought for the implementation of His will, for the establishment of His Kingdom. He has the initiative; He carries out His own will. The chief and decisive role in what happens to humankind and the whole universe belongs to God. A second interpretation sees God's will be done on earth through humankind's conformity with God's commandments (cf. Matt 7:21; 12:50 and John 9:31). Humankind is called to "do" the Father's will. This is the point that is expressed in the insight that permeates the Old Testament and in the continuity that is a dominant feature of Jewish literature. In it, our participation in the fulfillment of God's will and the necessity of obedience is emphasized.

There is, however, yet a third interpretation, a composite one, that sees as the subject of the action both God and human beings, that considers that the divine will is realized by divine-human cooperation. Thus, the two preceding views are intertwined. Certainly, so that His will may be done, God's intervention is essential. But we, by conforming to His precepts, God's will in the here and now, contribute to the foretaste and coming of the Kingdom in historical time, until its final consummation at the last day.

"On earth as it is in heaven." In the next verse we can perhaps distinguish various closely connected aspects: ethical, social, missionary, ecumenical, and a further one, which we will call ontological. They summarize descriptively most of what Chrysostom meant when he said: "For he did not say, 'Thy will be done in me or in us'; but 'everywhere on earth,' so that error might be done away with and truth established, all evil be cast out, virtue return and so nothing henceforth separate heaven from earth."[1] The prayer that our Lord put on our lips and in our hearts aims at a more radical change: the "celestification" of the earth. "That all persons and all things may become heaven" (Origen).[2]

By the phrase "Thy will be done," of the Lord's prayer, we beseech the Father that He will bring to completion His plan for the salvation of the whole world, and at the same time we ask for His grace that we may be freed from our own will and accept His will joyfully. Moreover, not only we as individuals, but that all of humankind may have fellowship in His will and share in its fulfillment.

2. After Pentecost this prayer on the Church's lips is highlighted by the events of the Cross and the Resurrection. It becomes clear that the divine will has been revealed in its fullness by the word, life and sacrifice of Jesus Christ. Each member of the Church is called thenceforth to advance in its realization, "So to promote 'the' Father's 'will,' as Christ promoted it, who came to do 'the will' of his Father and finished it all; for it is possible by being united with him to become 'one spirit' with him" (Origen).[3] Christ is made the leader of the faithful in realizing the divine will.

---

1. John Chrysostom, *Commentary on St. Matthew the Evangelist, Homily 19, 5, PG 57:280*, Paris. (J. P. Migne, ed., *Patrologiae Cursus Completus, Series Graeca*.)

2. Origen, *On Prayer*, 26, 6, ΒΕΠΕΣ 10:279, Athens. (*Bibliotheke Hellenon Pateron Kai Ekkesiastikon Syngrapheon* [Library of Greek Fathers and Church Writers].)

3. Origen, *On Prayer*, 26, 3, 10:277. Cf. John 4:34; 1 Cor 6:17.

The petition, "Thy will be done," is at the same time our guide in Gethsemane, at the decisive point in the history of the new Adam, our first-born brother. "My Father, if this cannot pass unless I drink it, thy will be done" (Matt 26:42). This prayer, in which the conformity of the human to the divine will reaches it culmination, illustrates *on a personal level* the meaning of the phrase "Thy will be done" of the Lord's Prayer. For all those who are determined to be conformed to God's will, who struggle for its realization on earth, the time will come to experience personally the pain, grief and humiliation that often accompany acceptance of God's will.

The repetition of "Thy will be done" by Christ in the context of His Passion sheds light on the second phase of our subject: Mission in Christ's way."

B
MISSION IN CHRIST'S WAY

By this expression we often tend to concentrate our attention on some particular point in Christ's life, such as, the Passion, the Cross, and His compassion for the poor. It is certainly not strange to put particular emphasis at times on one aspect, especially when it is continually being overlooked in practice. However, the theological thinking and experience of the catholic Church insist on what is universal (*to katholou*). The same is true of the person of Christ. This distinguishes the outlook and feeling of the "one, holy, catholic, and apostolic Church" from the schismatic, sectarian thought that adheres to that which is only a part. In this theological connection I would like to indicate five central points.

1. *Trinitarian relationship and reference.* Jesus Christ is seen in a continuous relationship to the Father and the Holy Spirit. He is the One sent (*Apestalmenos*) by the Father. The Holy Spirit opens the way for Him, works with Him, accompanies Him, sets the seal on His work and continues it from ages to ages.

Through Christ's preaching, we come to know the Father and the Holy Spirit. Nevertheless, even the preaching of Christ would remain incomprehensible without the enlightenment of the Holy Spirit, impossible to put into effect without the presence of the Paraclete.

In every expression of Christian life, but especially in mission, the work of Christ is done with the presence of the Holy Spirit; it is brought to completion within historical time by the uninterrupted action of the Holy Spirit. The Holy Spirit "recapitulates" all of us in Christ. He forms the Church. The source and bearing of our own apostolic activity resides in the promise and precept of the risen Lord in its Trinitarian perspective: "'As the Father has sent me, even so I send you.' And when he had said this, he breathed on them, and said to them, 'Receive the Holy Spirit'" (John 20:21–22).

The Christ-centeredness of the one Church is understandable only within the wider context of Trinitarian dogma. The one-sidedness of the Western type of Christocentrism was often caused by restriction of the image of Christ to the so-called "historical Jesus." However the Christ of the Church is the eternal Word, "the only Son, who is in the bosom of the Father" (John 1:18), who is ever present in the Church through the Holy Spirit, risen and ascended, the universal Judge, "the Alpha and the Omega, the first and the last, the beginning and the end" (Rev 22:13). The faith and experience of the Church are summed up in the phrase: The Father, through the Son, in the Holy Spirit, creates, provides, and saves. Essentially, mission in Christ's way is mission in the light of the Holy Trinity, in the mystical presence and working together of Father, Son and Holy Spirit.

2. *Assumption of the whole of humanity.* One of the favourite terms that Jesus Christ used to describe Himself was "Son of man." Jesus is the new Adam. The incarnation of the Word is the definitive event in the history of humankind, and the Church has persisted in opposing any Docetist deviation; "incarnate by the Holy Spirit and the Virgin Mary" insists the Sym-

bol of Faith. In His conception lies the human contribution, by the wholehearted acceptance of the divine will, in obedience, humility and joy, by His mother, the most pure representative of the human race. "Behold, I am the handmaid of the Lord; let it be to me according to your word" (Luke 1:38) was her decisive statement.

The absolute distinction between matter and spirit, as imagined by representatives of ancient Greek or Indian thought, is rejected, and humanity is raised up as a whole. Jesus Christ is not only the Savior of souls, but of the entire human being and the whole material-spiritual creation. This is as hard for classical thought to understand as the Trinitarian dogma. Often indeed, an attempt is made to simplify or pass it over, but then mission loses all its power and perspective. Christian mission does not mean taking refuge from our materiality, in one way or another, for the salvation of mere souls, but the transforming of present time, of society, and all matter in another way and by another dynamic. This perspective demands creative dialogue with contemporary cultures, with secular persons stuck in the materialism of this world, with the new options of physics about matter and energy and with every variety of human creation.

3. *The radical and eternally new element: Love.* Christ overthrows the established forms of authority, wisdom, glory, piety, success, traditional principles and values, and reveals that the living center of all is LOVE. The Father is love. The Son is love incarnate. The Spirit is the inexhaustible dynamic of love. This love is not a vague "principle." It is a "communion" of persons; it is the Supreme Being, the Holy Trinity. God is love because He is an eternal trinity, a communion of living, equal, distinct persons. The Son reveals this communion of love (koinonia agapes) in the world. In it He is not only the one who invites, but also the way.

Closely bound up with love are freedom, justice, liberation and the brotherhood of man, truth, harmony, joy and fullness of life. Every sincere utterance and endeavor for these things, anywhere in the world, in whatever age and culture, but above all in every loving, true expression of life, is a ray of God's grace and love. Jesus did not speak in vague and philosophical language about these great and holy things, but revealed them in power by clear signs and speech, and above all by His life.

Among the many surprises that Christ held in store was the fact that *He identified Himself with the humble*, the "least" of the people; from among whom He chose His companions and apostles. In the well-known saying about the universal Last Judgment He directly identified Himself with the despised, the infirm, the poor, the strangers and those in distress in the whole world. "As you did it to one of the least of these my brethren, you did it to me," He says, having "all the nations" assembled before Him (Matt 25:31–46).

This course remains determinative for His Church, His mystical body, for all ages. For this constitutes, in its authentic form, the most benevolent power that fights for human dignity, worth, relief, and the raising up of every human being throughout the length and breadth of the earth. Concern for all the poor and those unjustly treated, without exception—independent of race or creed—is not a fashion of the ecumenical movement, but a fundamental tradition of the united Church, an obligation that its genuine representatives have always seen as of first importance. "To the extent that you abound in wealth, you are lacking in love," declares St. Basil the Great, criticizing the predilection of many for a "piety that costs nothing."[4] He did not hesitate to call a "robber" not only the person who robs someone, but also the one who, though able to provide clothing and help, neglects to do so. Tersely he concludes: "You do injustice to so many, as many are those you could help."[5] The modern reality of the world's integration extends these judgments from the individual to the societal plane, from individuals to wider

---

4. St. Basil the Great, *Homily, To those who become wealthy*, 1, ΒΕΠΕΣ 54:67.

5. St. Basil the Great, *Homily, I will pull down my barns*, 7, ΒΕΠΕΣ 54:64–65.

conglomerations, to peoples, and the rich nations. The saints of the Church did not simply speak for the poor, but, above all, shared their life. They voluntarily became poor out of love for Christ, in order to identify with Him, who made Himself poor.

4. *The paradox of humility and the sacrifice of the Cross.* From the first moment of His presence in humanity, Christ makes "kenosis" (self-emptying) the revelation of the power of the love of the Triune God. He spends the greater part of His human life in the simplicity of everyday labor. Later, in His short public life, He faces various disputes and serious accusations. The power of love is totally bound up with humility. The opposite of love we usually call hatred, but its real name is egoism. This is the denial of the Triune God who is a communion (koinonia) of love. Therein also lies the drama of Lucifer, that he can do everything except be humble, and that is precisely why he cannot love. Christ destroys the works of the devil (1 John 3:8), and ransoms us chained in our egoism, by accepting the ultimate humiliation, the Cross. By the excess of this humility He abolishes on the Cross demonic pride and self-centeredness. It is in that hour that the glory of His love shines forth, humankind is redeemed.

Christian life means continual assimilation of the mystery of the cross in the fight against individual and social egocentricity. This holy humility, which is ready to accept the ultimate sacrifice, is the mystical power behind Christian mission. Mission will always be a service that entails acceptance of dangers, sufferings and humiliations; experiencing simultaneously human powerlessness, and the power of God. Only those who are prepared to accept, with courage and trust in Christ, sacrifice, tribulation, contradiction and rejection for His sake, can withstand. One of the greatest dangers for Christian mission is that we become forgetful in the practice of the cross and create a comfortable type of Christian who wants the cross as an ornament, but who often prefers to crucify others than to be crucified himself.

5. *Everything in the light of the Resurrection and eschatological hope.* The basic precept of the universal mission is given within the light of the Resurrection. Before the event of the Cross and Resurrection, Jesus had not allowed His disciples to go out into the world. Unless one experiences the Resurrection, one cannot share in Christ's universal apostolate. If one experiences the Resurrection, one cannot help bearing witness to the risen Lord, setting one's sights on the whole world. "All authority in heaven and on earth has been given to me. Go therefore and make disciples of all the nations" (Matt 28:18–19). The first sentence takes our thought back to "on earth as it is in heaven" in the Lord's Prayer. Authority over the whole world has been given to the Son of man, who fully carried out the Father's will. He is the Lord, "who is and who was and who is to come, the Almighty" (Rev 1:8). The faith and power of the Church are founded precisely on this certainty. The Cross and the Resurrection go together. Conforming one's life to the crucified life of Christ involves the mystical power of the Resurrection. On the other side, the Resurrection is the glorious revelation of the mystery and power of the Cross, victory over selfishness and death.

A mission that does not put at its center the Cross and Resurrection ends up as a shadow and a fantasy. As do simple people, so also do the more cultivated, who wallow in wealth, comfort and honors, come at some moment of crisis face to face with the implacable, final question: What happens at death? In this problem that torments every thinking person in every corner of the world the Church has the task of revealing the mystery of Christ's word: "For this is the will of my Father, that everyone who sees the Son and believes in him should have eternal life; and I will raise him up at the last day" (John 6:40).

I recall a personal experience, in an out-of-the-way region of Western Kenya. We arrived at night at a house that was in mourning. The little girl, stricken mortally by malaria, was lying on a big bed, as if sleeping peacefully. "She was such a good child. She was always the first to greet me," whispered the afflicted father in perplexity. We read a short funeral prayer, and I said a few words of consolation. Alone in the room of the school house where we were staying, by the light of the oil lamp, with the sound of rain on the banana leaves and zinc roof, I remembered the events of the day. Away in the darkness a drum was beating. It was in the house of mourning. In my tiredness I wondered. Why are you here? There came confusedly to my mind the various things that are spoken about in connection with mission: preaching, love, education, civilization, peace, development. Suddenly a light flashed and lit up in the mist of my tired brain the essence of the matter: You bring the message, the hope of Resurrection. Every human person has a unique worth. They will rise again. Herein lays human dignity, value and hope. Christ is Risen! You teach them to celebrate the Resurrection in the mystery of the Church; to have a foretaste of it. As if in a fleeting vision, I saw the little African girl hurrying up to greet me first, as was her habit; helping me to determine more precisely the kernel of the Christian mission: That is, to infuse all with the truth and hope of the Resurrection; to teach them to celebrate it. And this we do in the Church.

What our brothers and sisters in the isolated corners of Africa and Asia or in the outskirts of our large and rich cities long for, in their depression and loneliness, is not vague words of consolation, a few material goods or the crumbs of civilization. They yearn, secretly or consciously, for human dignity, for hope, and to transcend death. In the end they are searching for the living Christ, the perfect God-man, the way, the truth and the life. All, of whatever age and class, rich or poor, obscure or famous, illiterate or learned, in their heart of hearts long to celebrate the Resurrection and the "celestification" of life. In this the prospect of a mission "in Christ's way" reaches it culmination.

C

FULLNESS AND CATHOLICITY

The consequences of such a theological understanding are multifaceted. The important units, within which groups of critical problems for our time will be studied, have already been fixed: (a) turning to the living God; (b) participating in suffering and struggle; (c) the earth is the Lord's; and (d) towards renewed communities in mission. Before today much study, leavened with prayer, has taken place in small and larger groups, in conferences and congresses. The third part of this summary report will focus on only two points.

1. "Thy will be done," as it is repeated by Christ Himself in Gethsemane, helps us to overcome a great temptation: *The tendency for us to minimize the demands and cost of doing God's will in our personal life.* It is usually easier for us to rest in the general, in what concerns mostly others and in what suits us.

(a) The will of God, however, as it is revealed in Christ, is a single and indissoluble *WHOLE* (". . . teaching them to observe all that I have commanded you"). "Thy will be done" entirely, not by halves. The various so-called corrections that have at times been made to make the Gospel easier and the Church more acceptable or, so to speak, more effective, do not strengthen but rob the Gospel of its power. While waiting at a European airport a couple of years ago there came into my hands an impressive leaflet in which, framed between other things, was written: "Blessed are those who are rich. Blessed are those who are handsome. Blessed are those who have power. Blessed are the smart. Blessed are the successful, for they will possess the earth." I thought to myself: How many times, even in our own communities, do we prefer, openly or secretly, these idols, this worldly topsy-turvy representation of the Beatitudes, making them the criteria of our way of life?

The name of the city in which this meeting of ours is taking place reminds us not only of St. Anthony of Padua, to which the toponymy refers, but also of St. Anthony the Great, one of the universal Church's great personalities, who traced a model of perfect acceptance of God's will. This great hermit, in perfect obedience to: "If you would be perfect, go, sell what you possess and give to the poor, and you will have treasure in heaven;

and come, follow me" (Matt 19:21), went out in an adventure of freedom and love. This led to the outpouring of a new breath of the spirit in the Church at a time when it was in danger of compromising with secular power and the spirit of the world.

In the midst of our many sociopolitical concerns we have to bear in mind and act on the understanding that "this is the will of God, your sanctification" (1 Thess 4:3). Our *sanctification,* by following the divine will in all things, in our daily obligations, in our personal endeavors, and in the midst of many and various difficulties and dilemmas. The simplistic anthropology that encourages a naive morality, overlooking our existential tragedy does not help at all. Human existence is an abyss. "I do not do what I want, but I do the very thing I hate. I see in my members another law at war with the law of my mind and making me captive to the law of sin which dwells in my members" (Rom 7:15–23). Unfortunately, many of us, in critical situations, while we easily say "Thy will be done," in practice add: "not as thou wilt, but as I will." This overt or secret reversal of the divine will in our decisions is the main reason and cause of the failure of many Christian missions and initiatives. The hard inner struggle for purification and sanctification is the premise and mystical power of the apostolate.

The carrying out of God's will in the world will always be assisted by *continuous repentance,* so that we may be conformed to the model of Christ and be made one with Him. That is why in the Orthodox tradition monasteries have special importance, above all as centers of penitence. Everything that accompanies this struggle—worship, work, comforting the people, education, artistic creativity—follows, as a reflection of spiritual purification, of transformation, of a personal experience of repentance. The quest for new types of communities that will serve the contemporary apostolate must be closely bound up with the spiritual quest in the contemporary social reality for concrete forms of communities that will live out, profoundly and personally, repentance and longing for the coming of the Kingdom. The critical question for a mission in Christ's way is to what extent others can discern in our presence something, a ray, of His own presence.

(b) Conformity to God's will does not mean servile submission or fatalistic expectation. Nor is it achieved by a simple, moral, outward obedience. Joyful acceptance of God's will is an expression of love for a new relationship "in the Beloved"; it is a restoration of humanity's lost freedom. It means our communion in the mystery of the love of the Holy Trinity, communion within the freedom of love. Thus, we become "partakers of the divine nature" (2 Pet 1:4). Conformity to God's will is in the end a sharing in what the Orthodox tradition calls uncreated energies, by which we reach *theosis*, we become "god by grace."[6] The most blessed pages of Christian mission were written out of an excess of love for Christ, and identification with Him.

(c) The Church continually seeks to renew this holy intoxication of love, especially by the sacrament of the Holy Eucharist— which remains the pre-eminent missionary event—everywhere on earth. In the Divine Liturgy the celebrant, as representative of the whole community, prays: "Send thy Holy Spirit upon us and upon these gifts here present." Not "on the gifts only," but we beg that the Holy Spirit may be sent "upon us" also, so that we may be "moved by the Spirit." The whole prayer moves very clearly in a Trinitarian perspective. We beseech the Father to send the Spirit to change the precious gifts into Christ's Body and Blood, and in receiving Holy Communion we are united with Him; we become "of one body" and "of one blood" with Christ, that we may become fertile and bear the fruit of the Spirit, become "God's temple," receivers and transmitters of His blessed radiance.

The *enthusiasm for the acquisition of the Holy Spirit*, which is of late much sought after in the West, has always been strong in the East; but in a sober Christological context and in a Trinitarian perspective. The Church's experience is summed up in the well-known saying of St. Seraphim: "The purpose of Christian

6. St. Maximos the Confessor, *On various questions of Saints Dionysios and Gregorios, PG* 91:1084AC, 1092C, 1308.

life is the acquisition of the Holy Spirit." The saint continues: "Prayer, fasting and almsgiving, and the other good works and virtues that are done for Christ, are simply, and only, means of acquiring God's Holy Spirit."[7] This presence of the Holy Spirit has nothing at all to do with spiritual pride and self-satisfaction. It is at bottom connected with the continual exercise of penitence, with holy humility. "I tell you the truth," wrote a holy monk of Mount Athos, Starets Silouan, "I find nothing good in myself and I have committed many sins. But the grace of the Holy Spirit has blotted them out. And I know that to those who fight sin is afforded not only pardon, but also the grace of the Holy Spirit, which gladdens the soul and bestows a sweet and profound peace."[8]

2. The fact that the will of God refers to the whole world, the whole universe, *excludes isolating ourselves in an individualistic piety*, in a kind of *private Christianity*.

(a) The will of God covers the whole human reality; it is accomplished in the whole of history. It is not possible for the Christian to remain indifferent to historical happenings in the world, when faith is founded on two historical events: the Incarnation of the Word of God and the Second-coming of Christ. The social, the human reality is the place in which the Church unfolds. Every expression of human creativity, science, technology and the relationships of persons as individuals, peoples and various groupings are to be found among its concerns.

We are living at a critical, historic juncture in which a new universal culture, the electronic culture, is taking shape. The natural sciences, especially astronautics, biomedicine, and genetics are creating and posing new problems. Half of the earth's population is crushed into huge urban centers; contemporary agnosticism is eating away at the thought and

---

7. P.A. Botsis, *Philokalia of the Russian Vigilents*, Athens, 1983, p. 105 (in Greek).

8. Archimandrite Sophrony, *Starets Silouan, Moine du Mont-Athos.* (Traduit du russe par le Hiéromoine Syméon) Sisteron, 1973, p. 318.

behavior of the city-dwellers. The passage from the "written word" to the "electronic word" is opening up undreamed of possibilities for the amassing of a whole universe of increased knowledge and the creation of a new process of human thinking. A new world is emerging. A new sort of human being is being formed. The Church, the mystical Body of Christ who is "the one who is and was and is to come" has a pledge and a duty to the march of humanity in the future, the whole society in which it exists as "leaven," "sign" and "sacrament" of the Kingdom of Love that has come and is coming. Whatever the Church possesses, she has to radiate and offer for the sake of the entire world.

Nevertheless, if one temptation is for us not to see the universal duty when we pray "Thy will be done," the reverse is for us to be occupied only with universal themes and indifferent to concrete reality—to be too sensitive to certain situations and indifferent to others. To speak, for example, constantly about injustice in such-and-such a publicized region and be indifferent to injustice in Europe, as for example, in Albania, where four hundred thousand Christians are oppressed, deprived constitutionally from every expression of faith, even of the elementary right to have a Church: to believe.[9]

In various corners of our planet want, disease, oppression, injustice, the raw violence of arms oppress millions of our fellow human beings. All of these are cells of the same body—the great body of humanity to which we belong. Their suffering is the suffering of Christ, who assumed the whole of humanity, and the suffering of the Church, His mystical body. It is—must be—the suffering of us all.

The prophetic voice, both for the immediate and actual, and the whole world remains always the Church's obligation, even if it annoys certain people who do not wish to touch any unjust establishment. In many situations, "inside" and "outside," the Church is obliged today to speak in the way of biblical protest:

---

9. One is reminded that this report was given in 1989, before the totalitarian Communist regime of Albania was abolished.

Woe to those who talk about justice, but who in practice seek only their own rights and their own privileges. Woe to those who rejoice, crying "Peace, peace," but forget the fetters of the defenseless. Woe to the rich nations that continually celebrate freedom and love, but by their methods make the developing peoples poorer and less free. Woe to those who appear as God's lawyers and representatives, making a mockery—deliberately or unintentionally—of what is finest in humanity, the witness of Jesus Christ (cf. Isa 5:16–23).

(b) Still the Gospel cannot remain the possession of only certain peoples who had the privilege of hearing it first. By putting on our lips the prayer, "Thy will be done," the Lord "bade each one of us who prays to take thought for the ecumene" (the whole inhabited world) (John Chrysostom).[10] God's will, as it was fulfilled and revealed in Christ, has to be made known in every corner of the earth, in every cranny of the world, in every expression of our contemporary multi-centered civilization. A world missionary conference like our own cannot relegate to a footnote the fact that millions of our fellow men and women have not heard, even once in their lives, the Christian message; that hundreds of races still, after twenty centuries of Christian history, do not have the Gospel in their mother tongue.

Distinctions between Christian and non-Christian nations are no longer absolutely valid in our days. In all nations there is a need for re-evangelization in every generation. Every local Church finds itself in mission in its actual geographical and cultural territory and context. But its horizons, outside the place in which it is active, must extend in the catholic Church "from one end of the earth to the other." Despite cultural differences, all of us face more or less the same basic human problems. All the local Churches, expressing the life of the "one, holy, catholic and apostolic Church," are in a state of mutual interdependence and interchange, in both receiving and sending. The distinction between sending and receiving Churches belongs to the past. All should, and can, both receive and send. In proportion to the

---

10. Chrysostom, *Homily 19*, PG 57:280.

gifts (*charismata*) that every local Church possesses (personnel, knowledge, expertise, and financial facility), it can contribute to the development of the worldwide mission "to the end of the earth" (Acts 1:8). It is time for every Christian to realize that mission is our own obligation and to take part in it looking to the whole of humankind. Just as there is no Church without a worshipping life, so there cannot be a living Church without missionary life.

(c) Those outside the Christian faith, who still have no knowledge of the will of God in its fullness, do not cease to move in the mystical radiance of His glory. God's will is diffused throughout the whole of history and throughout the whole world. Consequently it influences their own lives, concerns them and embraces them. It is expressed in many ways— as divine providence, inspiration, and guidance. In recent time in the ecumenical movement, we have been striving hard for the theological understanding of people of other faiths; and this difficult, but hopeful dialogue very much deserves to continue at this present conference.

Certainly for the Church, God's will, as it was lived out in its fullness by Christ, remains its essential heritage and contribution in the world. It is not, therefore, a sign of respect for others to agree on a so-called common denominator that minimizes our convictions about Christ. Rather, it is an injustice if we are silent about the truth that constitutes the givenness of the Church's experience. It is one thing—imposition by force— that is unacceptable, and has always been anti-Christian and quite a different thing, a withholding or diminution, that leads to a double betrayal, both of our own faith and of others' right to know the whole truth.

Jesus Christ went about doing good among people of other faiths (let us recall the stories of the Canaanite woman and the centurion), admiring and praising their spontaneous faith and goodness. ("I say to you, not even in Israel have I found such faith" Matt 8:10.) He even used as a symbol of Himself a representative of another religious community, the good "Samaritan." His example remains determinative: beneficent service and sincere respect for whatever has been preserved from that which was made "in the image of God." Certainly in today's circumstances our duty is becoming more clear and extensive: a journey together in whatever does not militate against God's will; an understanding of the deepest religious insights that have developed in other civilizations by the assistance of the Spirit; a cooperation in the concrete applications of God's will, such as justice, peace, freedom, love, both in the universal community and on the local level.

(d) Not only the so-called spiritual, but also the whole physical universe moves within the sphere of God's will. Reverence for the animal and the vegetable kingdoms, the correct use of nature, concern for the conservation of the ecological balance, the struggle to prevent nuclear catastrophe and to preserve the integrity of creation, have become more important in the list of immediate ecclesiastical concerns. This is not a deviation, as asserted by some who see Christ as saving souls by choice and His Church as a traditional private religious concern of certain people. The whole world, not only "humankind," but the entire universe, has been called to share in the restoration that was accomplished by the redeeming work of Christ. "We wait for new heavens and a new earth in which righteousness dwells" (2 Pet 3:13). Christ, the Almighty and Logos of the Universe, remains the key to understanding the evolution of the world. All things will come to pass in Him who is their head. The surprising design, "the mystery of his will," which has been made known to us "according to his purpose," is "a plan for the fullness of time, to unite all things in him, things in heaven and things on earth" (Eph 1:9–10). The correspondence with the phrase of the Lord's Prayer is obvious. The transformation of creation, as victory over the disfigurement that sin brought to the world, is to be found in the wider perspective and immediate concerns of Christian mission. [. . .]

* * *

Through all the length and breadth of the earth, we millions of Christians of every race, class, culture and language repeat, "Thy will be done, on earth as it is in heaven." Sometimes painfully, faithfully and hopefully, sometimes mechanically and indifferently; but we seldom connect it intimately with the missionary obligation. The conjunction of the two phrases: "Thy will be done" and "Mission in Christ's way" gives a special dynamic to our conference. Understanding the missionary dimensions of this prayer will strengthen in the Christian world the conviction that mission is sharing in carrying out God's will on earth. Put the other way round, that God's will demands our own active participation, working with the Holy Trinity.

By sharing the life of the risen Christ, living the Father's will, moved by the Holy Spirit, we have a decisive word and role in shaping the course of humankind. The Lord is at hand. The history of the world does not proceed in a vacuum. It is unfolding towards an end. There is a plan. God's will shall prevail on earth. The prayers of the saints will not remain unanswered! There will be a universal judgment by the Lord of love. At that last hour everything will have lost its importance and value, except for selfless love. The last word belongs to Christ; the mystery of God's will reaches its culmination in the recapitulation of all things in Him. We continue to struggle with fortitude. We celebrate the event that is coming. We enjoy a foretaste of that hour of the last things. Rejoicing in worship —with this vision—with this hope.

Lord, free us from our own will and incorporate us in your own. "Thy will be done."

2

ORTHODOXY AND MISSION

(1964)

• Part of a report to the General Assembly of Orthodox Youth, "*Syndes-mos*," Kuopio, Finland, July 28–30, 1964. • "Orthodoxy and Mission" in *St. Vladimir's Theological Quarterly* 8 (1964), pp. 139–148, with an editorial note: "It brilliantly represents the growing sense of mission-ary responsibility among the younger generation of Orthodox youth leaders in Europe." • French: "Missions Orthodoxes," *Parle et Mission* 8 (1965), pp. 5–18. • Finnish: "Orthodoksisen Kirkon Lähetystyö": *Aamun Koitto*, Joensuu (1964), pp. 234–239. • Swedish: "Grekisk-ortodoxt Kurko-missionstänkande," B. Sharpe, trans., *Svensk Missionstid-skrift*, Uppsala, 53 (1965), pp. 15–27.• *Ἐλεύθερη ἀπόδοση στά ἑλληνικά, Ἀδι-αφορία γιά τήν Ἱεραποστολή σημαίνει ἄρνηση τῆς Ὀρθοδοξίας, Ἀθῆναι* 1971, 3ⁿ ἔκδ. 1973. • German: "Eine Kirche erwächt zur Mission." Re-printed from the *Yahrbuch Evangelischermission*, Hamburg, 1970. "Mis-sion aus der Sicht eines Orthodoxen," *Neue Zeitschrift fur Missions-wissenschaf—Nouvelle Revue des sciences missionnaires*, 26 (1970), pp. 241–252. • *Ἱεραποστολή στά ἴχνη τοῦ Χριστοῦ. Θεολογικές μελέτες καί ὁμιλίες, Ἀθήνα* 2007.

History shows that the awareness of the Church's call to mission was always alive in the Orthodox Church. However, external reasons, such as the Turkish occupation of the Balkans and Greece, which lasted four centuries; the Communist seizure of power in the twentieth century; and the immigration to countries which were predominantly of other religious beliefs have obliged the Orthodox to withdraw temporarily into themselves, in order to preserve their faith and form, to a certain extent, closed communities. This tactic, so understandable and perhaps necessary, became habitual with the years and often took the form of isolationism. Now, however, it has become the conviction of many people that indifference or stagnation in regard to the worldwide (*oikoumenike*) mission is equivalent to a denial of Orthodoxy itself.

A
MISSION: THE UNDOUBTED
OBLIGATION OF THE ORTHODOX

1. *Ecumenicity and apostolicity: Essential elements of Orthodox ecclesiology.* (a) "I believe in one, holy, catholic and apostolic Church" we repeat unceasingly in almost every worship service. This is the assurance, which the bishops, before their consecration, must give publicly. How, then, is it possible for the faithful and particularly for the clergyman to judge or to decide

in terms of "his own" province alone, "his own" needs only? The whole perspective of the *one* Church and her total needs are what we should always have before our eyes. Selfish absorption in "our own" needs and indifference to others denotes that our belief in the *one* Church is reduced to a mere verbal formality. [. . .]

Whenever we say "our Church," if we sincerely want to live as Orthodox, we are called to think in terms of the Church that extends "from end to end of the universe"; as we say in the offering of the Holy Eucharist (Liturgy of St. Basil the Great). There are not different Orthodox Churches, such as the Church *of* Greece, the Church *of* Russia, the Church *of* Romania, *of* Japan, *of* Uganda, and so on. There is but *one* Orthodox Church: The Church "which is in" Greece, *in* Russia, *in* Romania, *in* Uganda (cf. "The Church of God which is (in) Corinth" 1 Cor 1:2 and 2 Cor 1:1); the Church, which must extend everywhere. Orthodoxy is not a confederation of churches, but the "one, holy, catholic and apostolic Church," to which the Lord entrusted the continuation of His redemptive work, the salvation of the whole world in her true dimensions. The Church is "apostolic," not simply because of the apostolic succession, but also because she preserves the apostolic fire and zeal to preach the Gospel "to the whole creation" (Mark 16:15), and because she nurtures her members so that they may become "witnesses (of Christ) in Jerusalem and in all Judea and Samaria and to the end of the earth" (Acts 1:8).

(b) The realization that the Church "is his body, the fullness of him who fills all in all" (Eph 1:23) and that the plan of God is "to unite all things in him, things in heaven, and things on earth" (Eph 1:10) (ἀνακεφαλαιώσασθαι, to recapitulate, gather together), compels the believer to free himself from provincialism and narrow-mindedness so that he may live in longing and prayer for the recapitulation of all things in Christ. This deep longing cannot remain simply on the surface, as sentimentality and anticipation, but is expressed as active participation in a living call, in the continuous growth of the "mystical Body of Christ."

Thus, the universal, ecumenical mission from the Orthodox point of view is no less than an immediate result of a fundamental article of the Creed and of the basic understanding of the Church. If Orthodoxy does not embrace this definition of the ecumenicity of the Church—let us not hesitate to say it—she simply denies herself.

2. *Orthodoxy—Resurrection—Mission.* It is hard to understand genuine Orthodoxy apart from a vigorous pursuit of the worldwide mission, for it is impossible to conceive of an Orthodoxy which does not focus on the Resurrection of the Lord. Resurrection and the ecumenical mission are intimately related. The command concerning the mission to the world is directly related to the triumph of the Lord through His resurrection. The fact that He was given "All authority in heaven and on earth" (Matt 28:18) has to be proclaimed "to the whole creation" (Mark 16:15). Before the Resurrection, before the consummation of the work of salvation, the disciples were not allowed to pass the boundaries of Israel. Jesus advised them, "Go nowhere among the Gentiles, and enter no town of the Samaritans" (Matt 10:5). However, after His resurrection, they were no longer permitted to confine their preaching within these limits: "Go therefore and make disciples of all nations" (Matt 28:19; Acts 10:1–48, and 15:7–8).

The Resurrection of the Lord is the starting point for the expansion of the mission from Israel to the whole world. Those who continue to move solely within the boundaries of Israel—even the new Israel of grace —seem to insist that they live in the days before the Resurrection. The orientation of the mystery of redemption is beautifully expressed in the verse that electrifies the congregation in the Vespers Service of the Saturday before Pascha, "Arise, O God, and judge Thou the earth; for Thou shalt take all heathen to Thine inheritance." [. . .]

The Resurrection constitutes the backbone of Orthodox worship. In this framework, Orthodox hymnology—that of the period of Pentecost, as well as that of the Sunday Vespers and Matins—proclaims it as the very center *par excellence* of the salvation of all humankind and describes the missionary obligation that arises from this unique historical event. The Gospel texts that refer to the commandment: "Go therefore" are read very frequently, especially during the most prominent feast days (Matt 28:16–20; Mark 16:9–20; Luke 24:36–53; John 20:19–31, and Acts 1:1–8).

Therefore, one wonders how is it possible to think, to chant, to live so intensely the Resurrection, and yet remain reluctant in face of the call to worldwide mission, which is so closely interwoven with it. How can the Orthodox preach the doctrine of the Resurrection, if, in the believers' conscience, the duty to proclaim the triumph of Christ—the redemption of human nature—"unto all nations" is absent?

3. *Orthodox spirituality: "Being in Christ" and mission.* St. Paul, after meeting the risen Christ, first withdrew for several years into the Arabian wilderness, but after this preparation, he found it impossible to remain only in one place to contemplate and praise Him. His relationship with the living Lord was so agitating, that it constantly moved him into new adventures, new areas of action. "For necessity is laid upon me. Woe to me if I do not preach the gospel" (1 Cor 9:16), he wrote to the Christians of Corinth.

His passion for the mission to the Gentiles cannot be attributed to any simple extrovert tendency to escape the hardships of Israel, or to a self-deception that the missionary work there had been completed. Simply, he "knew" through revelation "the mystery of Christ" (Eph 3:3–4),". . . how the Gentiles are fellow heirs, members of the same body, and partakers of the promise in Christ Jesus through the gospel" (Eph 3:6). Consequently, he meant it when he said, "I am under obligation both to the Greeks and to barbarians, both to the wise and to the foolish" (Rom 1:14). He felt that he had to share with others the precious gift that he had received, namely, the personal experience of the risen Lord, the "life in Christ." This all-embracing life in Christ, which he proverbially expressed as, "I have been crucified with Christ; it is no longer I who live, but Christ who lives in me" (Gal 2:20), defined the spirituality of the Apostle Paul and should also be the source and criterion of the spirituality of Orthodoxy, in accordance with the Orthodox tradition of centuries.

(a) The command of the Lord, "Abide in me, and I in you . . . If you keep my commandments, you will abide in my love" (John 15:4, 10), remains the main goal of Orthodox spiritual life. Hence, "to abide in Christ" means that we try to think, feel and desire as Christ does. Likewise, it means that we have "the mind of the Lord" (1 Cor 2:16), "the affection of Christ Jesus" (Phil 1:8), and that our whole existence is rooted in the depths of His love.

Let us, therefore, recollect for a moment on the vision of our Lord. Is it possible for His horizon to be confined only to our town, to our nation, to the so-called "Christian world?" Has He not "made from one every nation of men" (Acts 17:26)? Does He not want "all men to be saved and to come to the knowledge of the truth" (1 Tim 2:4)? Does He not care for the millions of men who live as "strangers to the covenants of promise, having no hope, and without God in the world" (Eph 2:12)? We surely force the Apostle to repeat once more: "For some have no knowledge of God. I say this to your shame" (1 Cor 15:34). All this denotes very clearly that one may not confront, with a cold and indifferent heart, the drama of humankind estranged from God if one wants indeed to "abide in Christ." [. . .]

Finally, our concept of mission in the global perspective cannot be less than turning our hearts to Jesus in order that we may truly "abide in him." The true motive of the mission is to be found here. The conscientious believer *must constantly have in mind the evangelization of the whole world (the ecumene); he cannot do otherwise.* He cannot think contrary to the mind of the Lord. He cannot love in manner other than the Lord's. He cannot speculate about justice in terms other than those of the Gospel. He believes that there is no treasure at the disposal of every single man that is more precious than the truth, which was revealed by the Word of God. Therefore, he feels that the people who suffer injustice most in our times are those who have been deprived of the Word. He further feels that his "honor" and his "love" cannot be genuine, if he does not try something concrete—the best that he can, in this direction. His interest in the mission is so taken to heart that he cannot possibly do otherwise. It springs from the word of the Lord: "If you love me, you will keep my commandments" (John 14:15). "He who has my commandments and keeps them, he it is who loves me; and he who loves me will be loved by my Father, and I will love him and manifest myself to him" (John 14:21). The man who loves and is being loved obeys the whole Gospel, for he wants to live in Christ.

B
FUNDAMENTAL ATTRIBUTES
OF ORTHODOX MISSION

There are many points that should become the object of careful study in the Orthodox missionary effort, which is just beginning. Within the confines of this brief lecture we intend to stress some general and, in our estimation, fundamental features that must characterize this missionary revival.

1. *Expression of repentance and concern for the whole Church.* (a) The opinion is often expressed that since we have so many problems at home; missionary work in far away places is a "matter of luxury." On the contrary, we believe that it is a *matter of repentance* and it concerns every Orthodox community as well as every believer. The opening and broadening of our horizon is not less crucial to our own development than it is to the benefit of the people who receive the mission. It is a matter of

repentance, a change in thinking and action in accordance with a fundamental command of the Lord and in accordance with the true Orthodox tradition.

We have never been able to rid ourselves of internal problems, and we never shall be. When the Apostles went out "to the gentiles," (that is, to our ancestors) the problems of the Church in Palestine were far from being solved. St. Athanasius the Great, St. John Chrysostom and St. Photios had to contend with great problems within the Church, but were not thereby prevented from taking great personal interest in the Christianization of foreign countries. The most serious internal problem is whether we are ready "to observe all" that the Lord has "commanded" us (Matt 28:20), or whether we shall create our own interpretation of the Gospel adding and removing commandments according to our own conception of our contemporary needs.

It is certain that in every country there is today a wide field for missionary activity. But God is calling us all not simply for those who need us, but for those who need us most. As servants of the one Lord of this world, we must constantly be searching to discover in what place and in what concrete way we may be able to serve him.

(b) *The problem is not merely to create a few missionary groups.* The question is how the whole Church can be *mobilized by this worldwide missionary vision?*

The participation of every communicant must be sought with the same insistence and emphasis on his participation in worship. It must be sought as a consequence of the "Creed" which he continuously professes. Everyone can help; all have the responsibility as living members of the Church to help; this must be the motto. The particular form of assistance is a matter of organization.

It is urgent to assign a special day, or week, dedicated to mission each year, in all the Orthodox Churches, during which the missionary conscience of the Orthodox people will be stimulated through preaching, prayers and fund-raising efforts.

Special emphasis should be put on prayer and on financial contributions that result from sacrifice.

(c) In this missionary effort the *collaboration of all Orthodox Churches* should be sought. It is impossible to separately offer Orthodoxy in a world which is becoming a global neighborhood. The subject presents, of course, many complexities. However, this should urge us to a more systematic and persistent approach to the problem rather than to its neglect. Inter-Orthodox collaboration in many sectors is already a hopeful reality.

2. *Incorporation, not only adaptation.* (a) Much criticism, some of it justified, has arisen in the past of the tendency of many missions to establish spiritual colonies or annexes to their own Church rather than to create new, living churches, rooted in the soul and life of the people. The Orthodox tradition on this point has been, fortunately, very clear: *Sincere respect for the identity of the individuals and of the peoples, and sanctification of their characteristics in order that they may become truly themselves.* This is what happened with the Christianization of Ethiopia and the Slavic world. This is what the later Orthodox missionaries practiced in large nations (for example Nikolai Kasatkin in Japan) or small primitive tribes (like Innocent Veniaminov with the Aleutians of Alaska). These tactics were not the emanation of human wisdom. Rather, it was theological consistency, an extension of the fact that He who was sent by the Father "dwelt among us" (John 1:14), and became one with His people. The "incarnation" of the "Logos" of God into the language and customs of a country is the first task of every Orthodox missionary.

For the Orthodox, the great event of Pentecost (Acts 2:6–11), during which "each one heard them speaking in his own language" about "the mighty works of God," remains the basis for missionary tactics. The translation of the Bible and of the Divine Liturgy into the language of each people was the uninterrupted tradition of the Eastern Church. The Russian missionaries (as we have already seen) followed the same path and prepared translations into the languages of the smallest tribes of Siberia, the Kamchatka peninsula and Alaska. When, for a period of time, this method of work was neglected, the missionary effort came to stagnation.

The example of Nicholas Ilminski is very illuminating. He placed at the disposition of the mission the service and fruits of scientifically based linguistics and ethnology, to aid in the discovery of the most expedient methods to approach primitive tribes, and to translate the New Testament into their own language. This shows how much attention must be given by the Orthodox mission, especially among primitive tribes, to the field of descriptive linguistics which has made such astonishing progress in our times. The contribution of Greek linguistics and missionaries, who have a thorough knowledge of the language of the original text, could be of special importance in the translation of the New Testament. According to recent investigations there are about 1500 tongues and dialects in which there is still no extant translation of the New Testament.

(b) This is the first step. The end of the road of an Orthodox mission must however be: *the growth of an indigenous Church*, which will sanctify and make proper use of all pure elements in the popular traditions, and will uphold and support the people's personality. From this point of view, it is a missionary's duty to understand the civilization of other peoples. This, however, should by no means aim at a passive imitation or absorption. The example of the Thessalonian brothers, Cyril and Methodios, as well as the whole course of development of the Russian Church—which started with the assimilation of the Byzantine spiritual heritage, but proceeded along its own path of self-expression—is a guide of great importance.

First and foremost, we are to have respect for the past of every people. The Apostle Paul in Acts 14:16–17, while realizing that: "In past generations he allowed all the nations to walk in their own ways"; proceeds to complete his thought by saying that, "yet he did not leave himself without witness, for he did good and gave you from heaven rains and fruitful seasons, satisfying your hearts with food and gladness."

It is, therefore, not only a pedagogical command, but also a theological one to study how God bore witness concerning Himself to each particular people. Perhaps the combination of the phrases: "He did not leave Himself without witness," and "food and gladness" could help us gain more insight and understanding of the meaning and religious significance that some of the festivities have among people who live under primitive conditions.

3. *Worship and autonomy.* (a) Orthodox worship, wrote Professor Seeberg of the University of Berlin, is the only one that can be easily understood and embraced by the Oriental man. The mystical atmosphere of our worship appeals in a very profound manner to the whole of man, to every human person. When suitably translated and adapted to the character of each people, it can really help them in their approach to the mystery of redemption. Liturgical life played an essential role in the Christianization of Russia—witness the amazement of the Russian delegates before the splendor of the Byzantine Liturgy in St. Sophia and later the spiritual radiance of the monasteries throughout the vast empire.

(b) *The administrative autonomy* of the local Orthodox Churches is also of great importance in our times when the nationalistic feelings of the peoples of Africa and Asia are at high tide. The unity of the Orthodox Church is not based on a superficial uniformity of language or civilization, but on a unity of faith and of sacramental life.

It is very interesting from the missionary viewpoint that in the first centuries of the united Church, about forty different liturgies and about seventy liturgical languages were in use. The problem is not how to avoid the different voices, but how to make this variety a harmonious doxology to God. In the same way as every believer has his own personality which is sanctified, but not absorbed, likewise every nation has its own peculiar personality which must be developed autonomously on the basis, of course, of the precious tradition of the one Church. In God's garden there is a place—and there must be—for all kinds of flowers.

The development of an indigenous Church according to the Orthodox tradition presents us with many difficulties. These problems continually force us to examine and discern the eternal, that which is part of the tradition of the "one, holy, catholic and apostolic Church," from the temporal, that which is part of the traditions of a local Church and a particular people, and which therefore does not constitute a rule for all other peoples.

4. *Basic characteristics of the Orthodox missionary.* In addition to the general approach to mission, it is also necessary for us to look at the type of spirituality that should characterize the Orthodox missionary.

(a) Given that the work of the missionary is to continue the earthly ministry of our Lord, he should accept the way of life of his Teacher. He should follow the footsteps of the first missionary sent by God, He who "came not to be served but to serve, and to give his life as a ransom for many" (Mark 10:45); " . . . who, though he was in the form of God, did not count equality with God a thing to be grasped, but emptied himself, taking the form of a servant, being born in the likeness of men. And being found in human form he humbled himself and became obedient unto death, even death on a cross" (Phil 2:6–8). As He "dwelt among" His people and manifested His glory (John 1:14), so also the missionary is called to live among the people and manifest the glory of God and the mystery of the Incarnation.

(b) In order to *be* at all times a living witness of the presence of our Lord, the missionary must be in continuous personal relationship with Him. He must not only think or talk about Him, but "live in Christ" (Gal 2:20). This means a deep relationship with Christ of the whole human person, not merely of his intellect. It is the transformed life of the entire being in Christ that is the true characteristic of the missionary.

Our Lord defined the missionary work of His disciples as a direct continuation of His work. "As though didst send me into the world, even so I have sent them into the world" (John 17:18), He said in His High-priestly prayer; and after His resurrection He repeated the same truth to His disciples, saying: "As the Father has sent me, even so I send you" (John 20:21). Within the framework of this "as . . . even so" we must search for not only the contents, but also the means and methods of missionary work.

In the Gospel of St. John the fellowship and unity between Father and Son is emphasized. Every word and work of our Lord is dependent upon and connected with His Father. "I do nothing on my own authority but speak thus as the Father taught me. And he who sent me is with me; he has not left me alone, for I always do what is pleasing to him" (John 8:28–29). His *message* is nothing more than what He "had heard" and "had seen." "He who sent me is true, and I declare to the world that I have heard from him" (John 8:26). "I speak of what I have seen with my Father" (John 8:38). "I proceeded and came forth from God" (John 8:42; cf. John 12:49; 10:25; 5:36). His *will* is the same as the will of His Father. "I seek not my own will but the will of him who sent me" (John 5:30; cf. 6:38). His *works* are works of the Father. *Everything that He does, affirms that He was sent by the Father* (John 5:36). *The Apostles participated in the relationship of the Father and Son*: "He who receives anyone whom I send receives me; and he who receives me receives him who sent me" (John 13:20; cf. John 17:23). Therefore, the crucial problem for every missionary is how to maintain a close relationship with the Holy Trinity.

(c) There are substantially two things that will help this living relationship. First, the sanctification of the missionary in the truth of the Gospel: "Sanctify them in the truth; thy word is truth" (John 17:17; cf. John 15:7; 8:31). Second, conscientious participation in the sacraments, especially the sacrament of the Holy Eucharist: "He who eats my flesh and drinks my blood abides in me, and I in him. As the living Father hath sent me, and I live because of the Father, so he who eats me will live because of me" (John 6:56–57; cf. 6:53; 15:4–5).

It is clear that there is a direct relationship between "eating and drinking" and "sending"; that is, between participation in the sacramental life of the Church and missionary expansion.

***

In conclusion: Hence according to the affirmation of the Lord, "As the Father has sent me, even so I also send you" (John 20:21), *the mission of the Church is the continuation of His earthly ministry and participation in the living presence of our Lord in the world.* It is a participation in the life of our Lord who "gave us the ministry of reconciliation" (2 Cor 5:18).

Since the missionary is an "emissary," an "apostle of Jesus Christ by the will of God" (Eph 1:1), he will be talking in vain about mission if he does not try to be in constant "communion" with Christ. It matters not what he himself is going to say and do, but what the Lord will say and do through him.

So it is our duty to make the best use of all the opportunities and available facilities of the modern world for the extension of the Kingdom of God, but we should do this without falling into the temptation of superficial activism. Our supreme concern must be not *what we will DO, but how we will BE a living witness to the presence of the Lord in the world.*

3

THE PURPOSE AND MOTIVE OF MISSION

(From a theological point of view)
(1967)

• "The Purpose and Motive of Mission," *International Review of Mission* 54 (1965), pp. 281–297. 2nd ed., *Porefthendes—Go Ye* 9 (1967). Also as a separate pamphlet: *The Purpose and Motive of Mission—From an Orthodox Point of View*, Athens, 1968. • *Σκοπός καί κίνητρο τῆς Ἱεραποστολῆς (ἐξ ἐπόψεως θεολογικῆς)*, Ἀθῆναι, 1966. Reprinted from *Theologia* 37 (1966), pp. 434–452, 2nd ed. (1971). • *Ἱεραποστολή στά ἴχνη τοῦ Χριστοῦ. Θεολογικές μελέτες καί ὁμιλίες*, Ἀθήνα 2007.

Orthodox theological thinking about mission has not been systematically developed. Consequently when anyone is invited to speak from the Orthodox point of view about the purpose and motive of mission (a subject with which Western thought has been concerned for many years), there is a two-fold danger: Either he will limit himself to a repetition of the ideas of others or that, after studying the Catholic and Protestant conceptions, he will attempt to construct an Orthodox one distinct from the other two, merely in order to complete the familiar trilogy. There is a third way, more serious, more modest, and consequently more Orthodox. That is to avoid this controversial tactic—to begin with the general presuppositions and principles of Orthodox theology; to meditate upon Orthodox soteriology, ecclesiology and eschatology from the perspective of mission. Still, if it is to be done properly, this requires time and elaboration beyond the limits of this paper. This paper is offered merely as an introduction to the study of the subject.

A

THE THEOLOGICAL STARTING POINT

It will be useful for a better understanding of the points to be developed if we first recollect that, on the whole, the theological thought of the Eastern Church moves in a broader theological and cosmological framework, in which the dominant element is St. John's conception of the love (ἀγάπη) of the Trinitarian God, seen in the perspective of eschatology and in doxological contemplation of the mystery of God. A key to the Orthodox understanding of the process of history is, I think, the glory of the most holy God, viewed in the perspective of His infinite love: "the *Alpha* and the *Omega*, the beginning and the end" (Rev 21:6), "the first and the last" (Rev 1:17), remains God. He is the One "who is and who was and is to come" (Rev 1:8). He who is worthy to receive glory and honour and power, who created all things, and "by thy will they existed and were created" (Rev 4:11).

The development of human history, of which the Bible speaks, begins and ends with the glory of God. When our Lord says, "and now, Father, glorify thou me in thy own presence (παρά σοί, by, near thee) with the glory which I had with thee before the world was made" (John 17:5), He points us to His glory as a condition which existed before creation. As for the end of history, it is characteristic of the last book of the Bible that it says a great deal about the glory that God receives. In the description of the heavenly Liturgy, in which the redeemed by Christ participate "from every tribe and tongue and people and nation" (Rev 5:9), the basic theme is the doxology of the most holy God (Rev 4:5).

Let us analyze the theological data further. Creation was one more expression of the pre-eternal glory of God. But man rejected the absolute glory of God and, in seeking to create his own glory and in worshipping himself, he separated himself from the living God and provoked a cosmic catastrophe—the appearance of a new condition, death, in which the glory of the living God is overshadowed. The sin of men is a continual hindrance to the pouring out and manifestation of the glory. Amid the discord, the confusion and the disruption that human sin creates, the praise of God languishes.

However, God does not cease to reveal His glory to man (Exod 3:2–6; Isa 6:1f) and finally, "when the time had fully come" (Gal 4:4), He sends His Son, through whom He had "created" (πλάσσω) all things, in order to "recreate" (ἀναπλάσσω) "all things" (τά πάντα), so that "God is glorified in him" (John 13:32; cf. 17:1–10, where the work that the Son is given to accomplish is the glory of the Father on earth). His Incarnation is hailed with doxology, and is characterized by the angels as, "Glory to God in the highest, and on earth peace" (Luke 2:14). By His whole life and by His miracles He "manifested his glory" (John 2:11, cf. 11:4). By His transfiguration "He showed his glory to his disciples and they were able to receive it," as a "prelude to the future visible appearance of God in glory" (προοίμιον τῆς ἐν δόξῃ μελλούσης ὁρατῆς Θεοῦ θεοφανείας)[1] and as a sign of the transfiguration of man and of the whole creation.[2]

But above all, it is His Cross and His Resurrection that are the revelation of the glory of God. In Orthodox worship, the Cross is presented mainly as the symbol of victory and glory, and always closely connected with the Resurrection.[3] The distinction between the agony of the Cross and the glory of the Resurrection which is so common in the West is unusual in the

---

1. Grégoire Palamas, "In Defense of those who Practice Sacred Quietude, 1, 3." J. Meyendorff, ed., *Défense des Saints Hésychastes*, Louvain, 1959, p.193.

2. For the significance of the Feast of the Transfiguration in Orthodox spirituality and theology, see Andreas Theodorou, *The Essence of Orthodoxy*, Athens, 1961, p. 148ff. In the Vespers of this feast we sing, "Being transfigured, Thou didst free again the nature of Adam which had been dimmed—having transformed it into the glory and splendour of Thy divinity." (Τήν ἀμαυρωθεισαν τοῦ Ἀδάμ φύσιν μεταμορφωθείς ἀπαστράψαι πάλιν πεποίηκας, μεταστοιχειώσας αὐτήν εἰς τήν σήν τῆς θεότητος δόξαν τε καὶ λαμπρότητα.)

3. See the hymns sung at Matins on Sundays, where the praise of the Cross is interwoven with the praise of the Resurrection. See also the various expressions used to describe the Cross in Orthodox hymnology: "most illustrious" (ὑπερένδοξος), "life-bringing" (ζωηφόρος), "life-giving" (ζωοδώρητος), "Christ's divine glory," (Χριστοῦ θεία δόξα) "invincible trophy" (ἀήττητον τρόπαιον) and "the Cross, the thrice-blessed wood" (σταυρὸς ὁ τρισμακάριστος), "Thy Cross, O Lord, is life and Resurrection for Thy people" (ὁ Σταυρός σου, Κύριε, ζωή καὶ Ἀνάστασις ὑπάρχει τῷ λαῷ σου).

Orthodox Church; both are revelations and manifestations of the glory of God. In general, the Incarnation, the Passion, the Resurrection—the whole movement of the divine philanthropy in *kenosis*—are not only expressions of the divine love, but at the same time new manifestations of the glory of God. One could say that agape and glory are two aspects of the same thing: the life of God.

As He approaches His passion, the Lord says, "Father, glorify thy name. Then a voice came from heaven, 'I have glorified it, and I will glorify it again'" (John 12:28). Similarly, during the Last Supper, the ultimate revelation of the meaning of His mission begins with these words: "Now is the Son of man glorified, and in him God is glorified; if God is glorified in him, God will also glorify him in himself, and glorify him at once" (John 13:31–32). The same night, He begins His high-priestly prayer: "Father, the hour has come; glorify thy Son that the Son may glorify thee" (John 17:1). During the discourse at the Last Supper, two of the most central themes which recur with varying shades of meaning are *glory* and *love*—the two poles of redemption. In our Lord's prayer on this night, the glory of God is related to the perfect unity of the faithful in God: "The glory which thou hast given me I have given to them, that they may be one even as we are one" (John 17:22). And the "beholding" (θεωρία) of the glory of the Son is presented as the basic purpose of "being with Christ": "Father, I desire that they also, whom thou hast given me, may be with me where I am, to behold my glory which thou hast given me in thy love for me before the foundation of the world" (John 17:24).

The manifestation of the glory of God and the revelation, in *kenosis*, of the infinite love of God are linked together in the mystery of redemption. They constitute one single movement whose originator is God—a movement which makes a decisive change in the process of human history, which has been diverted towards separation and egocentricism, disregarding and obscuring the glory of God. In Christ, through His Incarnation, Crucifixion, Resurrection and Ascension, not only was human nature (τό ἀνθρώπινον) redeemed "from the bondage of decay," the universal order restored, which had been disrupted since the time of Adam, returning the entire universe once again to "cosmos" and the paradise it was created to be, thus fulfilling the will of the heavenly Father. Man, the king of the universe, the mind of nature, the sum of creation, began to participate by grace in the glorious life of the Holy Trinity—"he entered into glory."

With this event, history reaches its "goal" (τέλος). The "last day" (ἔσχατα), the great day for which God laid the foundations of the universe, has dawned; but this beginning of the eschatological era which leads to the final consummation does not mean the end of history. God's mission does not end, but receives its definite meaning and direction. Furthermore, the movement of history is now oriented to a definite goal. The Holy Spirit comes to continue and to complete the divine plan—with the participation of Christ's disciples, whom He authorized to proclaim redemption until the Second Coming when the glory of God will be fully revealed. So, in addition to a vertical movement from heaven to earth, the redemptive work of God now also has a dynamic horizontal direction on earth, though the participation of the Church.

B

THE ULTIMATE GOAL OF MISSION

Within the perspective that we have outlined, we can discern both the ultimate and the immediate purpose of our mission. Since Pentecost, when God's mission was revealed in its Trinitarian dimension, all who by faith and the mysteries "have beheld his (Christ's) glory, glory as of the only Son from the Father" (John 1:14) are incorporated into Himself and, having received the seal of the Holy Spirit, participate in this mission. "As the Father has sent me, even so send I you" (John 20:21; cf. 17:18). At this point, I should like to comment that it is not quite correct to say that "the mission is not ours, but Christ's."[4] It is also ours, inasmuch as we are incorporated into Christ: "All things are yours," St. Paul would say again in this case, "and you are Christ's; and Christ is God's" (1 Cor 3:22–23).

Since the Christian mission is incorporated into God's mission, the final goal of our mission surely cannot be different from His. And this purpose, as the Bible, especially the Epistles to the Ephesians and Colossians clarify, is the *"recapitulation (ἀνακεφαλαίωσις) of all things"* (Eph 1:10) *in Christ and our participation in the divine glory, the eternal, final glory of God.*

After His Resurrection and Ascension, Christ becomes "the rallying point of the restored unity, the reintegrating center of human and cosmic life."[5] "It is by him in his body and no more in Jerusalem or on Mount Gerizim, that the meeting of humanity with the Father will be realized in spirit and truth."[6] We could say that the centripetal tendency of the Old Testament, by which the nations are called to come to Jerusalem, and of which Professor Johannes Blauw speaks in the *Missionary Nature of the Church,*[7] is replaced not so much by the centrifugal movement of the disciples towards the nations, as by a new centripetal movement, whose center is Christ.

Furthermore, men are not called simply to know Christ, to gather around Him, or to submit to His will; they are called to participate in His glory. In the Old Testament, the ultimate goal of the eschatological period is the vision of God's glory, "They shall come and shall see my glory" (Isa 66:18); "They shall see the glory of the Lord" (Isa 35:2). The New Testament reveals that the call of God is to something more: to be "glorified with him" (συνδοξασθῆναι, Rom 8:17, cf. 1 Pet 5:10, Rom 9:23, 1 Cor

---

4. Lesslie Newbigin, *One Body, One Gospel, One World*, London, 1958, p. 28.

5. E. Roels, *God's Mission: The Epistle to the Ephesians in Mission Perspective*, Franeker, 1962, p. 67.

6. G. Khodre, "Church and Mission," *Porefthendes — Go Ye* 3 (1961), p. 40.

7. J. Blauw, *The Missionary Nature of the Church*, London, 1962, p. 40.

2:7). Our participation in this glory has already begun with our incorporation into Christ. "The glory which thou hast given me I have given to them" (John 17:22, cf. 1:14)—that is, the glory of the Sonship—and "those whom he justified he also glorified" (Rom 8:30; cf. 2 Cor 4:6).[8]

This glory will find its consummation in the Parousia. "When Christ who is our life appears, then you also will appear with him in glory" (Col 3:4; cf. 1:27, Phil 3:21, Rom 8:17, Matt 13:43, 2 Tim 2:10). Meanwhile, in spite of trials and suffering, we enjoy the pledge, the guarantee, of the glory—"The spirit of glory and of God rests upon you" (1 Pet 4:14)—and we walk in the "light of His glory"; "Beholding the glory of the Lord, [we] are being changed (μεταμορφούμεθα, being transformed) into his likeness from glory to glory" ("ἀπό δόξης εἰς δόξαν," [RSV—"from one degree of glory to another,"] 2 Cor 3:18). This phrase, "from glory to glory" *defines the process by which the faithful are sanctified during this present life, until the Second Coming.*[9]

---

8. St. Gregory Palamas, who speaks especially of the acquisition of God's glory by man, distinguishes clearly between the divine glory and the divine essence. In commenting on John 17:24 and 17:5, he writes: "So He gave to human nature the glory, but not the nature of deity. The nature of God is one thing; the glory of that nature, another—though they are inseparable from one another. And even though it is distinct from the divine nature it is not numbered among the things created in time; it is not so because of exceeding excellence, but it is united to the divine essence in an ineffable manner. And yet this glory, beyond and above all created beings, was not given only to Him who hypostatically was united with human nature, but also to his disciples, saying, 'The glory which thou hast given me I have given to them, that they may be one even as we are one, I in them and thou in me, that they may become perfectly one.' But He also wanted them to see it. This, then, is the glory by which we inwardly acquire and mainly see God." Palamas, *In Defense*, II, 3, 15, p. 419; cf. pp. 417, 645, 667, 705.

9. The prepositional usage of "from . . . to," which constantly recurs in the Pauline epistles (cf. "from faith to faith" ἔκ πίστεως εἰς πίστιν) expresses the idea of *having* and, at the same time, *not yet having*, which is the basic characteristic of New Testament piety. *Theologisches*

Moreover, it must be remembered that it is not only "human nature," but also the whole universe which participates in the restoration and finds its orientation again in glorifying God. The object of the phrases: "recapitulate" (ἀνακεφαλαιώσασθαι) (Eph 1:10), "who fills" (πληρουμένου) (Eph 1:23), and "reconcile" (ἀποκαταλλάξαι) (Col 1:20) is "all things" (τά πάντα). This is expressed emphatically in Orthodox hymnology: "The Cross sanctifies all things."[10] "All things have been illumined by Your Resurrection, O Lord, and Paradise is again opened, while all creation praises You and offers a daily hymn."[11] Elsewhere we have this joyful expression: "Now all things are filled with light, heaven and earth and regions below the earth; for all creation is celebrating the Resurrection of Christ, upon which it has been established."[12] "The condition of the world depends upon the condition of humanity, upon the relationship of man to God and to his brothers in Christ, who is the perfect Man; in the mystical life of the Church, through which Christ never ceases to be with us until the end of the world, the universe recovers its nature, becoming a new miracle and praise,"[13] as Olivier Clement has noted.

Again, however, we must remember this distinction: while the reconciliation of all things has already taken place "by the blood of his cross" (Col 1:20), yet creation waits with eager longing to be free "from its bondage to decay and obtain the glorious liberty of the children of God" (Rom 8:21). "Though this summing up and this reconciliation have taken place, the manifestation of this fact involves a historical process and awaits an ultimate eschatological fulfillment."[14] There is an eschatological

---

Wörterbuch zum Neuen Testament, ed. Gerhard Kittel, Stuttgart, 1950, vol. II, p. 255.

10. *Menaion*, Matins of September 14, Universal Elevation of the Holy Cross.

11. *Parakletike*, Vespers of Saturday, Mode Three.

12. *Pentekostarion*, Canon of the Resurrection, Ode 3.

13. O. Clément, *L'Église Orthodoxe*, Paris, 1961, p. 44.

14. E. Roels, *God's Mission*, p. 247.

aspect in every facet of the divine plan, and we find this eschatological dimension in the passages that speak of redemption.

The ultimate movement of history, however, goes beyond our incorporation into Christ and the "recapitulation" of all things in him. "When all things are subject to him, then the Son himself will also be subjected to him who put all things under him, *that God may be all in all*" (1 Cor 15:28). The subjection of all things in Christ is not the "end" (τέλος); it is connected with and oriented towards the ultimate and eternal glory of God. "And every tongue shall confess that Jesus Christ is Lord, to the glory of God the Father" (Phil 2:11). Finally, the last book of the Bible speaks clearly of "the holy city, Jerusalem," which has the glory of God (Rev 21:10), into which the glory of kings and "the glory and honour of the nations" are brought (Rev 21:24–26), and which is illuminated, not by the sun, but by "the glory of God." The absolute glory of God fills eternity and remains the ultimate goal of the universe; and into "his eternal glory in Christ" (1 Pet 5:10), God calls men by mission.

C
THE IMMEDIATE GOALS OF MISSION

The immediate goals of mission must surely follow the same line and direction as the ultimate goal; they must be the starting-point and preparation for that goal. In the march of the Christian mission, our eyes must constantly be fixed on the objective, on the "end" (τέλος), if mission is not to lose its ultimate direction. It is important to note that Orthodox spirituality is persistently oriented towards eschatological fulfillment, and has continually in view the "wholeness" (καθόλου) of the mystery of redemption. Its worship is preeminently doxological: "Heaven and earth are full of thy glory" (Holy Liturgy). This is its emblem.[15] The foretaste of the end, the transcending of time,

---

15. Every group of hymns ends and is linked together with, "Glory be to the Father and to the Son and to the Holy Spirit; both now and ever, and unto ages of ages, Amen." This is the most frequently recur-

the life in eternity, which is taking place through the mysteries in the Church, give the Orthodox theologian a new understanding. He does not see the "recapitulation" as something that will take place at a given moment in the future; he knows, he feels that it is already taking place. Mission is the participation of the faithful in the process of this "recapitulation." The period after the Ascension and Pentecost is not merely a time, but is "the time of the Lord"—not so much "time in years" ($\chi\rho\delta\nu\sigma\varsigma$) as "the season of the Lord" ($\kappa\alpha\iota\rho\delta\varsigma\ K\nu\rho\iota\sigma\nu$) in which the divine plan is fulfilled.

1. *Preaching the Gospel is a basic condition for this fulfillment, and is consequently the immediate objective and goal of mission.* The incorporation and participation of men in God's promises begins with the Gospel: "The nations ($\tau\dot{\alpha}\ \ddot{\epsilon}\theta\nu\eta$, nations, not *gentiles*, R.V.) are fellow heirs, members of the same body ($\sigma\dot{\nu}\sigma\sigma\omega\mu\sigma\iota$), and partakers of the promise in Christ Jesus through the gospel" (Eph 3:6), of which every missionary becomes a "$\delta\iota\dot{\alpha}\kappa\sigma\nu\sigma\varsigma$ (servant, rather than minister) according to the gift of God's grace" (Eph 3:7); ". . . the riches of the glory of this mystery, which is Christ in you, the hope of glory" (Col 1:27); must be made known to "the whole creation" (Mark 16:15). We should note particularly that the "service" ($\delta\iota\alpha\kappa\sigma\nu\iota\alpha$) of "the gospel of glory" constitutes, and already is participation in the glory of God, as it is analyzed in the third chapter of Second Corinthians, where it is compared with the service of Moses (2 Cor 3:5–11). [. . .]

So mission is not a question of proclaiming some ethical truths or principles, but the beginning of the transfiguration inaugurated by the "light of the gospel of the glory of Christ" (2

---

ring phrase in all Orthodox worship. The Holy Liturgy is a continuous series of exclamations of praise to the Holy Trinity, and prayers are nearly always concluded with phrases such as, "For to Thee belong all glory, honour and worship . . .", "For Yours is the dominion, and the kingdom and the power and the glory . . .", "For blessed and glorified is Your all-honorable and majestic name . . .", ". . . and to You be given the glory"—these and others are repeated as conclusions to the prayers of virtually all the services of worship.

Cor 4:4; cf. 4:6), through which we are called "so that [we] may obtain the glory of our Lord Jesus Christ" (2 Thess 2:14). This transfiguration is taking place "from glory to glory," so that it may end in "conformation" (συμμόρφωσις) to the image of the Son in His eternal glory (Rom 8:29). Accordingly, "the goal of preaching is," not only the gathering of the community to await the expected Lord in glory,[16] it is more of "a doxological movement," *an invitation to participation in the life of the glorified Lord, a mystical sharing in His glory, and a communion in the glory that is to be revealed at the Second Coming* (cf. Rom 8:18; 1 Pet 5:1).

This transformation, however, is not accomplished merely as a result of hearing the Gospel. In the first chapter of Ephesians, we read: "In him you also, who have heard the word of truth, the gospel of your salvation, and have believed in him, were sealed with the promised Holy Spirit" (Eph 1:13). The successive stages are "to hear," "to believe" and "to be sealed with the Spirit." Without this seal, salvation does not become personal. This is the "guarantee of our inheritance until we acquire possession of it, to the praise of his glory" (Eph 1:14). By His work of redemption, Christ redeemed human nature (τό ἀνθρώπινον); but personal participation in this salvation, the sanctification of human persons, is effected by the Holy Spirit in Christ, by "communion" with Christ, and the seal of the Spirit. It is therefore vital that after the preaching of the word of God, that those who accept the Gospel should become "a community of faith," "the Church." The basis is the creation of a new being through the presence of the Holy Spirit;[17] and this, in Orthodox thinking, is realized through the sacraments. It is "the sacraments" which "constitute the Church. They alone enable the Christian community to transcend human dimensions and make it into the Church."[18]

---

16. W. Freytag, "*Von Sinn der Weltmission,*" *Reden und Aufsätze,* eds. J. Hermelink and H. J. Margul, München, 1961, vol. II, p. 217.

17. Lesslie Newbigin, *One Body,* p. 20.

18. G. Florovsky, "L'Église, sa nature et sa tâche," *L'Église universelle dans le dessein de Dieu,* Neuchâtel, Paris, 1949, p. 65.

The Lord stressed that, "He who believes and is baptized will be saved" (Mark 16:16). Saint Paul, before assuring the Corinthians that ". . . you are the body of Christ" (1 Cor 12:27), had emphatically stated, "For by one Spirit we were all baptized into one body—Jews or Greeks, slaves or free—and all were made to drink of one Spirit" (1 Cor 12:13; cf. Rom 6:3, Eph 4:5; "You were buried with him (συνταφέντες) in baptism . . ." Col 2:12). Further, the Lord clearly stressed that only those who eat His flesh and drink His blood will have "life" in them, "eternal life"; they will abide in him, and He in them (John 6:53–58). The sacrament of the Holy Eucharist remains the center, the rallying point of unity in Christ, "until he comes" (1 Cor 11:26). This creates the visible unity of the Church: "Because there is one bread, we who are many are one body" (1 Cor 10:17). By her whole life, the Church "makes real—in a hidden way, but real—the glorious Body of Christ." As Olivier Clément says, "The Body of Christ, the Church, upon which the fullness of the Holy Spirit never ceases to rest, thus appears (through a legitimate extension of the dogma of Chalcedon) as a divine-human, (*theandric*) reality. It is not so much, in the proper sense, a continuous Incarnation; as it is the place where a perpetual "movement" of Ascension and Pentecost unites heaven and earth through the "veil" of the sacraments, the place where the Holy Spirit manifests the presence and the flesh of the glorified Savior."[19]

2. *The establishment of the "local Church"* which, through the mysteries and through her whole life, will participate in the praise and the life of the "one, holy, catholic and apostolic Church" whose head is Christ (Eph 1:22, 4:15, 5:23, Col 1:18), is surely the basic goal of mission, according to Orthodox tradition and theology. In each country, the Church is called to glorify God with her own voice. That means that in missionary work there must be a sincere respect for the identity of every nation; an investigation into the past of each particular people, of how God "allowed all the nations to walk in their own ways;

---

19. O. Clément, *L'Église Orthodoxe*, p. 65.

yet he did not leave himself without witness" (Acts 14:16–17). This means, we must endeavor not only to "adapt," but to "incarnate" the logos of God into the language and customs of the country; and the sanctification of the people's characteristics, so that they may become truly themselves, develop their own voice and add their own contribution to the common doxological hymn—always in harmony with the praise of the whole Church. Orthodox missionaries are always opposed to any monolithic, administrative concept of the Church, and for them the unifying factor in the ever-expanding Church has been the common doxology, multilingual in form, but one in the Spirit of the living God.[20] In the unity of the Church there is diversity in the Holy Spirit. This is the ecclesiological meaning of Pentecost. "They were all together in one place . . . there appeared to them tongues as of fire, distributed and resting on each one of them" (Acts 2:1–3).[21] [. . .]

It is within the Church that the incorporation of men "into Christ" is realized, that the glory of God is (ἀποκαλύπτεται) re-

---

20. See Anastasios Yannoulatos, «Βυζάντιον, Ἔργον Εὐαγγελισμοῦ», στή Θρησκευτική καί Ἠθική Ἐγκυκλοπαιδεία, Ἀθῆναι, 1964, Vol. 4, pp. 19–59. (Byzantium, Work of Evangelization) Idem, "The Missionary Activity of the Orthodox Church," in *Syndesmos VI Assembly, Finland, 1964*, Athens, 1964, pp. 36–52. F. Dvornik, *Les slaves, Byzance et Rome, au IXe siècle*, Paris, 1929. J. Glazik, *Die russisch-orthodoxe Heidenmission seit Peter dem Grossen*, Münster, 1954. N. Struve, "Orthodox Mission, Past and Present," *St. Vladimir's Theological Quarterly* 1(1963).

21. We shall not discuss here in detail the relation of Church and mission—whether mission is only an instrument of the Church or a goal, and *vice versa*. We would merely recall that the designations of the Church in the Letter to the Ephesians, "body," "bride," "dwelling," "holy temple" always refer to the Church as the objective or goal, and never as an instrument of mission (see E. Roels, *God's Mission*, p. 152). The Church is the recipient of all the blessings of Christ. The Church, "which is his body, the fullness of him who fills all in all" (Eph 1:23), fulfills and completes Christ. "He is the head, we are the body," writes St. John Chrysostom. "Is it possible for any interval to exist between the body and the head?" (*Homily 8 on First Corinthians*, Greek Fathers, 61, p. 72). The smallest interval would mean death.

vealed to us, and that the right doxology resounds. "A worshipping liturgical community is not only the image of the realized communion between God and man and of union of the human race in one Body in front of God, without any exception or distinction of individuals; it is not only the bulwark where the principalities of this world are weak and find no place. It is, basically, the missionary outcry of the Church triumphant to the whole world and the doxological announcement of the Kingdom, which is present and which is to come."[22] "To him the glory (ἡ δόξα, meaning *the* glory, not *be* glory) in the Church and in Jesus Christ to all generations, forever and ever. Amen" (Eph 3:21).

3. Incorporation into Christ must not, of course, be understood as an inner, mystical flight from the world, which finds its expression in the setting up of closed congregations, but as the starting-point for an active participation in the work of God, which is directed towards the recapitulation of all things in Christ, to the "glory of the Father." *The doxology of the redeemed must also echo beyond the limits of their own community and fill the universe.* Our Lord described His disciples as "light," "salt," and "leaven"; and we need to remember that light, salt and leaven all have a role and a meaning which is mainly concerned with the wider whole, which they serve. If

---

22. N. Nissiotis, "The Ecclesiological Foundation of Mission," in *Porefthendes—Go Ye* 5 (1963), p. 7. It is worth noting that the Russian Orthodox mission to the interior of northern Asia began as a worshipping, doxological march by Russian monks. They retreated into the forests for religious exercises and in search of a mystical vision and doxology of the holy God. They settled among the various wild tribes and enlightened the surrounding heathen. Later, from St. Stephen of Perm (1340–1396) to the great missionary to Japan, Nikolai Kasatkin (1836–1912), the doxology of God by the community of the faithful was the lung of the Orthodox mission which gave special power to its voice. See E. Smirnoff, *A Short Account of the Historical Development and Present Position of the Russian Orthodox Mission*, London, 1903, and footnote 20 of this present study.

leaven is left on its own, it will spoil and turn sour. Our inner union with Christ compels us to be as actively present in the history and development of society as our Lord, who is working in history and is also the Lord of history. We must have a positive attitude, not characterized by a superficial enthusiasm to impose the Kingdom of God by social and political means, or by anxiety and pessimism at the prevalence of sin and faithlessness. Redemption has already been achieved "in Christ"; the powers of darkness are decisively surrounded and the enemy, without doubt, has been totally defeated, but in desperation he still casts his last arrows; there are still the wounded, the dead, and the gloom of battle.[23]

We are still in the transitional period of "not yet." "It does not yet appear what we shall be" (1 John 3:2). We live in anticipation of the time "when his glory is revealed," knowing that they who "share Christ's sufferings . . . may also rejoice and be glad" (1 Pet 4:13), obtaining "the unfading crown of glory" (5:4). This anticipation, however, has nothing to do with the social passivity which characterizes the pietistic tendencies of some, who face the world with timidity and escape into the vision of the last days. It is a dynamic anticipation, marked by positive action and a positive attitude, derived from the certainty that, in the divine condescension, this eschatological fulfillment requires our participation. "And this gospel of the kingdom will be preached throughout the whole world, as a testimony to all nations; and then the end will come" (Matt 24:14). Our anticipation is also full of courage and peace, in the face of every present problem: "For whatever is born of God overcomes the world" (1 John 5:4). We know that, although we still live in the period of "not yet," "we are God's children now" (1 John 3:2). In the world, therefore, we move with the grace and freedom of the sons of God, just as the sons of noblemen behave and move on their fathers' property. "Whether . . . the world or life or death or *the present or the*

---

23. See W. Freytag, *Von Sinn der Weltmission*, p. 213.

future, all are yours; and you are Christ's; and Christ is God's" (1 Cor 3:22–23).

Mission is to cooperate "in the Holy Spirit" for the sanctification of all things, for their recapitulation in Christ and for "access" to the Father (Eph 2:18). We become "God's co-workers" in a broader sense, participating in the development of the unity, peace and love towards which God's plan is directed: "As children of God through grace," incorporated into Christ "for whom and by whom all things exist" (Heb 2:10), and united with him who not only "recreated," but "created" "all things." Christians study and share in the works of their Father and their first-born brother, "in the Holy Spirit." These are not only works of salvation, but also of creation. With joyful praise, they develop the abilities they have received from Him (mind, imagination, a sense of beauty), in the certainty that: "For from him and through him and to him are all things. To him be glory forever. Amen" (Rom 11:36).

In this perspective, we can include as an indirect goal of the Christian mission, everything that may help a people (and man in general) to develop all the possibilities received from God and to become truly themselves; including for example: education, works of civilization and social progress. These aims, of course, are second in importance and urgency to the preceding ones; nevertheless they have their own value and distinctive tones to add to the doxological symphony that the universe is called to offer to God.[24]

---

24. The intimate relationship between man and nature is very perceptible in Orthodox worship, and may be seen from its use of many natural elements and from the number of prayers made for various material objects; for instance, "the fields," "the vineyards," "the sanctification of the water," "the sick animals," "the silkworms," "the blessing of the flock," and so forth. The sense of creation and recreation of God permeates these prayers. Their starting-point as a rule is the fact that God is "the builder and creator of all things" (Prayer at the laying of foundations); "the One who created heaven and earth, and all things in them, who ornamented both with ineffable beauty for the glory (doxology) of His glorified name" (Prayer for the silk-

The first Christians brought the fruit of their labor to God (which were the products harvested from nature) not only for sanctification, but also as an offering of sacrifice and praise to God. Today we are also called to offer our fruits—from nature, of our mind and labor—as an offering of praise to Him who is the *Alpha* and *Omega*, by whose will all things "existed and were created" (Rev 4:11).

It should be underlined finally that, in the Orthodox understanding, the value of a work depends upon the extent to which it is done for the "glory of God." This is the criterion: it is the intention that matters. "Though a work be very humble," wrote St. Nicodemus the Hagiorite, "though it be very small" (and we would add, though it be entirely indifferent to mission), "yet if it is done for the purpose of pleasing God and for His glory, it is worth infinitely more than many lofty works, glorious—and magnificent—which are done without this intention."

Finally, Christians, upon whom "the spirit of glory and of God rests" (1 Pet 4:14) and who are "partakers in the glory that is to be revealed" (5:1), are called to proclaim redemption in Christ, glorifying him in every act and work (Matt 5:16, 1 Cor 6:20, 1 Pet 4:11). Moreover, beholding the face of the risen Lord and His glorious Presence, and being transfigured "from glory

---

worm). All these prayers conclude with the assertion that He is the One who "governs," "preserves," "blesses and sanctifies all things" (τά σύμπαντα), to whom by all means "we offer glory." Often the request for the sanctification of nature is interwoven with a reference to spiritual truths. For instance, in the prayer for the harvest of the vineyards, we say: "Thou should be called the Vine . . . grant that He who invited us may be a participant of the true Vine."

Everything is a *"sign"* related to the entire perspective of the mystery of redemption. The atmosphere of all our worship is filled with the certainty that the doxology of the redeemed is nothing other than our participation in the doxology of the universe. "Accept, O Lord, our doxology, which we offer according to our power, with all Thy creatures," we repeat every morning "for before Thee every knee bows, in heaven and on earth and under the earth, and every breath and creature praises Thine incomprehensible glory" (11th prayer of Matins).

to glory" (2 Cor 3:18), they are called to live, to be themselves—ontologically—"for the praise of his (God's) glory" (Eph 1:12).

D
THE MOTIVE OF MISSION

The question of the motive of mission can be studied from several angles: Love for God and men, obedience to the Great Command of the Lord (Matt 28:19), desire for the salvation of souls, longing for God's glory. All these, surely, are serious motives; and the last especially is in perfect harmony with those that have been developed already. However, we think that the real motive of mission, for both the individual and the Church, is something deeper. It is not simply obedience, duty or altruism. It is an *inner necessity*. "For necessity is laid upon me" said St. Paul. "Woe to me if I do not preach the gospel" (1 Cor 9:16). All other motives are aspects of this need, derivative motivations. Mission is an inner necessity (a) for the faithful and (b) for the Church. If they refuse it, they not only omit a duty, they deny themselves.

1. The Christian who is "incorporated" into Christ and who really lives in Him cannot think, feel, will, act or see the world in a different way from Christ. It is impossible for him to limit his horizon to his parish, his town, his nation, the so-called "Christian" world; it is impossible for him to be indifferent to the millions who still live as "strangers to the covenants of promise, having no hope and without God in the world" (Eph 2:12). He knows that God "made of one (blood) every nation of men" (Acts 17:26) and "desires all men to be saved and to come to the knowledge of the truth" (1 Tim 2:4). He knows also that: "The times of ignorance God overlooked, now (ταυῦν, now, without *but*, R.V.) he commands all men everywhere to repent" (Acts 17:30).

It is the sense of the importance of this "now" that urges on the missionary. It is this "all men everywhere" that compels him to see his duty in its worldwide dimension. This way of thinking has nothing to do with the cosmopolitan mind, which leads men to seek adventures outside their fatherland and their own culture, nor with a romantic disposition, which leads them to ignore the needs of the fatherland, the crisis of the "Christian nations." Living "in him" who is the Ὤν, the absolute reality, the missionary always remains realistic. He knows that every-where there is a mission field. Nevertheless, he can see that in some countries the needs are more urgent and "the workers"—not even—"few" and that there are territories in which the Gospel has never—not even once—been preached. "But how are men to call upon him in whom they have not believed? And how are they to believe in him of whom they have never heard? And how are they to hear without a preacher? And how can men preach unless they are sent?" (Rom 10:14-15). These four "how's" inflame his mind and heart.

The missionary believes that for every human being there is no treasure more precious than the truth that was revealed by the word of God. Therefore, he feels that the people who suffer injustice most in our time are those who have been deprived of the Word, not because they themselves refuse to listen, but for the simple reason that those who have known it for centuries have not been interested in passing it on. He further feels that his "honour," "justice," "faith" and "love" cannot be genuine, if he does not try to do something practical—the best he can—in this direction. Like St. Paul, he feels that he is "under obliga-tion" (ὀφειλέτης, debtor) "both to Greeks and to barbarians, both to the wise and to the foolish" (Rom 1:14). He cannot look upon the Cross by which the Lord "raised with Himself Adam and all of fallen nature,"[25] the Cross upon which He "stretched out his hands and embraced nations and peoples,"[26] as the Orthodox hymns constantly affirm, and at the same time simply confine

---

25. *Menaion*, Vespers, Universal Elevation of the Holy Cross, September 14.

26. *Parakletike*, Ode 1, Matins of Friday, Tone Two.

himself to praising the Crucified One and asking for His mercy, without sharing the universal purpose of this sacrifice and its cosmic meaning (see Col 1:20).[27]

When he contemplates the mystery of Christ revealed to and through "his holy apostles and prophets by the Spirit" (Eph 3:5); so that the nations are "members of the same body, and partakers of the promise in Christ" (εἶναι τά ἔθνη σύσσωμα καί συμμέτοχα) (Eph 3:6); when he sees the glory of God, though it be "in a mirror dimly" (1 Cor 13:12), he feels the need to cry everywhere, "Behold! Come!" These feelings, as well as the universal and cosmic meaning of the Passion and the Resurrection, are beautifully expressed in the following hymn, which is sung during Sunday Matins:

> O come, all nations; Learn the power of the awful mystery That Christ our Saviour, the Word in the beginning, Was crucified for us and willingly buried; Resurrected from the dead, To save the whole universe O let us worship Him![28]

---

27. The image of man and the universe being embraced on the Cross is very often repeated in Orthodox hymnology. For example, "Thy palms outstretched, O Merciful, Thou gatherest the nations that were far from Thee, in order to glorify Thy great goodness" (*Menaion, Kathisma* hymn of Matins, September 14th. Cf. *Parakletike,* Ode 1, Matins of Friday, Tone Eight and the *Aposticha* hymns for Lauds, Matins of Friday, Tone Seven). "Upon the Cross Thou didst extend Thine immaculate hands, gathering all the nations proclaiming: O Lord, glory to Thee!" (*Parakletike, Kathisma* Matins of Friday, Tone Two) and "Thy Cross today is lifted up and the world is sanctified; for Thou, who are sealed with the Father and the Holy Spirit, didst stretch out on it Thy hands; Thou didst attract the whole world to Thy full knowledge, O Christ" (Matins, September 14 Feast of the Holy Cross).

28. *Parakletike,* Lauds of Sunday Matins, Tone Three. Cf. Also the Sticheron hymn of Sunday Matins, Tone Two: "Nations and peoples must come to praise Christ our God, Who willingly endured the Cross for us, and the three days in Hades; and they must worship His Resurrection from the dead, through which all the ends of the earth have been enlightened."

Every member of the faithful, who consciously lives the spiritual life and thinks conscientiously, feels that the praise and doxology which he offers to God is deficient as long as there are still so many races and tongues that do not participate. He knows that these missing voices of the world must also be added; so that they may harmonize with the existing voices, and the whole doxology may acquire its melodic beauty and depth. For this reason, the missionary cannot keep quiet while there are still so many languages that are silent in the praise of God, and while the Lord does not receive the glory due to Him from and by the whole creation.

Lastly, when the missionary contemplates the final end, the goal of history, the "recapitulation of all things in Christ," "to the glory of God the Father," he feels a spontaneous, *inner necessity* to tune the plan of his life to God's plan, to orient himself to it, praising the Lord and being a living doxology to Him. With eyes fixed upon the eschaton, Orthodoxy maintains it vigor and this has provided a particular power to mission.

For all these reasons, we believe the participation in mission of those who think and live theologically is not simply a matter of "duty," of "practicality," a matter of "ethic"; it is more interior, more profound, an existential command. Incorporated into Christ and living in the Spirit, the missionary can think and live in no other way.

2. If this inner necessity is true for the believer, it is far more valid for the Church, which is not only "incorporated into," but actually "is" the Body of Christ, "the fullness of him who fills all in all" (Eph 1:23). A Church without mission is a contradiction in terms. The Church has been "anointed," "has been sent," as Christ was (Luke 4:18; cf. John 17:18), to continue His work: That is, "to proclaim release to the captives and the recovery of sight to the blind, to set at liberty those who are oppressed, to proclaim the acceptable year of the Lord" (Luke 4:18–19). Moreover, the Church has been sent to fulfill this work. We can see this meaning of fulfillment in the word πλήρωμα (Eph 1:23). She

is also catholic[29] (from the adjective καθολικός, which refers to wholeness, in opposition to everything sectional or partial), and this definition, too, with its theological, topical and metaphysical meaning, does not cease to stress the missionary dimension of the Church. [. . .]

Consequently, if the Church is indifferent to the apostolic work with which she has been "entrusted," the salvation of the world, she denies herself, contradicts herself and her essence, and is a traitor in the warfare in which she is engaged. A "static Church" which lacks a vision and a constant endeavor to proclaim the Gospel to the whole world could hardly be recognized as the "one, holy, catholic and apostolic Church" to whom the Lord entrusted the continuation of His work. She could not easily assert that she glorifies God and constitutes a "sign" of His glorious coming. The final cry of the Bible, "Come, Lord Jesus" (Rev 22:20), which resounds through Christian worship, cannot be separated from the eschatological vision; and that vision cannot be separated from the prophetic certainty that the Gospel "must first be preached to all nations, and then the end will come" (Matt 24:14).

There is one more point that may be noted from our liturgical life. The prayers, with which the faithful at every Divine Liturgy are called to pray "for the catechumen," "that the Lord may be merciful to them, teach them the word of truth, reveal to them the Gospel of righteousness, and unite them to His holy, catholic and apostolic Church,"[30] is not merely a relic of the life of the early Church, but indeed a constant reminder of the real structure of the Christian community in worship. Every local Church, in order to be organically connected with the one apostolic Church and faithful to her "catholic" tradition, worshipping in the Orthodox manner, is obligated to seek con-

---

29. John Karmiris, *The Orthodox Doctrinal Teaching on the Church,* Athens, 1964, p. 25ff.

30. "Prayer for the Catechumens," *Divine Liturgy of St. John Chrysostom.* Cf. *Liturgy of St. Basil the Great and Liturgy of the Pre-sanctified Gifts.*

stantly the extension of the doxology of God. She is obligated to have an uninterrupted flow of catechumens and to be praying: "That they too, together with us (the faithful), may glorify the most-honorable and majestic name"[31] of God. The strong desire to extend the doxology of God, the dynamic tendency of worship, is a basic element of Orthodoxy. The presence of these prayers in the Holy Liturgy is a continual remainder of the missionary dimension of every worshipping community, and calls for the revision of every static concept of Orthodox worship.

Finally, the following points should be stressed, especially for the Orthodox Church whose life and worship is centered in the Resurrection. The broadening of the horizon of the world-wide mission is directly related to the Lord's triumph through His Resurrection. The fact that He has received "All authority in heaven and on earth" (Matt 28:18) has to be proclaimed "to all nations" (28:19). It is, therefore, a complete contradiction then, on the one hand to sing and live the Resurrection so intensely, and on the other, to live in the days before the Resurrection; that is to confine our activity and interest to Israel—even to the new Israel of grace—without thinking of our imperative duty to proclaim the triumph of Christ "to the whole creation" (Mark 16:15).

The more one considers the mystery of the Church, her life, her worship and her tradition, the more one is persuaded that *mission—that is, the transmission of the word and the grace of God, and the manifestation of God's glory which "in Christ," is revealed and anticipated, "to the end of the earth" and to the end of time—is for her a profound inner necessity.*

When, in this perspective, we make a theological study of the purpose and motive of mission, it becomes clear that the Church's call to mission must be preached not only, or not so much, in terms of external reasons (such as the existence of still uncivilized tribes, the spread of hunger, the expansion of illit-

---

31. See footnote 30 above.

eracy), but precisely as a *call to repentance*, a call to rediscover the true meaning of the Church; for living out the mystery of our incorporation into Christ; for a true orientation in the face of both the immediate and the ultimate future, and for the right (ὀρθόδοξη) doxology of God.

4

THEOLOGY, MISSION AND PASTORAL CARE

(1976)

• «Θεολογία, Ἱεραποστολή καί Ποιμαντική», *Πρακτικά τοῦ Δευτέρου Συνεδρίου Ὀρθοδόξου Θεολογίας, Ἀθήνα, 12-19 Αὐγούστου 1976*, Ἀθήνα 1980, σ. 291–309. • "Theology, Mission and Pastoral Care," *Procès-verbaux du Deuxième Congrès de Théologie Orthodoxe à Athènes, 12-19 Août 1976, Athènes*, 1978, pp. 292–311. • Reprinted in *The Greek Orthodox Theological Review* 22 (1977), pp. 157–180. • French: "Théologie, Mission et Pastorale," reprinted from *Proche Orient Chrétien* 26 (1979). • *Ἱεραποστολή στά ἴχνη τοῦ Χριστοῦ. Θεολογικές μελέτες καί ὁμιλίες*, Ἀθήνα 2007.

Theological thought gives expression and direction to the practices of the Church. Whereas direct contact with life and specific problems that are of immediate concern to the Church militant constantly bring to light new matters for, and inspire new forms of, theological investigation. Although this would seem to be theoretically self-evident, it is not always clearly understandable in day to day reality. In many local Orthodox Churches there appears to be a veiled separation between ecclesial life and theological thought. Many theologians pursue their work without reference to the Church, while even more clergy hasten to exert their influence in every direction without adequate theological thought or even a suspicion that the problems with which they are dealing are not as simple as they might seem, but have theological correlations and interdependence. It is now time that we cease stopping short of the simple diagnosis of lack of coordination, theological research, and pastoral missionary activity. It is imperative that we move on rapidly to achieving, not only their harmonious, but also fruitful cooperation.

Furthermore, with regard to academic theology, its traditional division into four distinct fields (those of systematic, hermeneutical, historical and pastoral theology), as well as various specialized courses, tends to create the impression that missionary and pastoral work fall into exclusive domains and are the subject of only certain university departments. Whereas, in the Orthodox Tradition, the whole of theology is, and must be, oriented towards the expression of the self-awareness of the Church for a perfect fulfillment of her mission in the world.

The subject of this introduction is not Orthodox missionary and pastoral work in general, but an attempt to explore the main theme of our conference and more especially its second section: "Theology as a Manifestation of the Presence of the Church in the World," as it is related to missionary and pastoral work. I shall endeavor to emphasize, some crucial aspects of the problem, and to stress their practical implications, with a view to: (a) Clarification of the significance and the unity of missionary and pastoral care for the Church in today's context. (b) Pinpointing certain sensitive and painful areas in the reality of the life of the Church today. (c) Stressing the basic characteristics of Orthodox presence and witness.

A

SIGNIFICANCE AND UNITY
OF MISSIONARY AND PASTORAL
WORK IN TODAY'S CIRCUMSTANCES

1. In the past, the boundaries between "Christian" and "non-Christian" worlds were relatively well-defined. Hence, we had the classical distinction between missionary work and pastoral care. The former referred to the non-Christian world and involved preaching and conversion to the faith, whereas the latter was concerned with the spiritual edification and sanctification of the members of the Church.

In our times, however, these simple patterns have been profoundly altered by new factors. The boundaries between "Christian" and "non-Christian" can no longer be represented by lines drawn across geographical maps. Moreover, the boundaries between belief and unbelief are no longer as permanent and steadfast as they once seemed. Indeed, they even cut across the midst of so-called "Christian" communities, in which among these Christian masses there exists, indifference and unbelief. Often boundaries even are found within the very heart of men and their personal history and development. Many "believers" of yesterday, waver today between belief and unbelief; while other "unbelievers" struggle on in hope, wavering between unbelief and belief. The cry of the possessed child's father expressed in the Gospel: "I believe, help my unbelief!" (Mark 9:24), is typical of the cry of many Christians today.

The religious morphology of the modern world is very complex. From the Christian viewpoint we can distinguish diagrammatically a number of layers:

(a) The multitudes that have long belonged to other religious systems and whose cultures and consciences have been influenced by them. These are the hundreds of millions of people who live by the standards dictated by the great religions, such as Hinduism, Buddhism, Islam, Shintoism, and so forth. This composite body displays a number of important phenomenological differences, particularly between monotheistic, prophetic religions, and the great Hindu systems, or the expressions of a primitive religiosity.

(b) The vast masses that reject all religious experience as something unnecessary, useless or harmful. Here again we can easily distinguish the more fanatical and aggressive groups, who hate and fight every form of religious expression, from the larger masses who simply despise religion as obscurantism and even anachronistic.

(c) A particularly numerous strata is made up of those who have become uprooted from their old religious beliefs and live within the rhythm of the modern technological era with ever lessening reference to, or relationship with, religious ideas. They do not despise them, they simply have no interest in them; they do not consider them an indispensable, essential foundation of life. This group also includes a variety of those holding attitudes dependent on the origin, form, and intensity of their existing religious subconscious. A particularly large group among this category includes the religiously indifferent, those with Christian roots and family backgrounds. They are not seriously interested in any other faith. They are suspended between a little faith and unbelief, still enjoying some Christian traditions as folklore.

(d) Finally, and not to be overlooked, are a group of people who have accepted the Gospel and are struggling, with frequent failures, to live by it. The more general crisis and confusion of the modern world extends into the Christian realm, giving rise to a peculiar "faithlessness of the faithful." [. . .]

The Church is "under obligation" (Rom 1:14) to all these categories of people "to testify to the gospel of the grace of God" (Acts 20:24). The special problems which are connected with the dialectic relationship between faith and lack of faith in each of the above cases call, of course, for different frames of reference, methods and approaches in regard to missionary activity. A basic chapter for theological development is the correct understanding of man's universal religious experience, as well as the interpretation of the great religious systems which still influence nearly half of humankind. The attitude adopted by Christians towards these religious systems has varied greatly, ranging from the entirely positive to the categorically negative. To most Orthodox, religions represent humankind's persistent search for the highest reality and the profound mystery of his existence.[1] They bear some traces of

---

1. For a historical outline and detailed bibliography see: A. Yannoulatos, *Various Christian Approaches to the Other Religions: A Historical Outline*, Athens, 1971. There is a more general theological consideration of the matter by the same author and in light of present day discussions in "Towards World Community," paper presented at the *Multilateral Dialogue between Men of Living Faiths*, held in Colombo, Sri Lanka, 17-24 April, 1974, *Ecumenical Review* 16 (1974), pp. 619-36; see also the augmented edition of "Towards a Koinonia Agapes" in S. K. Samartha, ed., *Towards World Community; The Colombo Papers*, Geneva, 1975, pp. 45-64. See also my book: *Facing the World. Orthodox Christian Essays on Global Concerns*, New York-Geneva, 2003. For other characteristic Orthodox perspectives see: L. Philippidis, *Religionsgeschichte als Heilsgeschichte in der Weltgeschichte*, Athens, 1953. *Idem, Contempo-*

God's manifestation *(theophany)*, but also many signs of deterioration and demonic influences. They are, to my mind, akin to accumulators of vital experience, intuitions, and sublime inspirations that have been charged with the rays of the Sun of Righteousness. They have helped many people to have a little light, or at least brought a reflection of the light on their path.

But the most crucial subject for modern Orthodox theology is the phenomenon of secularization, the absorption of man by the enticements of "the world" and of "this age." Egocentric anthropocentrism, by ignoring all transcendental values, draws into its whirlpool the universal thought and consciousness, the criteria for evaluating life, and all social, political, economic and cultural structures.[2] This is a new type of "heresy" which radically alters the whole meaning of the world and of man, and which requires thorough analysis, evaluation and confrontation.

---

rary Religious Movements for the Unity of All Humanity, Athens, 1966. N. Arseniev, *Revelation of Life Eternal*, New York, 1965, primarily pp. 27-59. G. Khodre, "Christianity in a Pluralistic World—The Economy of the Holy Spirit," *Ecumenical Review* 23 (1971), pp. 118-128. E. Vasiliescu, "La théologie orthodoxe roumaine dans ses rapports avec les religions non-chrétiennes," *De la théologie Orthodoxe roumaine des origines à nos jours*, ed. par l'Église Orthodoxe Roumaine, Bucharest, 1974, pp. 376-391.

2. For an analysis of the meaning and character of secularization from a Western perspective see among others: Harvey Cox, *The Secular City—Secularization and Urbanization in Theological Perspective*, New York, 1965; Symposia: *Secularization and the Protestant Prospect*. J. F. Childress and D. B. Harned, eds., Philadelphia, 1970. J. Morel, Hrsg., *Glaube und Säkularisierung*, Innsbruck-Wien-München, 1972. For Orthodox essays on various aspects of the issue see: S. Agourides, *The Gospel and the Modern World*, Thessaloniki, 1970. K. Papapetrou, "Die Säkularisation und die Orthodoxe Kirche Griechenlands," *Kyrios* 3 (1963), pp. 193-205. O. Clément, *Theology after the 'Death of God.'* Essay for a Response of the Orthodox Church to Contemporary Atheism, Athens, 1973 (in Greek).

2. Orthodox theological thought in recent years has pointed out and underlined some *basic truths regarding the duty of Christians to bear witness* "to all nations,"[3] specifically that:

(a) Mission belongs to and is an essential part of the nature of the Church. It is the offering of salvation to humankind, the continuous transfusion of a new quality of life into human society, "that they may have life, and have it abundantly" (John 10:10).

(b) The Gospel is addressed to all peoples, and therefore the work of the Church remains incomplete as long as it is

---

3. See articles published in *Porefthendes—Go Ye*, from 1959-1969. See also A. Schmemann, "The Missionary Imperative in the Orthodox Tradition," in G. H. Anderson, ed., *The Theology of the Christian Mission*, New York, 1961, pp. 250-257. N. Nissiotis, "The Ecclesiological Foundation of Mission," *The Greek Orthodox Theological Review* 8 (1962), pp. 22-52. A. Yannoulatos, *Indifference for Mission Means Denial of Orthodoxy*, Athens, 1972 (reprinted from the periodical *Ecclesia*); see also other chapters in the present volume. E. Voulgarakis, *Love as Contemporary Interpretation of the Mystery of Salvation*, Athens, 1974. See also *Reports to the Second International Conference of Orthodox Theology: "The Catholicity of the Church," St. Vladimir's Seminary, September, 1972," St. Vladimir's Theological Quarterly* 17 (1973), Nos. 1-2. Basic positions on mission are summarized in the conclusions of various Orthodox theological conferences organized by the WCC: "Salvation in Orthodox Theology," Athens-Pendeli, May, 1972; "Confessing Jesus Christ Today," Bucharest-Cernica, June, 1974; "Confessing Christ through the Liturgical Life of the Church Today," Etchmiadzin-Armenia, September, 1975. For the first two see the pamphlet: Orthodox Contributions to Nairobi, (Papers compiled and presented by The Orthodox Task Force of the World Council of Churches) Geneva, 1975, No. 92. The three studies were also published in French in the periodical *Contacts* 27 (1975). For a summary of the positions on mission and Christian witness in general in ecumenical circles, see *Reports of the Bangkok Conference on Salvation Today: Bangkok Assembly 1973*, Geneva, 1973. "Symposium on Evangelism," *International Review of Mission* 63 (1974), January. D. M. Paton, ed., *Breaking Barriers. Nairobi, 1975: The Official Report of the Fifth Assembly of the World Council of Churches, Nairobi, 23 November—10 December, 1973*, London-Grand Rapids, 1976, especially pp. 41-57, 70-85. "The Nairobi Assembly - Implication for Mission," *International Review of Mission* 65 (1976), January.

restricted to certain geographical areas or social spheres. The whole inhabited world is its field of action, both where the joyful message is welcome and where those at first sight may reject it.

(c) Mission is not the duty of only one generation, for example, the apostolic age, but it is the duty of Christians of all ages. The Church continues its mission despite the wounds inflicted upon her by heresies and the tribulations imposed by persecutions. Mission is the expression of the vitality of the Church, as well as a source of renewal and renewed vigor.

(d) Even though missionary work in its most absolute form is undertaken by charismatic people, in the final analysis it remains the duty of all members of the Church; everyone should contribute to and participate in it, whether directly or indirectly. It is an essential expression of the ethos of Orthodox spirituality, whose basic points of reference are the Resurrection and Pentecost.

(e) The purpose of mission is not the conquest of the world or the imposition of a Christian state which exercises control over all, but the transmission of the word and grace of God, revealing His glory which, in Christ, "is and is to come." Its aim is not to increase the power of an organized religion, but to constitute a ministry offered to the world in all humility and aiming at "its salvation." Its aim is the realization of the presence of God, who is Love.

(f) Since the coming of the Kingdom of God constitutes the end of history, and a prerequisite of the Second Coming is that the Gospel will have been "preached throughout the whole world, as a testimony to all nations" (Matt 24:14), mission constitutes a basic function of historical reality and one which has eschatological dimensions.

3. The continuous offering of the Gospel everywhere, however, refers not only to the length and breadth of the earth, but also to the depths of each soul for its essential reformation. The Church grows both by acquiring new members and by

enabling those already baptized to acquire a deeper experience of the mysteries of life and love. If in the first case there is a type of growth that is quantitative, in the second the growth could be called *qualitative*. It is to this case in point that the *pastoral responsibility*[4] of the Church is concerned, "to equip of the saints, for the work of ministry, for building up the body of Christ" (Eph 4:12–13).[5] Without pastoral care the new life of believers, born through the acceptance of the Gospel and baptism, remains anemic and withers away. Life in Christ, like every form of life, must conquer death daily. Grace and sin, progress upward, new and tragic backslidings are conditions well known to us all. The character of Christian life remains dynamic; continuously over-coming the profane elements within ourselves by means of the adhering of the soul to the Holy of Holies; by the mystical participation in His Death and Resurrection; and by commending ourselves to Him. In the words of St. Basil: "This is the definition of Christianity: the imitation of Christ according to the measure of His incarnation and in accordance with each man's vocation."[6] Since pas-

---

4. Among the more general works on pastoral care see in Greek: Nectarios Kefalas, *Lessons in Pastoral Care*, Athens, 1898. Jerome Kotsonis, *Lectures on Pastoral Care*, Thessaloniki, 1961. K. Mouratides, *Christocentric Pastoral Care in the Ascetic Treatises of St. Basil the Great*, Athens, 1969. In the area of Pastoral Psychology see: J. Kornarakis, *The Problem of the Relationship between Pastoral Care and Psychotherapy, from the Orthodox Perspective*, Athens, 1957. Idem, *Elements of Neptic Psychology*, Thessaloniki, 1963. W. L. Northriddle, *Psychology and the Work of Guiding Souls*, S. Agourides, trans., Thessaloniki, 1959. G. Kapsanes, *Themes of Ecclesiology and Pastoral Care*, Thessaloniki, 1975. Idem, *Pastoral Care According to the Holy Canons*, Piraeus, 1976. A. Stavropoulos, *Premarital Pastoral Care*, Athens, 1973. For tendencies in Romanian theology see: A. L. Moisiu, "Problèmes de théologie pastorale dans la littérature théologique de ces dernières décennies," *De la théologie Orthodoxe roumaine des origines à nos jours*, Bucharest, 1974, pp. 440-52.

5. The text of Ephesians 4:11-16 expresses in a clear and deeply moving manner the orientation of "apostolic," "evangelical," and "pastoral" work.

6. St. Basil the Great, *The Long Rules* 43, *PG* 31:128B.

toral care has as its specific aim the continuous transformation in Christ of the faithful, "from one degree of glory to the other" (ἀπό δόξης εἰς δόξαν 2 Cor 3:18), their acquisition of the Holy Spirit, and finally, their "theosis,"[7] pastoral care constitutes the vertical dimension of the Christian struggle—in both height and depth.

The "qualitative" growth of the local Church has immediate missionary implications. This is so not only because it is conducive to the creation of a healthy and dynamic body which transmits the Gospel spontaneously to its environment, but also because the genuine faith and love of one man has beneficial effects on the whole of mankind who share in the same human nature. In the characteristic expression of the Russian ascetic, Seraphim of Sarov, "Achieve peace within yourself and a thousand souls around you will find salvation."[8] Mission and pastoral care characteristically go hand in hand in all Orthodox communities, which are the so-called "missionary." At this point in time, the patient work being carried out by the Orthodox in Korea, or in various African countries, combine harmoniously both of these practices; that means, strengthening and spiritually assisting the few faithful, as well as attracting new Christians. The increase and strengthening of the Orthodox community are two parallel and concurrent activities and one assists the other. St. Paul, on the one hand, epigrammatically told the elders of Ephesus that he was "testifying

7. Among various works on the subject see: V. Lossky, *Théologie mystique de l'Église d'Orient*, Paris, 1944. A Theodorou, *Theosis in the Teachings of the Greek Fathers of the Church up to St. John Damascene*, Athens, 1956 (in Greek). P. Bratsiotes, *Die Lehre der orthodoxen Kirche über die Theosis des Menschen*, Brussels, 1961. M. Lot-Borodine, *La déification de l'homme selon la doctrine des pères Grecs*, Paris, 1970. G. Mantzarides, *The Doctrine of the Theosis of Man According to Gregory Palamas*, Thessaloniki, 1963 (in Greek).

8. Irene Gorainoff, *St. Seraphim of Sarov*, P. D. Skouteris, trans., Athens, 1975, p. 255 (in Greek). Cf. The comment of St. Cyril of Alexandria: "For that which is owed to the believer ought to be a more suitable gift for all of nature." *Commentary on the Gospel of St. John*, 7, 24, *PG* 73:696.

both to Jews and to Greeks of repentance to God and of faith in our Lord Jesus Christ," and on the other hand, that "for three years" he "did not cease night or day to admonish every one with tears" (Acts 20:21, 31).

It is noteworthy that terminology and imagery from "pastoral" life are also used in the New Testament with missionary overtones: "And I have other sheep, which are not of this fold; I must bring them also, and they will heed my voice. So there shall be one flock, one shepherd" (John 10:16; cf. 1 Pet 2:25). These other sheep—men imprisoned in other systems and other "folds" of thought—already belong to the Lord of all, and they must "return" to His fold, the Church. Words like "the return" (ἐπιστροφή) or "they return" (ἐπιστρέφουσι) are used to designate conversion [of the Gentiles] (Acts 15:3, 15:19). The category of the "lost" and "gone astray" (Matt 18:12–13), include not only those who once came to the Church and then rejected it, but also those "wandering," deluded in the dark woods and dense paths of instinctive religions. The basic duty of the Church, therefore, remains first to "search" in each and every direction, and second to "save that which was lost."

It is now evident that from the outset mission and pastoral care are interdependent and mutually fulfilling. They both constitute one and the same task. Consequently, polarizations such as "inside," "outside," "we first, and others afterwards," between mission and pastoral care are, especially today, totally unjustifiable. It is not possible to overlook the need for serious internal pastoral care, but neither is it possible to allow immediate pastoral work to paralyze Christian witness throughout the world, nor to justify missionary inertia. The correct formulation of the problem is not "either this or that," but "so much for this . . . so much for that." "And you shall be my witnesses in Jerusalem and in all Judea and Samaria and to the end of the earth" (Acts 1:8).

B
TRAUMATIC SITUATIONS
INHIBITING ORTHODOX WITNESS

When, however, after taking account of the theological considerations and analyses, we come to present-day reality, we find that our ecclesiastical life displays many traumatic situations which dangerously inhibit both her mission and her pastoral activity. At ecumenical meetings many Orthodox theologians often tend to gloss over these situations in silence, and to idealize conditions within the Orthodox Church. In a Pan-Orthodox theological conference like this, however, we must soberly acknowledge the reality and proceed to self-criticism. What follows does not necessarily apply to everyone. There are, fortunately, some blessed exceptions. On the other hand, I shall not propose to go into any of the root causes in the few brief paragraphs of this presentation; because this would require a long historical and sociological analysis. I shall, therefore, limit myself to a few broad issues.

1. A certain spiritual malaise can be detected in the body of the *clergy*, the principal bearers of the message. There is usually an enormous gap between descriptions of the greatness of the sacerdotal mission and the reality we live with. Many of the clergy seem able to preach one thing and to live another; they appear to maintain a superficial, ceremonial type of religiosity, absent of love, spiritual sensitivity, or freedom. Critical questions are anxiously awaiting responsible theological confrontation. What is it that prevents many workers in the Church from blossoming as personalities? What leads others to discouragement and despair? Why do serious people shrink from the priesthood? It is a common secret that many priests live under conditions of oppression and lack of freedom, because despite the sacramental character of the Church, within her organizational structure are also several secular powers which often

transform the relationships between bishops and priests into something more like the relationships between feudal lords and serfs.

My point is not to level charges against group A or group B—indeed, we bishops are usually the products of an established mentality—but to review the situation in the light of the authentic Orthodox tradition. The most painful aspect of the matter is that although many causes of the malady in question have long since been identified, the situation with regard to the clergy, instead of improving, is deteriorating. It is imperative that we investigate in depth, adopting even daring solutions, so that we may no longer be left with no alternative but the ordination of persons of low educational standards,[9] and, unfortunately, not only educational.* [. . .]

Finally, it is wrong to overlook the human qualities of the priest and natural frailty of his character. We know what society expects of the priesthood and we know its severe judgments. In addition to giving descriptions of ideal models, theology

---

9. Some very interesting statistical data are given in A. Youssides, *Ordinations in the Church of Greece during the Years 1950–1969* (A Statistical and Sociological Investigation), Thessaloniki, 1975 (in Greek). Cf. An analysis by D. Savramis, *Die soziale Stellung des Priesters in Griechenland*, Leiden, 1968

*As a way to kindle the discussion, I mention a few undeveloped proposals: (a) The systematic on-going education of the clergy regarding the new realities of the world and the abundant experience of the Church, so that we do not become mere celebrants of religious ceremonies. (b) Essential preparation of clergy and laypeople to do mission work in difficult areas in and out of the country. (c) Develop a group of clergy with lay professions (e.g. doctor), without the present restrictions of the external dress code. (d) Ordination of deacons or sub-deacons at a younger age with the opportunity to choose marriage later. The period of 20 to 35 years of age could be utilized without restraints for missionary service in more demanding areas. (Cf. *The Impediments of Marriage*—A Report of the Church of Greece to the Pan-Orthodox Great Council, Athens, 1971 (in Greek). (e) The reactivation of certain lower level degrees of ordination in the Early Church in order to serve the missionary and pastoral care needs of the contemporary Church.

should treat each member of the clergy "with loving kindness," see him as a human being who has his personal struggles and is subject to weakness and disappointment, and concern ourselves seriously with the problem of how he may be supported and assisted. Pastoral care for the clergy is the most neglected area of pastoral activity. Without the proper, continuous renewal of the clergy, all our plans for pastoral care and mission are destined to remain ineffective.

2. Further, modern theology is often characterized by a certain *spiritual languidness* (ἀτονία). It is often embodied in sterile academic forms and technical language. It fails to go deeply into the problems posed by the new currents of thought, by science, by politics, or by the reintroduction of the philosophies of Asiatic peoples and cultures, which in our era exercise a peculiar enchantment. At other times, we are unconsciously held back, without knowing it, by a fear of waking sleeping dogs, lest we incur the displeasure of the high and mighty, lest we jeopardize established privileges. Obsessions and personal conflicts sometimes lead to polarizations; these become stumbling blocks to fruitful dialogue that could transcend personal opinions in the interests of a higher synthesis. We often express views on subjects without sufficient study, views that have not been allowed to mature through protracted reflection and under the influence of worship in the silence of the Holy Spirit.[10] Too often "we technologize, we do not theologize."[11] We forget that a plethora of

---

10. "In the Holy Spirit (are found) the riches of the knowledge of God, the contemplation (of the divine) and wisdom; for in Him (the Holy Spirit) the Word reveals all dogmas concerning the Father" (Theodore Studites, Gradual Antiphons, *Paracletike*, Sunday Martins, Third Antiphon, Fourth Tone).

11. "People therefore technologize and do not theologize; for the wisdom of the world becomes primary overlooking the boast of the Cross." St. Basil the Great, *Epistle 90*, PG 32:473B. With regard to the patristic view in general, see K. Scouteris, *The Meaning of the Terms 'theology,' 'theologize,' and 'theologian' in the Doctrine of the Greek Fathers and Ecclesiastical Writers up to the Cappadocian Fathers*, Athens, 1972 (in

words, an intellectual theology, leaves the people of God un-moved.

Finally, an important question arises. From where stems the right and the possibility of theologians to theologize? Does it come from our theological degree or from our studies? The im-placable words of the psalmist, "But to the wicked, God says: `What right have you to recite my statutes?'" (Ps 49:16). These words, which induced Origen to descend in contrition from the pulpit, are of particular significance for many of us, who so eas-ily pronounce theological judgments, without awe and with a naive self-confidence. In the patristic tradition, "purification" (*katharsis*) is defined as a prerequisite of theology, of the "speak-ing of divine things."[12] Surely our theological thinking would be of a different depth, quality, and warmth, if it developed in a climate of continuous metanoia, which is a transformation of the mind, of its liberation from prejudice, a "purification of the heart," "vigilance" (*nepsis*), and a "sharing in" (*methexis*) the universal experience of the Church in humbleness and sobriety.

3. Local and international living conditions, the pace of life in large cities, global communications and mass media net-works, and the close interdependence among cities and nations have long since transformed the presuppositions upon which various ecclesiastical organizational patterns were based. Thus *many administrative structures* prove *insufficient* and are unable to meet present-day requirements. I will refer to two examples.

First, the structure and the nurture of the parishes in the Diaspora and in the big cities: In the former case, the parish extends over dozens of square kilometers. While in the latter

---

Greek), especially pp. 89-99, 155-174; cf. critical essay: *Theology, Truth and Life, Spiritual Symposium,* Athens, 1962.

12. St. Gregory Nazianzus, *Logos*, 43, *PG* 36:581A. Cf. "A great thing it is to speak of God; but a greater to cleanse one's self for God. For into a soul that is ill-cultured wisdom cannot enter. *Orations* 32, 12, *PG* 36:188C. Cf. "It is by purification that purity is to be achieved." *Orations*, 20, 12, *PG* 35:1080B.

case a parish in a big city, for example in Athens, may include 30,000–50,000 inhabitants and remains virtually without pastoral care. It is not only a problem of excessive numbers. The main difficulty arises from the pace of life, from our great mobility, from the possibility of forming relationships irrespective of one's place of residence. The parishioners remain strangers to one another, and unknown to the priest. The character of the Eucharistic community has been radically altered and only a few symbolic rituals remind them of family life and communion in Christ.

Second, the problem of different jurisdictional areas sometimes has an inhibiting effect on missionary initiatives. The Churches with the largest numbers of believers and, surely, those with the most means and personnel, often regard the duty of mission as something not under their direct responsibility and prefer the security of a discreet silence rather than interfering with the responsibilities of others. This, however, gives rise to a theological problem: Is worldwide mission *the exclusive obligation of certain local Churches alone*? Should not some form of essential and effective cooperation be sought? What is the meaning of jurisdiction? Do the Buddhists or the Moslems "belong" to the jurisdiction of Church A or Church B? Or will they belong to these only as and when they are converted to Orthodoxy? Is the indifference as to whether or not they become Christians to be construed as respect for another jurisdiction?

I hasten to state that I am at present unable to suggest a satisfactory solution to these questions, because every "solution" virtually means the creation of a new problem. It is just as inconceivable that national Orthodox Churches should intervene arbitrarily in any region of the world, as it is to consider the creation of autonomous missionary societies based on Western models. What is now imperative is that we should realize that solutions do not turn up by themselves, and that, humanly speaking, opportunities continue to be lost. Solutions must be sought by means of systematic theological work and clear ecclesiastical planning. Under the leadership of the Ecumenical Patriarchate and with participation of all the Orthodox Churches, respecting the canonical order, a Pan-Orthodox Committee for Mission might be established. Its duty would be to study, plan and promote realistic proposals—utilizing the combined Orthodox dynamism and effort—to witness Orthodoxy on a worldwide scale. It is an established fact that each local Church contributes more willingly and more generously to missionary work when it sees itself as a responsible participant, rather than as the financial sponsor of some distant, unknown and isolated parish.[13]

4. More generally, there is a tendency for the *membership of the Church* as a whole to display a kind of somnolence, which results *in inertia and passivity*. It is very doubtful whether the faithful are aware that the Church saves and transforms lives in the Holy Spirit. Their religious feelings often include elements of primitive awe when confronted with that which is mysterious, with the numinous. Their religious psychology in relationship with the Divine is reminiscent of *do ut des*. Especially the confusion that is cultivated by many Churches that only the clergy could be considered the Church—and, indeed, only the clergy of a certain rank—creates one of the most dangerous misunderstandings. This leads to indifference in ecclesiastical matters and to irresponsibility. Thus, laypeople who represent

---

13. There are many related activities which might be usefully developed at a pan-Orthodox level. These include: (a) the introduction of a "Week of Pan-Orthodox Witness" during Lent. (In 1968 the Church of Greece began dedicating a "Week of Foreign Mission," with remarkable results.) The specific contents of this week would be adapted to local conditions. (b) The introduction of a "Week for the discussion of missionary and pastoral problems" in Orthodox Theological Schools. (c) The organization of a system under which certain priests, theologians, and specially trained laypeople, would be assigned for a period of time by the more affluent Orthodox communities to serve the poorer ones—in the mission field or in the *diaspora*—the cost of the work being carried by the wealthier communities. The present ease of travel from one place to another must be exploited with creative thinking to provide a global witness for Orthodoxy.

the overwhelming majority within the Church, instead of becoming co-workers in Christ in the common task of mission and edification, are reduced to the role of spectators, judges and critics. Theological thought is called upon "again and again" to proclaim and clarify the fact that all believers are responsible for the life of the Church. They are participants in its work, are limbs of the body that continue the work of Christ, the salvation of the whole world. The presence of faithful laypeople within the structures of social life offers inexhaustible opportunities for witness, ministry, and the glorification of God.

A matter of resurgent interest today is the more active participation of women (who represent more than half the members of the Church and more than three quarters of those who attend Church regularly). Some examples include: The revival of the institution of deaconesses and more extensive utilization of social workers, nuns, and so forth. The enormous contribution of women is particularly noticeable in areas under regimes hostile to the Church. The position of the Virgin Mary in the work of divine economy and the multi-faceted role of women saints in the life of the Church may open up vital new horizons for both reflection and action.[14]

5. The limited time allotted to this presentation precludes any lengthy analysis. I must confess that I have not had the courage to touch on serious, hidden or very sensitive wounds that exist in the life of the Church, and that in what I have said I have tried to use discreet formulations. (Perhaps this kind of mildness is in itself a sign of a "post-traumatic" theological attitude.) At any rate, the fact remains that there are still many aspects of the ecclesiastical reality which might be considered "traumatic." Such traumas include:

(a) The various small or large compromises in matters of conscience with those in power, with the economic, political, or other "establishments" of this world.

---

14. For more on the subject see P. Evdokimov, *La Femme et le Salut du Monde*, Tournai-Paris, 1958.

(b) The use or abuse of the material resources and possibilities that are at the disposal of the Church; the arbitrary and high-handed administrative practices (on various pretexts) of some Church authorities.

(c) The difficulty of cooperation between those working for the Gospel; our inability to predict and to plan programs and our failure to understand the new conditions of human life.

(d) Our sluggishness and carelessness in implementing decisions.

(e) The indifference of young people who regard the Church as slow in thought and slow to act, as being a religious "establishment" lacking inspiration, sensitivity or hope; the excessive inconsistency in the behavior of "devout Christians," which causes "outsiders" to seriously doubt the effectiveness of the Gospel.

(f) The divisions which have become a permanent characteristic of the Christian world and include not only the broad confessional clashes, but also antipathy and obstinacy within smaller Orthodox groups.

It is far healthier to make a courageous and sincere confession of the wounds and errors that in reality afflict our ecclesiastical history than to adopt the attitude that currently prevails among us: namely, that of embellishing and idealizing that reality in order to justify ourselves in our own eyes, as well as in the eyes of "others." [. . .]

Naturally, there is also a risk that the recognition of these regrettable facts may well lead to intense or latent melancholy and numerous inhibitions. Over and above the diagnosis of the illnesses and the remedy, our theological thinking is called upon to interpret further their significance, to offer guidance as to how to heal the wounds. The nature of the struggle of the Church goes beyond the social and physical realms and involves spiritual-metaphysical dimensions: "For we are not contending against flesh and blood . . ." (Eph 6:12). As history proceeds towards its eschatological fulfillment, the confrontation between the powers "of darkness" and the Disciples of Christ grows more dramatic. In our apocalyptic age, the powers of evil appear to be on the rise, and it is no wonder that their actions strike at especially sensitive, neuralgic areas of the body of the Church. The tragic remains a basic dimension of history, and the Cross pinpoints and manifests its poignancy. There is, of course, the possibility of a failure of faith: "Nevertheless, when the Son of man comes, will he find faith on earth?" (Luke 18:8). Yet this thought must not lead us to "discouragement" but rather to "vigilance."—"Watch therefore" (Mark 13:35, 37). The final word belongs to God, not to His opponents and those who are His betrayers: "And the Lamb shall conquer them, for he is Lord of lords and King of kings, and those with him are called and chosen and faithful" (Rev 17:14). [. . .]

C

DYNAMIC PRESENCE
AND WITNESS IN THE WORLD

The eschatological insight and certainty that are underlined again and again in Orthodox worship grant power to resist, tranquility, and spiritual equilibrium to the faithful, and in particular those who actively take part in the missionary and pastoral work of the Church, so that they may continue, in spite of tribulations, their course and service within the world.

In this final section I will attempt to outline some basic characteristics of what would be a dynamic Orthodox presence and witness. Naturally, it is evident that the considerations put forward here do not cover the whole spectrum of relevant problems. They simply throw a few rays of light on the most crucial aspects of the subject so that they may eventually facilitate further investigation.

1. In the terrible confusion which marks our age, the Christian message (*kerygma*) should be conceived of *as a joyful proclamation*—"the good news" to each person *in the specific circumstances of his life,* a message that meets his immediate existential

needs and experiences. Although the message itself is one, universal and eternal, each man or woman who receives it lives in a specific situation and has different associations of ideas. In the past, in order that the mystery of salvation in Christ should be made available to the men and women of the early Christian era, it was necessary, for the presentation of the Gospel, to assimilate and make use of the categories of thought that were at that time familiar to all. This was accomplished mainly through theology.

Today's city dweller is faced with the new horizons opened up by the rapid advances of science and the possibilities provided by technology, new social structures and political articulations. He moves within problematics that are far larger, more intricate and complex than the citizen of the Greco-Roman or the Byzantine worlds. His sensitivities have changed. The old symbols of thought have lost their immediate significance; to men familiar with frequent sacrifices, as for example in the Judaic and Greco–Roman religions, the emphasis on atonement was existentially relevant. It is no longer so today.

Theology today then is faced, together with the old problem of how to express the Eternal, also with the new problem of how to do so in a way that is meaningful to modern man. But in order to tune into the wavelength of modern thinking, it is essential to comprehend the depths of the changes brought about by science, and to gain an understanding of the new dimensions that they have opened.

Of most immediate importance are the sciences which deal with man and his history, and which reveal significant aspects of his psychosomatic structure, i.e. medicine with it various branches, anthropology, sociology, and most important of all, psychology and psychotherapy. A serious evaluation and utilization of the findings of modern science—God's gift to man— is an obligation of missionary and pastoral theology. However a sober evaluation and use of modern knowledge cannot be achieved by fragmentary or individual work. This will necessitate collective seeking and critical evaluation of the findings, thinking "in ecclesia," but also delegation of the work involved (such as the creation of specialized research centers in the various theological schools). Our theological schools will need to put forth a great effort in order to confront the basic questions, with the assistance of scientists and specialists in other fields. We will also need to organize interscholastic cooperation, in order that our research may acquire a worldwide perspective and may benefit from the collective experience.

There are certain bridges that could be used to help us approach people of different religious customs and ideas, referred to in a preceding paragraph (A1). These remain:

(a) Maintaining sensitivity to the existence of a transcendental reality, the vibration of our response to the tremors of man's religious experience in worship, of man's spiritual introspection, of his desire for salvation, of his encounters with the supra-rational, the Holy.

(b) We can "get on to the same wavelength" as modern, secularized man by concerning ourselves with the problematics that deal with issues such as: social justice, equality and freedom, the transcending of individualism through a sense of social responsibility, and control over the continued pollution of the physical—and spiritual environment.

(c) The search for fulfillment of life before the eternal enigma and chilling horror of death.

(d) The infinitely broad theme of love that, in spite of all the deviations, misconceptions and perversions to which it is subject, fills the foreground of human interest.

Yet, any effort to understand "others" often remains indistinguishable and incorrect unless it is implanted in a specific, localized and particular *life situation*. There is a revealing passage regarding the missionary and pastoral approach used by St. Paul: "For though I am free from all men, I have made myself a slave to all, that I might win the more" (1 Cor 9:19–23; cf. 10:33). The rendering specific of the Gospel message and its "incarnation" in a local situation remain basic elements of Christian witness. Worldwide mission cannot be successful unless it becomes highly specific, i.e. adapted to the specific environment.

Furthermore, the Christian message can retain both its eternal significance and current relevance only when it does "not rest in the wisdom of men but in the power of God" (1 Cor 2:5); when it is presented as a call to repentance and as judgment, when it forms a bold protest against specific concrete, illegitimate situations that conflicts with the will of God and "his righteousness" (Matt 6:33). A message of good news which ignores tragedy and sin in personal and social life and refers to the salvation of the world only in generic terms is of questionable sincerity and credibility. "For the word of God is living and active" and penetrates the deepest roots of evil, "piercing to the division of soul and spirit, of joints and marrow, and discerning the thoughts and intentions of the heart" (Heb 4:12).

2. The term Gospel (good news) also means a *word of life and consolation*. At the beginning of His activity the Lord stated, in the words of the messianic prophecy: "The spirit of the Lord is upon me, because he has anointed me to preach good news to the poor. He has sent me to proclaim release to the captives and recovering of sight to the blind, to set at liberty those who are oppressed" (Luke 4:18; cf. Isa 61:1). And then, as He went about preaching "the Gospel of the kingdom," Christ also relieved human suffering, both physical and mental, "healing every disease and every infirmity" (Matt 4:23). In that way, He thus revealed by His acts that the quintessence of His teaching and life is LOVE. The giving of comfort, consolation, and the support of souls became the perpetual task of the Holy Spirit, of the Comforter.[15]

---

15. "And he is called 'Paraclete' (Comforter) because he comforts and consoles and supports our weakness," St. Cyril of Jerusalem, *Catechetical Homilies for those Being Illumined*, 16, 20, *PG* 33:948A. Elsewhere the 'Paraclete' is referred to as "the guardian and sanctifier of the Church, the ruler of souls, the governor of the tempest-tossed, the enlightener of the lost, the one who sets the goals for those who

Giving comfort to people, both in times of great upheaval and in the difficulties of everyday circumstances, has always been one of the main tasks of pastoral care; a task revealing in concrete terms the charity and love of God which is thus manifest in the Church. All the great saints of our Church, the "imitators of Christ" (*Christomimetoi*) the "bearers of the Holy Spirit" (*Pneumatemphoroi*) in addition to their prophetic preaching for an overall change in society, have taken pains to comfort specific individuals, to console the suffering, the humble, and victims of injustice.

The oppression, suffering and tribulations of man continue in our day, sometimes under the mask of obvious or concealed slavery by unjust social structures, at other times from circumstances arising from the human condition itself—sickness, death, failure, passions of the soul. Wherever we look, we find hunger and thirst for a word, an act of comfort: "Comfort, O comfort my people, says your God. Speak tenderly to Jerusalem, and cry to her" (Isa 40:1–2). No amount of government initiatives and measures in the area of social welfare will ever erase the problems of human suffering. Every kind of sorrow, melancholy, inner conflicts, feelings of guilt following on the intricate circuits of sin, will continue to afflict human existence in various forms and from diverse directions. It is not only the deprivation and bitterness of the poor; there are also many wealthy people who are starved for authentic love and the meaning of life; the need for balance, for liberation from the tyranny of the ego.

Therefore, whoever truly follows Him, who "went about doing good and healing all that were oppressed by the devil" (Acts 10:38), must keep continuous vigil, so that he may always be ready to offer comfort and help to any person permanently or accidently set on his path, and to be ready for broader action to alleviate the open or concealed wounds of society as a whole.

---

struggle, and one who crowns the victors," St. Cyril of Jerusalem, *Catechesis*, 17, 13, *PG* 33:985B.

Such an active attitude towards contemporary life will give new impulses towards the radical revision of our theological themes.

3. The work of Christ, which is continued by the Church, has always been the dissolution and destruction of the works of the devil (1 John 3:3–8). Self-sacrifice (*kenosis*) and the Cross have always been prerequisites for the elimination of evil. The willing and patient *acceptance of pain and the cross* (Mark 8:34), in complete obedience to the will of God, in love and the hope of the resurrection are persistently emphasized in the Orthodox tradition and constitute the secret of profound knowledge of Christ: "That I may know him and the power of his resurrection, and may share his sufferings, becoming like him in his death" (Phil 3:10); this kind of "knowledge," "power," "communion and likeness" has always been the foundation for a life of "sobriety," "vigilance," humility, love, and freedom.

It is true that the *ascetic* ideal and *experience* was intensively expressed in Orthodox monasticism, but it had a wider effect, in that it influenced the conscience of the members of the Orthodox Church, ensuring their power of resistance in times of adversity, and in the difficulties of daily life. It was not the product of any dualistic concept which holds the body in contempt or of any reservations concerning the value of present day life—such as we find in Hinduism and Buddhism, nor was it moralistic in nature. The ascetic ideal remains deeply theological, radically based on continuous reference to the events of Kenosis, Crucifixion, Resurrection, expectation of the end, and contemplation of the One. Undoubtedly some of the more serious weaknesses of our time are: the virtual absence of the ascetic spirit in everyday Christian life; the very superficial guidance of the faithful with shallow moralistic literature, ignoring the vital experience of the saints which often remains undeveloped and under-utilized by theologians. The wisdom of the ascetic spirituality (*Philokalia*) of the Orthodox Church needs to be more closely assimilated and incorporated into everyday life and thought. This wisdom contains treasures of the highest psychological significance for modern man.

The ascetic ethos of Orthodoxy is also of extreme relevance in this age, because alongside the current strong tendencies towards hedonism, an appreciation for the value of ascetic discipline has been cultivated in many other areas of life. Spectacular achievements in the sciences, sports, and the arts, for instance, have been the result of systematic, persistent, and intense ascetic self-discipline. In this connection, the multifold importance of monasteries is very evident. Monasteries have always been beacons of missionary radiance, and invaluable powerhouses of pastoral care for the faithful. If people in general, and clergy and theologians in particular, made a regular practice of retiring every now and then into silent retreat, meditation, ascetic practice and prayer, to refresh their thinking and renew their mental and spiritual health, the results would certainly be of great benefit. All those who have made a significant contribution to mission and the pastoral ministry of the Church lived in ascetic vigilance, compunction and repentance, in unceasing struggle against the dark abysses of the human ego; some pursued their ascetic struggle in the desert, others in the solitude of the cities. Continuous, relentless, persistent personal struggle in the Holy Spirit has always been the source of the spiritual radiance of the people of God.

4. The crowning point of the dynamic, transfiguring presence of the Church in the world lies in the event that mystically exalts human life to become an offering and sacrifice to God. *The worshipping experience of Orthodoxy has immediate and direct pastoral and missionary implications.* It liberates the believer from narrow patterns of thought, from passions, and most of all from his suffocating egoism. Worship unites him with Christ, and with the entire Church of the faithful, with all those who have lived and conquered, who live now and who will live in the future. In other words, with all those whom He, "who is who was and who is to come" holds and enfolds in His love. It trans-

figures him into a living member of the body of Christ, ready to behold the world and to act in the same way as Christ did.

Orthodox theology can contribute, with the cooperation of all responsible clergy, to the development of new expressions and enrichment of the Church's forms of worship and this with a view to achieving a direct existential relationship between worship and the Word, to safeguarding worship as *logike latreia* (Rom 12:1); that is, preserving its existential relationship with the Logos, so that worship does not degenerate into mere religious emotion. Rather, that it foster instead dynamic expressions of doxological exaltations of "today," of awaiting the "tomorrow" of the *eschaton,* so as not to be transformed into a nostalgic escapism into "yesterday."

Above all, theology is called upon to complete Orthodox worship by highlighting the inner connection that exists between the liturgical experience and the dynamic presence of the Christian in the world. Any division between the experience of worship and everyday life leads, in effect, to a falsification of Orthodox Christianity and to schizophrenic tendencies in the faithful. Inasmuch as conscious participation in the life of worship of the Church constitutes participation in that specific act which liberates man, through the crucifixion and resurrection of Christ, from the demonic powers, *prolongation of the Divine Liturgy into everyday life—"the liturgy after the Divine Liturgy"*—implies a continuing struggle against the negative powers that are always active within us, as well as within society. That which is experienced during worship should find its expression in everyday personal and social life. Thus the Liturgy is transfigured into life, and life become worship, praise, and the glorification of God. [In regard to the phrase "liturgy after the Liturgy," see the appendix at the end of this chapter entitled: *Clarification of the Phrase . . .*]

During difficult periods for Christianity (such as that of the Turkish occupation, or the oppression by atheistic regimes) the liturgical life of the faithful strengthened their powers of resistance and brought new vigor to local Churches undergoing suffering. Through the Holy Eucharist *par excellence*, the faithful experience the "Pascha of the Lord," realizing a continuous "exodus" from weakness into the experience of the power in Christ; from disillusionment to joy, and "the expectation of hope"; from inactivity and irresponsibility to responsible witness and a dynamic presence in the world.

***

Vincent of Lerins's classical definition of "catholic," that is orthodox, is "that which is believed everywhere, always and by all" (*quod ubique, quod semper, quod ab omnibus creditum est*).[16] Basing ourselves on this definition, we may say that the missionary ideal is "everywhere, always, by all." The local Church surely is responsible first for the witness of faith in her area. But she must not overlook the injustice perpetrated when so many other parts of the world remain starving for the word of God. It is an elementary principle of justice that all men always have equal right to spiritual goodness.

Mission and pastoral care are closely interrelated functions of the ministry of the Church and have as their aim to "seek and save the lost." Since the Church is carrying on the work of Christ, she cannot confine "saving" to circumscribed areas and structures. She must seek all those who have "gone astray." And seeking involves an *exodus*, a "passing over"—after experiencing the "Pascha" of the Lord—from static patterns, inhibitions, and conventional situations to a patient advance into the infinite multifold situations and areas of activity of the world. The perennial task of the Church remains her duty to be present and to bear witness, in the eternal "here" and "now," in the power of God, thus constituting in herself, as it were, an incarnate *paraclesis*, an incarnated Eucharistic hymn, constantly chanted among men, with sobriety and ascetic vigilance, on behalf of the whole world.

---

16. *"Id teneamus quod ubique, quod ab omnibus creditum est, hoc est etenim vere proprieque catholicum,"* Vincent of Lerins, *Commonitorium prim*, 2, *PL* 50:640.

A CLARIFICATION OF THE PHRASE:
"THE LITURGY AFTER THE LITURGY"
(1975)

In the course of missionary meetings and conferences of the World Council of Churches during the last decades of the twentieth century various ideas and definitions were proposed from time to time. These were later adopted in missionary discussions and with frequent repetition became "code definitions." In certain cases the person who originally proposed the definition was overlooked—that is the father of the idea—and paternity was appropriated by another, who adopted and frequently repeated the phrase. This is precisely what happened with the Orthodox phrase used to understand mission as "the liturgy after the Liturgy." I had occasionally proposed this phrase in inter-Christian circles and particularly in the missionary meeting at Etchmiadzin, Armenia in 1975, which had as its theme "Confessing Christ through the Liturgical Life of the Church."

The idea and proposal to continue the Liturgy by the faithful after the conclusion of the Divine Liturgy in Church, with each believer as the celebrant—using the code phrase: "the liturgy after the Divine Liturgy"—was developed for the first time in 1963 in Athens, in my sermon to the members of the Christian Union of Scientists, on the Second Sunday of Lent, the Feast day of St. Gregory Palamas. In point of fact, among other things, I emphasized the following: "This event (of the Divine Liturgy) must not be lost as an instantaneous emotion, *but the Liturgy must be extended into daily life. And all of life must be transfigured into a liturgy.* Our office, our altar, our factory or our home becomes our temple; our work becomes our liturgy, where our soul and body will be offered as "a living sacrifice, holy, and acceptable to God" (Rom 12:1).

In Etchmiadzin, at the end of the Conference, I used part of this sermon as a "Meditation" in order to promote further what the Committee was seeking, and I emphasized the need to continue the Liturgy in daily life (using the phrase "liturgy after the Liturgy"). A summary, with excerpts quoted from my text was published by Fr. Ion Bria, my successor since 1973 at the Desk for Orthodox Studies and Relations of the World Council of Churches. In subsequent years Fr. Ion Bria repeated this phrase in various conferences and publications of the WCC, adopting precisely the original idea. At my request to restore the truth about the origins of the phrase, Fr. Bria published a section of my text from Etchmiadzin with the observation: "An idea, truly summarizing the original discussion, was formulated by Bishop Anastasios Yannoulatos, Professor at the University of Athens. Here is the text in a free and revised form":

"The Liturgy is not an escape from life, but a continuous transformation of life according to the prototype of Jesus Christ, through the power of the Spirit. If it is true that in the Liturgy we not only hear a message, but we participate in the great event of liberation from sin and of *koinonia* (communion) with Christ through the real presence of the Holy Spirit, then this event of our personal incorporation into the Body of Christ, this transfiguration of our little being into a member of Christ, must be evident and be proclaimed in actual life.

"The Liturgy has to be continued in the personal, everyday situations. Each of the faithful is called upon to continue a personal "liturgy" on the secret altar of one's own heart, to realize a living proclamation of the good news "for the sake of the whole world." Without this continuation the Liturgy remains incomplete. Since in the Eucharistic event we are incorporated in Him who came to serve the world and to be sacrificed for it, we have to express in concrete *diaconia*, in community life, our new being in Christ, the Servant of all. The sacrifice of the Eucharist must be extended in personal sacrifices for the people in need, the brothers for whom Christ died. Since the Liturgy is the participation in the great event of liberation from the demonic powers, then the continuation of the Liturgy in life means a continuous liberation from the powers of evil that are working inside us; a continual reorientation and openness toward insights and efforts aimed at liberating human persons from all the demonic structures of injustice, exploitation, agony, loneliness, and at creating real communion of persons in love.

"This personal everyday attitude becomes "liturgical" in the sense that: (a) It draws power from the participation in the Sacrament of the Holy Eucharist through which we receive the grace of the liberating and unifying Holy Spirit. (b) It constitutes the best preparation for a new, more conscientious and existential participation in the Eucharist. (c) It is a living expression—in terms clear to everybody—of the real transformation of men and women in Christ."[1]

[We have returned repeatedly to this idea (see Chapter 6: "Discovering the Orthodox Missionary Ethos," p. 105; Chapter 8: "Eucharist—Service—Witness in Mutual Reciprocity," p. 127; Chapter 13: "The Global Vision of Proclaiming the Gospel," p. 205).]

---

1. "The liturgy after the Liturgy," *International Review of Mission* 67 (1978), No. 265. See also I. Bria, ed., *Martyria-Mission. The Witness of the Orthodox Churches Today*, Geneva, 1980.

5

"THY KINGDOM COME"
ORTHODOX WITNESS
IN THE MODERN WORLD

(1977)

• Keynote address at the 9th General Assembly of Syndesmos, Chambésy, Switzerland, 19–25 July, 1977. • «Ἐλθέτω ἡ βασιλεία Σου—Ὀρθόδοξη Μαρτυρία στή σύγχρονη οἰκουμένη», *Πάντα τά Ἔθνη* 2 (1983), no. 7, pp. 4–5, no 8, pp. 4-6, no 9, pp. 4–6. • "Confessing Christ Today," in *The Bond of Unity*, ed. H. Bos, Athens, 2003, pp. 177–190. • *Ἱεραποστολή στά ἴχνη τοῦ Χριστοῦ. Θεολογικές μελέτες καί ὁμιλίες*, Ἀθήνα 2007.

One serious disadvantage in our various missionary efforts is the lack of a general vision of apostolic work. Only when these efforts are placed within a broader theological and universal realm do they acquire their proper dimension. An attempt for such a vision is undertaken in this text by using as an axial value the dynamic Christian truth to which our prayer unceasingly returns: the coming of the Kingdom of God. In what follows, three areas will be studied diagrammatically: (a) the biblical and hermeneutical facts. (b) The proclamation of the Kingdom in various zones of the globe. (c) The proclamation of the Kingdom and our personal responsibility.

A

BIBLICAL AND HERMENEUTICAL FACTS

Can it be considered in any way appropriate today to refer to a kingdom—even if it be the Kingdom of God—at a time when criticism of, and hostility to, the institution of a monarchy has reached a state of paroxysm in many parts of the world? What kind of response is likely to be aroused today by such preaching or by the raising of such expectations? And yet, the coming of the Kingdom of God means precisely the surpassing of every other type of kingdom and authority. "Thy Kingdom come," writes Origen, "that every authority and power and force and every kingdom of the world and sin which reigns in our mortal bodies be abolished, and that God reign over all of

99

these."[1] "Thy kingdom come," that the hypostatic Love (1 John 4:16) may reign absolutely in us, and in the universe.

1. To those concerned with the interpretation of Holy Scripture it is clear that the "kingdom of God" or the "kingdom of heaven," which lies at the core of Christ's teaching, refers first to an eternal event, second to a new reality that is inaugurated by the life and work of Christ in the history of humankind, and third to something that is to be fully realized in the future.

We are concerned here with a central motif that dominates the so-called "synoptic tradition." Luke and Mark predominantly use the expression the "kingdom of God," whereas Matthew usually refers to the "kingdom of heaven" and the "kingdom of the father." This difference has given rise to not a few discussions, but, finally, nearly all have agreed that the same event of the "divine Kingdom" is referred to in all instances. The same reality is also described as "life" (Mark 9:43, 46; Matt 7:14), "eternal life" (Mark 10:17)—which in John is the central motif of Christ's teaching—and these terms are associated with the ideas of "redemption" (Luke 21:28), and "glory" (Mark 10:37).

Jesus begins His preaching with the assurance that the "kingdom" has already been inaugurated by His presence and the work He is doing. All His wondrous acts, especially the liberation of man from conditions of disease and privation, and the driving away of the demons that harass men are "signs" of the presence of the Kingdom (Matt 12:28; cf. Luke 11:20). When the Pharisees asked "when the kingdom of God was coming," Jesus assures them that, "the kingdom of God is in the midst of you" (Luke 17:20–21 ff). That is, it is among you.

The confines of this spiritual Kingdom are unimaginably broad and embrace the whole world. Invited into it and expected to come "from east and west" (Matt 8:11) are former sinners and tax-collectors, the despised and insignificant of this world (Matt 9:10); this is something never before conceived of

---

1. Origen, *Fragments from the Gospel of Luke*, 45, ΒΕΠΕΣ 15:79, 33-36.

in Judaic thought. The requirements for admission to the Kingdom presuppose neither race nor social class, but are clearly spiritual and moral in nature. The characteristics of those that shall enter the Kingdom are revealed and conditioned upon the "Beatitudes."

The manner in which the "kingdom of God" is referred to in the Gospels demonstrates that this reality surpasses established and rational limits; therefore, the "mysteries" of the Kingdom are announced by parables, by images, by poetic language.

A schematic review of the meanings attached to the "Kingdom of God" in Christian thinking, leads us to discern three basic viewpoints: (a) that it implies the visible Church founded by Christ and carrying on His redeeming work until the Second Coming; (b) that it is the Kingdom of Christ on earth between the Second Coming and the Final Judgment; and (c) that it refers to the eternal Kingdom of God after the Final Judgment.

To these classical perspectives, some interpretations with more dominant social elements were subsequently added: that the Kingdom of God is a Christian transformation of social reality, organized in accordance with God's will for humanity.

In the twentieth century, interpreters of the Bible have confronted more radically the question of how precisely Jesus Himself understood the Kingdom of God.

(a) Some have spoken of an immediate expectation of the end, leading Him to an unreserved acceptance of death.

(b) Others have transposed the *"eschaton"* to the historical "present," maintaining that the Kingdom has already been realized by means of Christ's work.

(c) Still others have attempted to highlight a synthesis of these two points of view; that each, to a different degree, experiences the "Kingdom of God" in the present, and that it will be universally fulfilled, by a sudden and surprising act of God, in the future.

(d) Most investigators today tend to accept the view that the Kingdom of God began with Christ's manifestation in the life of mankind and is "now in the process of fulfillment."

Another important theological contribution in our time has been the underlining of the "tension" existing between the "already fulfilled" and the "not yet fulfilled." That is, that the Kingdom is coming in time and will be fully accomplished at the end of time; while, within time there is a tension between the present reality and the delayed Second Coming.

It is of decisive importance that Jesus inseparably associated His own person with the Kingdom. The certainty of the apostolic Church that after the Resurrection God "has highly exalted" Christ, that "at the name of Jesus every knee should bow . . . and every tongue confess that Jesus Christ is Lord, to the glory of God the Father" (Phil 2:9–11), led her to speak of the "Kingdom of Christ." Thus the Christological interpretation given by Christ Himself to the "Kingdom of God," namely that only in Christ is the Kingdom present. According to Origen: "The kingdom of heaven is Christ Himself, urging all men to repent and drawing them to Himself by grace."[2]

In the Orthodox theological tradition, the starting point and basis of the "Kingdom of God" is Trinitarian. It is the Kingdom of the Father and of the Son and of the Holy Spirit. After the Resurrection and Pentecost, it is the Kingdom of God and the "kingdom of his beloved Son" (Col 1:13), that enters into history, by the power of the Holy Spirit. It is an eternal reality coming "into our midst" and into the world through divine grace and the sacraments, and whose fulfillment is the goal and end of history.

2. It is within this framework of the "already begun and expected Kingdom of God," that mission—the *proclamation* of *the Kingdom* "unto the end of the earth," to the whole of humankind, with the perspective of its eschatological fulfillment—holds a fundamental position. It is the continuing duty of all disciples of all ages to proclaim the Kingdom of God and the incorporation of men of all nations into the mystical Body

---

2. Origen, *On the Gospel According to Matthew*, 11, 12, *PG* 17:293, 26-29.

of His Church—which is the prelude and the "image" of His Kingdom. The duty to preach to the whole world remains the prerequisite for the consummation of the historical process of the maturation of humankind: "And this gospel of the kingdom will be preached throughout the whole world, as a testimony to all nations; and then the end will come" (Matt 24:14). [. . .]

Through the sacraments of the Church, the faithful see and experience the event of the Transfiguration which presages the coming in glory of the kingdom of Christ. And it is through mission that all men are invited to communion in the new life, by participating in the joyful paeans of praise of the risen Christ, and by participation in the Liturgy, where the present and the coming of the Kingdom are experienced.

B

PROCLAIMING THE "KINGDOM" IN VARIOUS REGIONS OF THE WORLD

In every generation, the preaching of the Kingdom continues, but each period has its peculiarities and its particular circumstances. In the following brief review a few particular features, which have been observed over wide areas of the earth, are emphasized with a special reference given to the responsibilities and role of the Orthodox. [. . .]

1. In the regions inhabited by most of the traditionally Orthodox peoples, *"the Eastern world,"* the Church continues (1977) its sacramental presence under the circumstances of societies which are often fundamentally organized as anti-Christian ideologies. In an environment which exalts in and boasts of the achievement of social equality and justice in the historical realm, Christians must reiterate the complexity of the human person, to man's metaphysical quest, and to the steps that still have to be taken for human existence to be fulfilled.

Discreetly, but unequivocally, the presence of the Church continues to point to the problem of death, to the meaning of life, and to the purpose of history. The Orthodox communities in these parts of the world are like ever-burning vigil lamps, contributing to the awakening and vigilance of the conscience of humanity for the final coming of the "Kingdom of God." It is seen especially by their life of worship, by their humble confession of Christ, by their "martyrdom" (*martyrion*) and the lived experience of the fruits of the Holy Spirit (Gal 5:22), and in the doxological expectation of the eschaton.

In "*the Western world*," the galloping technological development, free market economy, and free movement of ideas tend to form a lifestyle that is mainly characterized by a whirl of "worldly aspirations" and an enthrallment in the immediate delights of this century and of this world. Rationalistic currents have penetrated even traditionally Orthodox countries like Greece inciting young people, thinkers and artists to dispute the meaningfulness of Christian faith, and especially that of the organized Church.

Our times call for inspired Church leaders, a living theology, related to our time, to serious monastic centers, elders and spiritual leaders to assist the people in the practice of vigilance, and to the envisioned goal and "end" of history.

The Orthodox communities that are scattered as minorities throughout the Western world are centers of spiritual life for their members; "signs" of the mystical Body of the Church, humble "images," "old"—and, therefore, particularly precious—of the Kingdom. They are called to develop the Orthodox experience in their environment in a living and timely manner for the contemporary social conditions, by creatively fusing the depths of the Orthodox tradition with the practicality of Western society.

The Western Christian communities are making sustained efforts to resist the various currents of this era, such as: technocratic development, social adjustment, philosophical reorientations, and global interdependence. At the same time, they are also striving to understand the meaning of all these changes so that they can rethink their positions and present a more suitable witness to Christ.

We Orthodox too, in both socialist and free-economy countries have a duty to take up theologically, with love, wisdom, and spiritual courage, the problems of modern man; to become aware of the radical changes that brought about the flowering of the sciences and technology, to both their positive and negative messages, and to soberly evaluate and utilize the new theories of life and social organization. [. . .]

The longing for justice and brotherhood on a universal scale cannot be abandoned to the monopolistic exploitation of others; for these ideals are at the very heart of the proclamation of the Kingdom. Indeed, they define the basic ingredient thereof: "For the Kingdom of God is not food and drink but righteousness and peace and joy in the Holy Spirit" (Rom 14:17). The "sons of the kingdom," often referred to by the synonymous expression "the righteous" (Matt 13:38, 43), must be factors of "righteousness and peace and joy in the Holy Spirit" in their immediate or broader environment. The new and ever revolutionary idea they have to offer is the unique value of the human person, which has been virtually overlooked by both Capitalism and Communism.

One particularly characteristic note in our era is the explosive protest of the youth against every kind of "establishment": their longing for fullness of life, for deep experiences, their quest for forms of spirituality that go beyond the traditional individualistic morality, their searching in the field of Eastern religions and their attempts at a more direct escape by the use of drugs. The latter phenomenon resembles a return to a kind of religion practiced among primitive peoples; where witch doctors administer herbs with narcotic properties to men afflicted by obsessive ideas and desires so as to induce a kind of "release," an ecstatic state, a leap into another world.

A living Orthodoxy has to present the process of inner transformation and renewal through the acceptance of the Word and the life-giving power of the Holy Spirit and introduce people into the "deifying" realm of the mysteries of the Kingdom. They can transmit another quality of life, "eternal" in its intensity. They can transmit the fullness of life,—"that they may have life, and have it abundantly" (John 10:10),—that the Christian faith can give by emphasizing the transcendental nature of man, the "divine image," and the existentialist communion with the Holy Trinity which is activated in and by the Holy Spirit and leads to a substantial transformation of life.

2. In the immense expanses of the so-called *"third world,"* the presence of Christians is very limited and especially that of the Orthodox, very slight, indeed, no more than a token presence. Nevertheless, there are minuscule Orthodox communities (in Eastern, Central and Western Africa, in Japan and in Korea), as a reminder of the existence of Orthodoxy. They are humble candles that witness to the fact that Orthodoxy is not identified with any particular place or culture and that there is a forgotten commandment (Matt 28:19) that awaits our attention. These communities are also ambassadors representing the Eastern Christian tradition in countries where people have become accustomed to looking upon Christianity as a sort of spiritual foreign trade commodity of Western Europe, forgetting that Christianity was born in Palestine and that it first spread to Asia and Northern Africa.

Despite this all but nonexistent presence of Orthodoxy in this enormous geographical area, it is imperative that, as members of the wider Christian family, we should be aware of the spiritual fermentations taking place in these regions, as well as the missionary efforts being made by other Christian confessions.

A significant development in recent years has been that the more responsible participation of the Orthodox in the Ecumenical Movement has resulted in a continuous invitation and challenge to share in the problems of the Christian communities of the so-called "third world." Moreover, we have been offered an opportunity to transmit theological experiences from the historical consciousness and subconscious of Orthodoxy, and, thus, "indirectly" to contribute to a correct orientation of world-wide missionary activities. The primarily Orthodox minority in the Islamic world could play an important role in promoting mutual understanding between Christians and Moslems in the context of the theological dialogue that is just beginning.

From another point of view, the sensitivity of these new Christian communities to the historical development and progress of their own people and to significant social and concrete issues, can teach us a great deal about the historical aspects of the Kingdom, the dimension of "now," so that we may avoid any one-sidedness in our view of the eschatological mystery of the "Kingdom of God." This is a mutual give-and-take process. For this reason it is useful to follow, in a serious way, the problems that preoccupy these new Christian communities.

In *Africa*, new movements, partly of a nationalist or totalitarian political nature on the one hand, and partly of a religious nature on the other, are bursting forth and spreading with a rapidity akin to the luxuriant growth of the African virgin forest. In parallel with Christian mission, two other worldwide movements electrify the Africans: Islam and the Communist ideology in its various forms. The Orthodox certainly have the opportunity, but also the obligation, to develop a more active and systematic struggle in this area, where a few Orthodox outposts are already in existence. [. . .]

The slogan of "indigenization"—initially signifying the liberation from Western structures and ideas that had been introduced along with Christianity by Western missions—must not lead to new forms of servitude, to an exclusively "African" totalitarianism or to a naive African "messianism."

The "Kingdom of God," to which all men are called regardless of color or race, has universal human dimensions in the now and in the future. The Trinitarian theology of the East remains the best theological foundation for the development of the significance of the human person and its harmonious co-existence with other persons in a communion of love in the mystery of the Trinitarian God. In this way it overcomes both the egotistical "individualism" cultivated by the capitalist mentality of the West, and the risk of "massification"—a melding together of the masses into a dehumanized throng—under the kind of arid and ruthless black dictatorship which afflicts and is the scourge of many African countries.

In *Latin America*, the striving for national identity and a more just society are burning issues, inflaming the will of the people, and it is natural that direct theological problems are posed for Christians living in this politically explosive region. The fervent longing for a healthier social structure and the idea of the "Kingdom of God" in "the world" and in history, leads to an urgent socioeconomic, militant attitude, and to a "theology of liberation" all characterized by various tendencies toward an earthly messianism.

The Christians of Latin America are reluctant to leave the initiative for a dynamic transformation of society exclusively to political forces, and indeed political forces with a negative attitude to the Faith, as happened once in Eastern Europe. This shows sensitivity to the historical process which is undoubtedly highly significant. However, as Olivier Clément has correctly pointed out, "the risk in this theology is that it may come to focus exclusively on the Old Testament and Jesus, overlooking the mystery of the Holy Spirit and the mystery of the Trinity." In the tension of struggle, one-sidedness is always a possibility.

In concert with so many other Christians with vigilant consciences in Latin America, the Orthodox presence and theological thinking must serve as a reminder of the need to preserve the whole, the historical and the eschatological meaning of the Kingdom. This truth upholds the conscience and demands the social struggle towards "justice, peace and joy" in historical time, but without losing sight of the perspective of the eschatological consummation of the Kingdom.

In Asia, the great religious systems (Islam, Hinduism, Buddhism, Taoism, and so forth) with their many faces continue to be dominant. The Christian Churches constitute a small—in many countries, tiny—but often dynamic and important minority. In recent times the need for an essential and visible dialogue with people of other religions and confessions, apart from efforts in terms of missionary activities, has made itself felt. Even though in some Christian circles this "dialogue" gives rise to suspicion, it is true that its significance is becoming increasingly clear and its importance recognized. [. . .]

Nevertheless, the encounter with other religions is seen to be strenuous and difficult and admittedly, I find it hard to share the optimism and the expectations put forward by some Orthodox scholars who believe that: "The religions themselves ought to be converted to Christ now"; or speak about an effort "to awaken the Christ who is asleep in the night of the religions."[3]

These views overlook in part the tenets of the history of these religions, and do not see that the great world religions are complex systems with structures and conditions that make it very difficult to hope for a "discovery" of Christ from within. However, surely these religions are not closed lakes, but great searching rivers, enriched not only by their main sources, but also by the melting of snow on other mountaintops along their courses, and by rainfalls that allow waters coming from nearby or far-off seas to flow into them.

The dialogue and Christian witness on a worldwide scale, will not only enable Christians to better understand the religious experiences and achievements of other peoples, it is hoped that it will also open windows through which the latter may catch a glimpse of the Kingdom. Orthodox worship, ascetic experience and discipline are, in some aspects, attuned to the same wavelength with the ethos and experiences of the Eastern world. While traveling in Thailand, Ceylon, Korea and Japan, I felt that many of the external elements of the popular

---

3. Fr. George Khodre, "An Orthodox Perspective, Christianity in a Pluralistic World: The Economy of the Holy Spirit," in S. J. Samartha, ed., *Living Faiths and the Ecumenical Movement*, Geneva, 1971.

Buddhist religion were very close to our own expressions of devotion, even though their theoretical, religious associations are entirely different.

China is a special case. It would seem that Communism here has acted as a bulldozer to the religious *flora* of the past. It has destroyed the sacred patriarchal structure in the family and society (which had been solidified in Confucianism), many of the magical elements (cultivated by popular Taoism), and in general given very strong emphasis to Chinese realism. However, it would be risky to say that no vestige of popular religious feeling survives in China. Great trees may be destroyed in a forest fire, but the roots of smaller plants, such as grasses, are more resistant. The survival of Chinese religious thought is still evident in continental China, and in the Chinese populations living in Formosa (Taiwan), Hong Kong and Singapore. There are many who look forward to the day when the Chinese, with all the facts before them, will freely recreate its own religious experience, choosing from among the elements of their own religious patrimony, as well as those of other cultures, including the Christian culture in particular. The message of the "Kingdom of heaven" will be of vital importance for this immense population that has always lived by the vision of a cosmic harmony where man is the mediator between heaven and earth. [. . .]

My aim in presenting this sketchy review has been to point out that our increasingly unified world, in which the Kingdom of God must continue to be preached, includes a wide variety of forms; and that the Christian witness must keep a watchful eye for the "signs of the times," meditating on their meaning and making creative use of the circumstances of historical reality. The "Kingdom of God," it is true, will only be complete at the *eschaton*, but let us not forget that it has already entered into history and that the activation of the "leaven" (Matt 13:33) of its presence in the ecumene (*oikoumene*) in geographical space and in historical time remains for Christians an urgent apostolic task.

C
PREACHING OF THE KINGDOM OF GOD
AND OUR PERSONAL RESPONSIBILITY

A view of the global landscape and general information about it are surely essential elements for understanding the context of Orthodox witness in the contemporary world. But this vision becomes cerebral and lifeless if it is not complimented with a more direct reference to the personal life and responsibility of each Orthodox believer. To proclaim the "Kingdom of God" is not something that refers generally and indefinitely to everyone under the sun. It carries direct experiential consequences for each one of us, which broadens the horizon of our spiritual life and brings hope, light and the breath of life.

1. Our personal contribution to the advent of the Kingdom begins with the actual *development of its "signs" within ourselves.* When a human being submits consciously to the criteria and the requirements of the "Kingdom of God," when he becomes a "dwelling place of the Holy Spirit," then he gradually comes to be a "sign," a living signpost, indicating the expected full realization of the Kingdom; and thereby the Kingdom penetrates more deeply into the human community. Its image and brilliance are reflected in the faces of the saints who have accepted it with all their hearts. St. Macarius of Egypt made the following comment regarding the passage "the Kingdom of Heaven is within you":

> That the Kingdom is within, what else can this mean but the heavenly bliss of the Holy Spirit being activated within worthy souls, just like the spiritual delight and joy and bliss in eternal light that the saints will have in the Kingdom? A pledge and a beginning of this will be given to worthy and faithful souls to possess even now through active communion with the Holy Spirit.[4]

---

4. Macarios of Egypt, *First Letter to Monks*, ΒΕΠΕΣ, vol. 42, p. 161.

2. For anyone conscientiously living the "mystery of faith," the "Kingdom of God" *has come and is coming*. For the believer, this is the most certain thing in human history. It is a blessed reality which will be fully consummated in the end no matter what delays or human reactions may intervene. The awareness of its nearness, the vision of its fulfillment "in glory," has been not only the content, but also the most vital nerve of mission. This vision fills the souls of the faithful with courage, optimism, vigilance, serenity and peace. No labor undertaken for the sake of the Kingdom is ever lost. The vision of Him who exists beyond history, the projection of the *eschaton* into the present activates the will to make right use of the present moment.

3. The "Kingdom of heaven" is *a gift of God*, an offering from Him, *but also* requires *intense human effort*, for it "has suffered violence, and men of violence take it by force" (Matt 11:12; cf. Luke 16:16). "Nor is the kingdom of God for the sleeping and the foolish . . ."[5] There are certain conditions that need to be consistently fulfilled; there are heights that must be conquered. The journey begins with repentance (Matt 3:2), the right attitude before God, with whose person the Kingdom is consummated through union with Him. The Kingdom cannot be gained by mere lip-service: "Not everyone who says to me, 'Lord, Lord,' shall enter the kingdom of heaven . . ." (Matt 7:21). Nor can it be conquered by conventional religious practices: "Unless your righteousness exceeds that of the scribes and Pharisees, you will never enter the kingdom of heaven" (Matt 5:20). Violence and grace complement each other.

Christian life has a dynamic, evolutionary character. The believer already in possession of something precious, continuously discovers more and more. It is a process of transformation from "from one degree of glory to another" («ἀπό δόξης εἰς δόξαν» 2 Cor 3:18) through the presence and the energies of the Holy Spirit. The believers unceasingly receive, discover and offer.

---

5. Clement of Alexandria, *Logos on What Rich Man is Saved*, ΒΕΠΕΣ 8:361, 36-38.

The believers who convey the message of the Kingdom are not perfect. They are like thirsty men who, knowing where the "living water" is, tell others where they too may quench their thirst.

4. Our personal Christian experience is made steadfast and strengthened through our *incorporation into the mystical Body of Christ*. Our confession draws strength from the experience of the Church. Therefore, in the final analysis, the individual, personal witness for Christ is *ecclesiastical*. When we confess the Lord, we do so mainly as members of a community, the Church which carries on His work. "Because it is only in the Church that the kingdom of heaven is preached, and every goal of the Gospel of salvation looks thereto."[6] Orthodox missionaries do not act as individuals. If they go in twos and threes, if their immediate aim is to form a worshipping community with the local people, they do not do so merely for mutual support, but in order to constitute a "sign," a "revelation" and an "instrument" of the "Kingdom of heaven" that has come and is yet to come.

It is possible that in her historical exterior the Church may present wounds, in one place or another, but in her inner depths she remains, nevertheless, a "divine institution" and of divine substance. The presence of "scandals" in this field of history does not negate the existence of the Kingdom; on the contrary, it confirms its historical authenticity. During her time on earth, in the interval between the founding, and the fulfillment of the Kingdom, between the sowing of the seed and the harvest, "the good seed," and the weeds "grow together (Matt 13:24–30); next to the "sons of the Kingdom," are also the "sons of the evil one" (13:38). There is nothing surprising in this. "All scandals" will be swept away together "at the end of time," upon the fulfillment of the Kingdom. Until then there is a need for patient acceptance of this and to strengthen "the good seed" in every way.

------

6. Eusebius, *On the Inscriptions of the Psalms. A Brief Interpretation of Some*, PG 23:1045, 35-37.

5. The culmination of the experience of the Kingdom on earth, and the essential announcement of its advent, resides in the *life of worship* for the Orthodox conscience. This is the "type" and image of the heavenly liturgy, a reflection of the doxology of the angels and saints who see the glory of the King of the universe. The nature of the Kingdom is beyond verbal description. In the Eucharistic assembly, together with the believers of all times and places, we partake of the holy Body and the precious Blood "to augment the divine grace and appropriate the Kingdom." We sense the Kingdom with our whole being, we receive a foretaste of it. The experience of the already founded and yet still expected "Kingdom of heaven" gives us a different sense of life and a different kind of dynamism. It brings within us the dawn of the Kingdom. [. . .]

6. The "Kingdom of God" is already present in the world, but *"is not of this world"* (John 18:36). The "principalities" and "the powers . . . of this present darkness" (Eph 6:12) have been dethroned after the redeeming work of Christ, but have not yet been totally destroyed. In the historical process of humanity, they will continue stubbornly to launch their counterattacks even though they know that the battle has already been decided by the Cross and the Resurrection of Christ. The lot of the "sons of the Kingdom" remains to be in conflict with these powers, and is a continuation of the work of Christ who came "to destroy the works of the devil" (1 John 3:8). In the dialogue with the contemporary social movements there exists many elements we Christians must evaluate and utilize. While remaining sensitive to the temporal, the "political," we must keep our eyes fixed intently on and never cease to point to the eschatological, the eternal.

7. Whoever lives in the light of the "Kingdom" and senses its importance, cannot fail to feel the *urgency of its announcement*. The code phrase "Confessing Christ today," which has been extensively used in recent years, does not lead us to think only

of present circumstances and the problems of today's mission, but calls to mind the immediate demand to confess Christ, to announce the Gospel of the Kingdom not tomorrow, but today. Men can—and must—enter the Kingdom today (Matt 5:20; 18:3; 20:1–16). Moreover, the effort to live the principles and the spirit of the Kingdom must be made in the "today" of every "present" moment. The devil relies heavily on the great resolutions of today which are postponed until tomorrow. And perhaps, being a modern devil, he may take satisfaction in the endless discussions in committees and assemblies in which action is often drowned.

8. Participation in the Kingdom implies *jubilation, but also tribulations*. The parables of the "treasure in a field," and the "pearl of great value" (Matt 13:44–45), refer to exceeding joy at the discovery and the acquisition of the great gift of God. "Peace and rejoicing in the Holy Spirit" is the atmosphere of the Kingdom; but at the same time, readiness for self-denial and sacrifice is demanded. Entry will be made through the "narrow gate." The apostolic experience and the lives of the saints emphasize that ". . . through many tribulations we must enter the kingdom of God" (Acts 14:22).

To clear the way for the advent of the Kingdom in the hearts of men is by no means a simple or easy task. There is a price to pay. Whoever wants to work effectively for the propagation of the Gospel must be prepared to accept pain and hardship. There is no Christianity without the Cross; nor is there Christian and missionary life without crucifixion with Christ. Those who look for comfort, for the power of this age, for worldly riches and privileges cannot be true "sons" and preachers of the Kingdom. They only contribute to misunderstanding its meaning. The ascetic tradition of the Orthodox Church is a continuous existentialist protest against an easy and comfortable Christianity, which pays lip-service to the cross of Christ, but in reality avoids or even hates it (Phil 3:18).

***

"Blessed be the Kingdom of the Father and of the Son and of the Holy Spirit . . ." It is with this doxological invocation of the Kingdom that the Church begins the celebration of the fundamental sacraments of our Church. This Eucharistic invocation and doxological gazing fulfills within our daily routine, the transformation of our lives into the mystery and image of the Kingdom.

DISCOVERING THE ORTHODOX MISSIONARY ETHOS

(1978)

• "Aspects de l'Orthodoxie—Structure et spiritualité." Basic lecture to the Colloqué organize par le Commité des Recherches d'Histoire des Religions. • French: "A la redécouverte de l'éthos missionnaire de l'Église Orthodoxe," *Aspects de l'Orthodoxie*, Strasbourg 1978, pp. 78–96. • «Τό ὀρθόδοξο ἱεραποστολικό ἦθος,» *Φῶς Ἐθνῶν* 1978, with various additions. • "Discovering the Orthodox Missionary Ethos," *Martyria–Mission. The Witness of the Orthodox Churches*, ed. I. Bria, Geneva 1980, pp. 20–29. • «Ἀνακαλύπτοντας τό ὀρθόδοξο ἱεραποστολικό ἦθος», trans. I. Roelides, *Jesus*, Nicosia 2000, pp. 26–38. (There were some variations in each of the three languages.) • *Ἱεραποστολή στά ἴχνη τοῦ Χριστοῦ. Θεολογικές μελέτες καί ὁμιλίες*, Ἀθήνα 2007.

During the last two decades (1978) we have seen a rekindling of missionary interest in the Orthodox Church. First, there is a new missionary self-awareness, second, a clearer realization of the historical reality of the Orthodox Churches, and third, an active concern with problems related to Orthodox missionary presence in the contemporary world.

A
THEOLOGICAL SELF-AWARENESS

1. *The obligation of mission.* This missionary interest is no longer presented as a novelty, an innovation within the Orthodox Church, but as a rediscovery of the sources of tradition. Recently, in varying tones and theological contexts, mission is being emphasized as an essential characteristic of the nature of the Church; it is the extension in time and space of the work of Christ. The apostolicity of the Church does not refer to apostolic succession alone, but to the fact that it preserves the unextinguished apostolic spirit, so that the Gospel may reach "the end of the earth."

Mission is viewed as a necessary expression of the ethos of Orthodox spirituality whose two poles are the Resurrection and Pentecost. The basic commandment, "Go therefore and make disciples of all nations" (Matt 28:19) is a consequence of the risen Lord's triumph. The Resurrection is the starting point for extending the disciples' mission throughout the inhabited world (*oikoumene*) so that Christ's victory, the salvation of human nature, can be preached "to the whole creation."

2. *The meaning of mission.* After the obligation of mission was stressed in the reawakening of the Orthodox missionary conscience, theological thought also focused on the meaning of Christian mission. Basic themes of thought and experience in the theology of the Eastern Church are, on the one hand, the love of the Trinitarian God in an eschatological perspective, and on the other hand, a doxological view of the mystery of God and of human existence. According to Holy Scripture, the unfolding of history begins and ends with the glory of the Father. God's interventions in history were a series of *theophanies;* the definitive manifestation of God's glory reached its culmination in the Cross and Resurrection.

The vision of the glory of the Trinitarian God is the ultimate purpose of "being" with Christ. Through the Lord's work of redemption the dawn of the last day approaches, namely man's participation in divine nature—*theosis,* by grace, in the glorious life of the Holy Trinity. Until then, the Holy Spirit continues to fulfill the divine plan with the participation of the Lord's disciples, to whom He gave authority to preach salvation to all creation, and to prepare for the *Parousia* in which the glory of God will be fully revealed.

All those who "have beheld his glory" through faith and the sacraments, and who have become members of His body, partake in a mission that has one goal: the recapitulation of all in Christ, and their participation in the divine glory. The purpose and aim of the missionary activity of the local Churches and the faithful are set forth in this broader theological spectrum. The preaching of the Gospel is a doxological movement. The foundation of a local Church is a prelude of the Kingdom of God; the creation of a Eucharistic community, which will, through the sacraments and the whole of her life, participate in the praise and life of the entire Church. Moreover, she contributes to Christ's presence becoming perceptible in a specific place and time, "until He comes" in His final *Parousia*.

If the missionary is unable to transmit this sort of glory—which is not of the world, and thus not a reflection of civilization, wealth and knowledge, but the glory of God as it is revealed in the mystery of *Kenosis*, of Resurrection and of Pentecost—then he has nothing essential to offer.

B

REALIZATION OF ORTHODOXY'S HISTORICAL REALITY

In the West there has been a widespread notion that historically the Orthodox Church has been rather indifferent to mission; that she has been preoccupied with theological disputes and an introverted liturgical life, and that through monasticism she has cultivated a static spirituality, indifferent to the world and historical events. A more careful and in-depth study of the history of the Orthodox Church reveals that their contribution in spreading Christianity has been very important throughout the ages and that Orthodoxy has lived by the theological principles mentioned above in multifaceted and multidimensional forms.

1. *The Byzantine Church*, following the missionary tradition of the first three centuries, continued to be interested in spreading the Gospel. We cannot go into historical details here,[1] but it

---

1. For a brief history of Orthodox missions see A. Yannoulatos, "Les missions des Églises d'Orient," *Encyclopaedia Universalis*, vol. XI, Paris 1972, pp. 99–102. For further information concerning Byzantine missions see by the same author, «Βυζάντιον, Ἔργον Εὐαγγελισμοῦ», στή Θρησκευτική καί Ἠθική Ἐγκυκλοπαιδεία, Ἀθῆναι 1964, Vol. 4, pp. 19–59. Ἔως ἐσχάτου τῆς γῆς, (*To the end of the earth*), Ἀθήνα 2009. Among many specific studies, see in particular: C. Diehl, *Justinien et la civilisation Byzantine au VIe Siècle,* Paris, 1901, and *Le grand problème de l'histoire Byzantine*, Paris 1943. F. Dvornik, *Les Slaves, Byzance et Rome au IXe Siècle*, Paris 1929 (in French).

would be useful to highlight some basic principles which characterized the Byzantine Orthodox missionary activity.

(a) The Byzantines were simultaneously concerned with internal mission, that is, within the empire's geographical boundaries, where there were various pockets and bulwarks of idolatry, as well as with spreading the Gospel outside the borders of Byzantium.

(b) Orthodox missionaries attempted to create an authentic local liturgical community and to translate the Holy Scripture and liturgical texts into the local languages. Whenever they did not apply this principle—as, for example, in the case of the Arabic tribes—the consequences were catastrophic. The uprooting of Christianity from the life of the Arabic people is attributed also to the fact that they did not have the biblical and liturgical texts in their own language.

(c) The building of a beautiful church has always been a priority, not only for practical purposes, but also because it is a visible symbol of God's presence in the midst of the people, the place where the sacraments of the "Kingdom which has come and is coming" would be celebrated.

(d) Emphasis on liturgical life and the ascetic ideal did not inhibit interest in the social, political, and cultural dimensions of life. Along with religion, the Byzantines offered the peoples they attracted to Christianity their experience in matters of government, education; the foundation for cultivating their own literature, and the first teachers and artists, who then instructed the future leaders in various cultural fields. They gave them all the necessary prerequisites to develop into true nations; to define themselves, and to formulate their particular identity.

(e) In accordance with Byzantine theological tradition, Christian unity was not harmed by a variety of mentalities, languages, customs, cultures and national identities. They did not, therefore, carry out a colonial policy, but helped these new peoples shape their own personalities and develop as autonomous entities.

(f) Missionary activity was never the work of so-called "missionary experts"; people from every social class and group contributed. Monks and clergy carried the main weight of the task, but many laymen, laywomen, politicians, military men and even prisoners contributed spontaneously to spreading the Gospel.

2. *The Russian Church* adopted the Byzantine missionary tradition. With originality and daring, they continued and developed missionary methods inherited from the Byzantines. For example, catholicity in their view meant that the missionary obligation extended within and outside the borders of the empire; participation of both clergy and laity, and an even broader mobilization of the faithful; education and formation of native clergy; translation of liturgical and religious texts into native languages in a systematic and deliberate manner; the celebration of the Divine Liturgy in the language of the people; and emphasis on the meaning of the temple's beauty as a visible symbol of God's glory in space.

From the beginning of the 19th century until the Marxist revolution, the Russian Church developed systematic internal missionary activities as well as external ones in China, Japan and Korea.[2]

In the immense Russian territory, the monasteries were strongholds and centers of Christian expansion and steadfastness. During the nineteenth and twentieth centuries institutions were created such as the famous "Spiritual (Theological) Academy of Kazan" which was dedicated to linguistic, religious and missionary studies. "The Orthodox Missionary Society," was also founded in 1870 by the famous missionary, Innocent Venia-

---

2. A. Yannoulatos, "Orthodoxy in China," *Porefthendes—Go Ye* 4 (1962), vol. 14, pp. 26–30, vol. 15, pp. 52-55. Idem, "Orthodoxy in Alaska," *Porefthendes—Go Ye* 5 (1963), vol. 17-18, pp. 14–22, vol. 19-20, pp. 44–47. *Idem,* "Orthodoxy in the Land of the Rising Sun," *Orthodoxia 1964*, Pan-Orthodox Symposium, Athens 1964, pp. 300–319, 338–440. *Idem, Ἕως ἐσχάτου τῆς γῆς, (To the end of the earth),* Ἀθήνα 2009.

minov, the Metropolitan of Moscow, for the purpose of educating and supporting missionaries, producing and disseminating missionary publications and providing economic aid for Orthodox missionary groups.

3. *Other Orthodox Churches*. From the middle of the fifteenth century until the middle of the nineteenth century, the Orthodox Churches in Asia Minor, Greece, Yugoslavia, Bulgaria, and parts of Romania were confronted with the problem of surviving the oppression of Islamic-Turkish domination. Under these conditions it was impossible to speak of any missionary activity. Despite this, certain Greek texts exist which refer to a considerable number of Moslems who were converted to Christianity and died as martyrs. During this prolonged period of Turkish occupation, many outstanding figures (such as St. Kosmas Aitolos, St. Nikon Metanoeite, and so forth) struggled to restore the Christian faith to those populations that had undergone the influence of Islam. In those difficult years monasteries were always centers of spiritual encouragement.

If we exclude the case of certain phases of Russian mission, the other Orthodox Churches, as a rule, did not take part in the visions and the plans of Western Christianity which, during the last centuries, combined missionary activity with the political objectives of the great powers. On the contrary, the local Orthodox Churches, living under the oppression of states with another religion, found themselves anew in the atmosphere of the early Church, of persecutions and martyrdom. This is the reason we Orthodox do not share the peculiar feeling of guilt and the expressions of "repentance," made today by certain Christians in the West for their "politics of Christian colonization"; expressions which are exploited by the various representatives of other religions. On the contrary, we feel that socially and politically we belong on the side of those oppressed by the followers of other religions and Christian confessions, and not on the side of the oppressors and spiritual colonizers. Thus, in the contemporary discussion about mission tactics, we are obligated to remind others that the erroneous mission of the so-called Christian nations did not represent the Christian position, but rather a political policy, which utilized means and masks, and even Christianity itself.

C
PROBLEMS AND ACTIVITIES OF CONTEMPORARY ORTHODOX MISSION

1. *Contemporary problems of mission:* (a) The new local Orthodox Churches which came into existence after the various Balkan nations gained their national independence were faced with a variety of internal problems. At the same time, numerous groups immigrated to western countries where different religious creeds were prevalent. In an effort to preserve their own religious traditions, the Orthodox were often forced to form closed groups. In order to confront different waves of atheism or secularization which began to infiltrate traditionally Orthodox lands, specialized missionary societies, created in the regional Churches by the initiative of bishops, priests and lay leaders, began developing programs for domestic mission.

(b) The new conditions prevailing in our day (1978), the radical restructuring of society, and other profound changes, present the Orthodox Churches with extremely difficult problems. With the communist regimes in power in Eastern Europe and the continuing erosive effect of secularism in traditionally Orthodox countries, such as Greece, the field of internal mission is clearly becoming more critical.

The faithful are called upon to participate in a universal, multidimensional, spiritual struggle at home and abroad. Thus any polarization of interest between "internal" and "external" mission should be avoided; each reinforces and stabilizes the other. The worldwide missionary duty is increasingly evident.

The whole Church must offer the whole Gospel to the whole world, to those near and to those far away, and concern itself with the whole of man and the whole of human life.

(c) The participation of the Orthodox Churches in the World Council of Churches and sustained contacts with the Roman Catholic Church have enabled many Orthodox to obtain a better view of the worldwide missionary landscape—the thought, the organization, and the activities of the Western Churches—and a broader awareness of missionary problems. Thus, a disposition of cooperation can be observed in such endeavours as the translation of the Sacred Scriptures, missionary training, Christian radio and TV programs, common research, as well as efforts to dialogue with persons of other faiths and ideologies. However, there remain serious ecclesiological problems in the way of full cooperation which cannot be silenced. When we reach the heart of these matters, we Orthodox feel that the quest for Love is inseparable from the quest for Truth and that the essential critical theological dialogue, even in this area, is not simply a right, but an obligation.

Although full participation in common missionary activities present serious difficulties regarding both Canon Law and the lack of people and resources; nevertheless, there remains a vast area for joint theological research and for laying sound spiritual foundations for mission. Therefore, the Orthodox do not hesitate to face these problems with the faithful of the Western Churches, in humility and with courage born of love, contribute to a better understanding of the meaning of Christian witness in the modern world.

2. *Activities of Orthodox mission today.* The revival of interest in the "external mission" of the Orthodox Churches originated in recent years from two unexpected quarters.

The first was the emergence of indigenous Orthodox Churches in Eastern Africa which were not the result of any European missionary activity. This was the case with the Orthodox nuclei of Uganda and Kenya, whose members came mainly from the so-called "African Independent Churches." The Church had arisen around the 1930's as a reaction to the policies of certain Protestant missions.[3]

Care of these Churches was undertaken by the Patriarchate of Alexandria, which in the 1960's created a Diocese to oversee the pastoral work in these communities. Another effort, on virgin ground, was begun a few years ago by Greek missionaries in Zaire. It must be admitted that this awakening of African interest occurred, unfortunately, at a time when Orthodox missionary consciousness was at a low point; and for this reason was not ready to respond to the possibilities presented. Thus, the African Orthodox Church was, at first, left without substantial help and developed with all the advantages and disadvantages of the spontaneous growth of a self-sown plant.

The second thrust came with the initiative of a group of young people in 1959. The "General Secretariat of the Executive Committee for Mission," of the World Fellowship of Orthodox Youth—"*Syndesmos*," began publishing the periodical "*Porefthendes—Go Ye,*" in Greek and English. In 1961 it decided to establish an autonomous Inter-Orthodox Missionary Center. This was also called "*Porefthendes*" and its goals were defined as follows: The investigation of the theoretical and practical problems associated with external Orthodox mission; cultivation of a missionary awareness in Orthodox Churches; to help the small Orthodox missionary nuclei in Asia and Africa; and to contribute to the training of missionary personnel. The Center continued the publication "*Porefthendes—Go Ye*" during the entire decade of 1960–1970 (See further analysis in Chapter 11, Paragraph B, of this book). [. . .]

---

3. D. E. Wentink, "The Orthodox Church in East Africa," *The Ecumenical Review* 20 (1968), pp. 33–43. Cf. Doens, "Information Supplémentaire sur l'Église Orthodoxe en Afrique Orientale," *Revue du Clergé Africain* 25 (1969), pp. 543–576. In both these articles, reservations and different views are presented.

D
THE ORTHODOX ETHOS IN CHRISTIAN WITNESS

I should like to add a few basic "missionary categories of thought" that exist in Orthodox theological self-awareness and experience and which determine the Orthodox ethos in Christian witness.

1. Christian mission does not seek to "conquer" the world; neither does it aim to spread and project a Christian commonwealth that controls everything. Its purpose is not to increase the authority of an organized church, but to serve the world with love and humility, to offer it salvation. It is not simply a matter of transmitting religious teachings, but the *"incarnation" of the Word* in new geographical areas and new circumstances with a view to the establishment of new "churches," of new nuclei of truth and grace, where the sacraments of the Kingdom will be celebrated and where its coming will be experienced in thanksgiving and praise.

2. The universal view of the world and of man *in the light of Trinitarian theology* presupposes correct action on the local, concrete level. A basic characteristic of Orthodox theological thought and action is the constant reference, with an attitude of praise, to the doctrine of the Holy Trinity; where human thought, humbled and transfigured, becomes a faithful recipient of the reality of love. For Orthodox, the so-called practical affairs of the Church are, in the final analysis, an extension of her dogmatic tenets. Thus, we believe that the Trinitarian theology of the East remains the best theological infrastructure for appreciation of the importance of the human person and the harmonious coexistence with other human persons in a community of love (*koinonia agapes*).

This theological perspective and certainty makes it possible to overcome both the selfish individualism cultivated by the capitalist mentality of the West and the danger of massification, reducing persons to dehumanized masses, under the various forms of dictatorship that harass and burden so many countries. The Christian message, by revealing the immense value and potentiality of the human person, seeks to transfigure life through "communion" in the life of the Holy Trinity. Thus, this becomes a witness of the manifestation of the glory of God in the contemporary world; a world which is burning with the desire for divine transfiguration.

3. In the Orthodox tradition, special emphasis is laid upon the *inner genuineness* and the dynamic significance of the holiness of life of each believer in order to radiate the Gospel. When a person submits consciously to the criteria and demands of the Kingdom of God, when one become a dwelling place of the Holy Spirit, then that person becomes a living "sign," of the anticipated fulfillment of the Second Coming. The Kingdom of the God of love is illuminated and reflected and its image is mirrored in the faces of the Saints who embrace it with their whole soul.

In the history of Orthodoxy, the greatest missionaries were those who, with the cry of the revelation, "Come Lord Jesus," vibrating in their hearts, lived the Gospel uncompromisingly. The constancy of the lives of the monks with the evangelical precepts of poverty, chastity and love gave an amazing reassurance to their mission. We are referring, of course, to the consistent heroes of the monastic ideal and not to the poorly fashioned copies.

In the Orthodox Church, this ascetic ethos did not remain limited to the monasteries, but permeated more generally the conscience of the believers. For the married life as well has its own asceticism, and each believer is called to a spiritual struggle for the establishment of the Kingdom of God within oneself, independent of the external conditions under which one lives.

In general, the Orthodox tradition is profoundly nurtured by the intuition that life has priority over speech. "Life without speech can be more beneficial than speech without life. For the former even when silent, can be beneficial, but the latter, even when shouting, will only disturb," wrote St. Neilos (430). By overcoming any polarization, the Orthodox conscience sees clearly her ideal in the combination of these two elements. "And if life and the world of reason happen to go together, they become an image, an example of all (true) philosophy."[4]

The whole tradition focuses attention on "being" in Christ or on ceaselessly "becoming" in Christ by an unremitting effort of repentance and transformation. Inner purification is placed above that of preaching. Therefore, in Orthodox spirituality the Saints have always exercised a stronger influence than preachers. As St. Gregory Nazianzus says, "It is great to speak of God; but it is greater to purify oneself in and for God."[5]

4. *The axis* around which the Orthodox community revolves and the source from which she draws spiritual strength for her mission is the liturgical life and above all the *Divine Liturgy*. The Orthodox contribution to mission is determined by the theological, sacramental message and meaning of the Liturgy. "The Liturgy is our thanksgiving for and on behalf of the created world and the restoration in Christ of the fallen world. It is the image of the Kingdom; it is the transformation of the world into the Church."[6] In the Holy Eucharist, the vigilance of the Spirit is intensified, the "coming age" is announced in glory, the meaning of the historical nature of time is transformed and the present day is bathed in the reflection of eternity. Mission does not mean just the announcement of redemption in Christ, but its revelation, an invitation to a doxological participation in the event of salvation in Christ, through the Holy Spirit.

---

4.   St. Neilos, *Epistle* 3, 242, *PG* 79:496D. Cf. *Epistle* 2, 103, *PG* 79:245BC.

5.   St. Gregory Nazianzus, *Homily* 53, *PG* 36:581A.

6.   Remarks at the Meeting on the theme "Confessing Jesus Christ Today," in Bucharest-Cernica, 4-8, June 1974, Report No. 3, paragraph 2, published in *Orthodox Theology, The Orthodox Contribution to Nairobi*, papers compiled and presented by the Orthodox Task Force of the World Council of Churches, Geneva, 1974, p. 18.

The faithful by experiencing in the Liturgy: communion with God, sanctification in truth, inclusion in Christ and through Christ in the Father, and incorporation into the Church of the past, present and future broaden the horizons of their thoughts and interests, and acquire inner strength enabling them to prolong the experience of the Liturgy into life. That is, to work for the essential promotion of brotherhood in the world, the bridging of the separated, and the elimination of all forms of cultural, linguistic, or political barriers. There is another kind of liturgy (λειτουργία means the work of people); the "liturgy after the Divine Liturgy" that each believer ought to carry on after the celebration of the Liturgy in Church. The Divine Liturgy is continued with each one as celebrant before the mystical stone altar of reality, of daily obligations. Thus the Liturgy becomes life and the whole of life is elevated as Divine Liturgy; that is, to thanksgiving, love, doxology of God, and communion with Him and with the whole world. (See "Clarification of the Phrase . . ." at the end of Chapter 4.)

5. Such a liturgical spirituality does not imply a negative attitude towards the world, but, on the contrary, an *admirable freedom and ease* facing the world, an attitude of affection and love towards man. The closer one is to God, the nearer one is to the world; and vice versa. "He, therefore, who has lost the likeness with God has also lost the intimacy with life," said St. Basil.[7] If the Church Fathers have been so important in the life and thought of the Orthodox, it is because, by drawing ever closer to God, they became more familiar with life and its problems, both personal and social.

There is a special sensitivity in patristic thought to justice, truth, compassion, and a pronounced sense of communion with all men. Even the ascetics, who have been so misunderstood by the mentality of activism, do not live for themselves but have an intense awareness that they belong to the broader society of the Church. In the *"Philokalia"* we read the following amazing defi-

---

7. St. Basil the Great, *Ascetic Homily*, PG 31:869.

nitions: "A monk is one who is separated from all and in harmony with all." "A monk is one who is separated from all and joined (*συνηρμοσμένος*) with all." "A monk is one who considers himself to be just one among the many, for he sees himself in every other person without exception,"[8] "Blessed is the monk who considers all men as God after God."[9] The matter of social justice assumes Christological dimensions in the thinking of the Saints. In their eyes, the person who is wronged, poor, sick, despised is the person of Christ. "As long as there is time, let us visit Christ, serve Christ, feed Christ, clothe Christ, offer hospitality to Christ, honour Christ," wrote Gregory Nazianzus.[10]

The struggle of the Saints for freedom from the bonds of personal egotism is directly connected to "being joined (*συναρμογή*) with all men," to the sense of unity in society where one affects all, for the improvement of its structures. The demand for justice is interwoven with the proclamation of the Kingdom. "For the kingdom of God is not food and drink but righteousness and peace and joy in the Holy Spirit . . ." (Rom 14:17). On behalf of the righteousness which makes man, more than anything else, to resemble God, the faithful are obligated to struggle with word, with silence, with their active or passive resistance, with their martyrdom. But it would be naive and superficial to identify the coming of the Kingdom of God with sociopolitical struggles and romantic messianic conceptions.

6. In the Eastern Church, one finds a strong existential understanding of the concept *"my power is made perfect in weakness"* (2 Cor 12:9). This leads to a serene freedom from "power" complexes and anxiety-for-success which often torment "missionaries" and "missionary societies." There is awareness that often what may appear as failure is only the death of the seed of

---

8. St. Neilos the Ascetic, *On Prayer, 153 Chapters*, 124, 125, *Philokalia of the Holy Neptic Fathers*, vol. 1, ed. E. Papademetriou, Athens 1974, p. 187 (in Greek).

9. St. Neilos, *On Prayer*, 121, p. 187.

10. St. Gregory Nazianzus, *On Charity*, 50, *PG* 35:909.

wheat that falls on the earth and brings much fruit later. If the unsurpassed missionary epic of the brothers from Thessaloniki, Cyril and Methodios, were to be judged, for example, by the direct fruits of their work at the beginning of the tenth century, we would have to characterize it as a failure. Their work collapsed in Moravia. Later, however, with the dispersion of their disciples to the land of the southern Slavs, to Bulgaria, and then with the spread of their work into Russia, their life sealed the history of the Slavic lands and to a great extent the history of the world.

For centuries many local Orthodox Churches have lived under political oppression. There is in Eastern Christendom a familiarity with the tragic, with poverty, with sickness, with external weakness, with the internal experience of the Cross. At the same time, however, these local Orthodox Churches demonstrated extraordinary endurance and the power of renewal. And following long periods of oppression or even of internal decline, new forces and inspired men arose and contributed to the creation of new periods of spiritual flourishing.

Each day, at the time of prayer, we Orthodox direct our thoughts and hymns toward concrete persons: apostles, confessors, martyrs. Many of them, according to the criteria of their time, had completed their lives in some tragedy. And yet in the apparent "failure" of their lives, the Church found support. There is a direct relationship between witnessing for Christ and the acceptance of the external powerlessness of martyrdom for His sake, for the love of His Church, and having always the living hope which "does not disappoint"(Rom 5:4–5).

Seeking no worldly influence or glory, many saints have remained entirely unknown to history. But the genuineness of their lives and their unyielding love of God profoundly affected the souls of the anonymous people who knew and loved them. Many carried on missionary work without being aware of it. They did immense good just by simply existing. They lived in freedom: freedom from the desire for wealth, for fame, for power and from the fear of human failure. The daily contact of the Orthodox believer with all these saints, who lived constantly and doxologically with Christ's first and final coming, with a spirit of joyful praise, gives shape and form to the Orthodox ethos.

This liturgical, ascetical, social and martyr-like ethos is still at work. It is the kind of ethos that offers to missionary work a special quality of expression and presence, an invincible endurance and joyful freedom.

7

THE ASCENT OF HUMAN NATURE

(1980)

• Homily at the main event of worship at the World Missionary Conference of the World Council of Churches in Melbourne, 1980.• "The Ascent of Human Nature," *International Review of Mission* 69 (1980), pp. 202–206. • *Your Kingdom Come. Mission Perspectives*, Geneva 1981, pp. 237–242. • French: "L'élévation de la nature humanine," *Que ton Règne Vienne! Perspectives missionnaires*, Genève 1982, pp. 101–105. • «Ἡ ἀνύψωση τῆς ἀνθρωπίνης φύσεως», *Πάντα τά Ἔθνη* 6 (1987), vol. 22, pp. 3–5. • *Ἱεραποστολή: στά ἴχνη τοῦ Χριστοῦ. Θεολογικές μελέτες καί ὁμιλίες*, Ἀθήνα 2007.

A
THE ULTIMATE SIGN OF
GLORY FOR HUMAN NATURE

With the development of the sciences and technology in the Twentieth century, many have spoken about the amazing capabilities of man. Indeed, sometimes boastful expressions have been heard, such as: "God is dead." "We are gods." These voices sound like a direct echo of the ancient assertions of the Devil in Eden: "And you will be like God, knowing good and evil" (Gen 3:5).

But the Devil cannot create something new. He cannot create; he can only pervert creation. With that ancient proposal of his, he distorted the truth, and turned it into a lie. Just as in Eden, he began with a basic truth, but he expressed it in such a way that set humanity in a wrong direction; pushing humanity towards the way of arrogance, and self-realization.

In the same way, the desire of man to elevate himself to the throne of God is not altogether wrong. It is primarily a *distortion* of a predisposition that has a divine origin, in that God created man "in His own image" in order to be with Him.

Humanity has finally found the right direction towards the throne of God through Jesus Christ, the "second Adam." This is exactly the main point of the Christian message that culminates in the feast of the Ascension. The final destination of humanity is precisely deification—to be made divine (what in Eastern theology we call *theosis*). But this is only possible in Jesus Christ who "emptied himself, taking the form of a servant" (Phil 2:7).

This basic theological message is transmitted by the Feast of the Ascension. In accordance with the Christological conscience and the worshipping subconsciousness of the ancient undivided Church, we see in the Ascension the consummation, "the end" of all the other decisive phases of the course of the life of Christ, the God-Man. The descent of the Logos of God from heaven to earth began with the Annunciation. The ascent of the same Logos of God from earth to heaven is fulfilled through the Ascension. The Annunciation was the prelude to the Incarnation, while the Ascension is the conclusion of it. In the Annunciation then, He descended from heaven to earth naked, without flesh, while now He ascends from earth to heaven, raising the human nature He had assumed with Him. Forty days after His birth, He was taken to the temple and as the "first-born" was dedicated "to God," according to the Law. Forty days after His Resurrection from the dead, which is a rebirth of the human race, He ascends to the celestial sanctuary above the heavens as the "first-born of the dead" in order to present His human nature, "holy and pure," to God the Father.

> God the beginningless, Who did exist before all ages, Who took man's nature on Himself, deified it mystically, was taken up on this day. Hence, the Angels ran before the Apostles, did indicate Him as He rose with great glory to Heaven's heights; and as they worshipped Him they cried out and said: Glory be to God Who was taken up.[1]

The basic key to the theological understanding of the message of the Feast of the Ascension remains the biblical concept of Christ as the "second Adam" and as "the first-born" of creation. The whole divine plan in Christ not only brings reconciliation between God and man, but reunites that which

---

1. The *Kathisma* hymn from Matins of the Feast of the Ascension, Third Tone, "Awed by the beauty."

the sin of the first Adam had separated: humanity and heaven. The divine "glory" is once again given to human existence. Just as the fall of Adam opened for humanity the way to Hades, thus the Ascension of the "second Adam," Jesus Christ, opened the way for our entrance into heaven, where the presence and the will of God prevails absolutely.

With His birth, Christ became the "first-born among many brethren" (Rom 8:29). His presence and work have cosmic dimensions. He is "the first-born of all creation" (Col 1:15), the "beginning, the first-born from the dead, that in everything He might be preeminent." (Col 1:20). [. . .]

The central purpose of the redemptive mission of the Lord was not to add a few moral principles or to clarify certain aspects of the Old Testament, but to ontologically renew "all things"; to raise up everyone who had fallen, to make them incorruptible, to glorify the condemned, to deify human nature. It is precisely this which remains as the heart of the Gospel message; that Christ became incarnate "and dwelt among us," that He preached the Kingdom of God in word and power, that He suffered for us, that He arose from the dead and ascended into heaven, opening to mankind the Kingdom of God. Christ transfigured the human nature that He had assumed. That is, our own nature, and ultimately raised it with the glorified Body of His divine-human Person to heaven, where God is absolutely present, above and beyond our ability to comprehend, and yet so very close to us.

The old classical language, bound within static concepts of space and time—"above," "below"—threatens to compartmentalize us into false and dangerous dilemmas regarding the presence of Christ in heaven and at the same time "with us." Nevertheless, the contemporary advances in the natural sciences emphasize that space is not static, that the universe is in motion and that space is continually expanding; space and time are mutually interdependent.

The assumption of human nature and its elevation has been ontologically completed by our "first-born brother," our God-

Man Lord. It is precisely this event which constitutes the ultimate sign of glory for human nature. But for us it remains an enormous potential, still underdeveloped. Everyone, as a free person, is called to freely accept this possibility, to activate it through the power of the Holy Spirit, who brings the Kingdom of God into our midst, who leads us to the "bosom of the Father."

B

IMPLICATIONS FOR DIRECT MATTERS

All these things, while at first sight may appear to be theoretical, have in fact, like all the dogmas of the Church, direct relevance to the concrete and practical problems of our life; much in the same way that mathematical equations offer solutions to many practical problems in physics.

1. This view of the significance of the elevation of the human body with the Ascension of Christ emphasizes precisely the enormous *value of the material world and of the human being* as a psychosomatic unity. It constitutes a most surprising affirmation for the whole person. Christ sanctifies the human body; it is this body that He transforms, resurrects and elevates to heaven. This is the body of the God-Man which, before His Resurrection worked, walked, served, suffered and bears "the marks of the nails." The Christian revelation does not speak about liberation of the soul and spirit from the prison of the body like other philosophical or religious systems. It is opposed to vague idealisms and to every form of atheistic humanism. It preaches the resurrection and elevation of the whole human nature. After the presentation to the Father, the "regenerated" human nature reached the height of its development. *Humanity and the world acquire an indescribable dignity and significance.*

Those who take an authentic interest in human beings, in the protection of their health, their freedom, and justice and dignity of the human person, find themselves in harmony with the great purpose of the elevation of human beings which was realized by the risen and ascended Christ. In order to be truly human one must be "God-like." Jesus Christ remains always the measure of the fullness. Captive—as we often are—to a post-Augustinian theological tendency to devalue human existence, it is necessary to rediscover respect for human nature and to understand the amazing possibilities, and unimaginable horizons which were opened to it by the ascended Jesus.

2. The missionary work we serve is not simply the proclamation of some moralistic message or an invitation to salvation for only a few individuals. Rather, it is an *invitation to a journey, to a liturgy of transformation of the whole world,* to the activation of human potentiality for the elevation, the "ascent," of the whole of human nature to "the throne of God," to deification by grace through participation in the life of love of the blessed Holy Trinity.

Through the mission of the Church, people are invited to participate in the fullness of life, so that they may have "life and have it abundantly" (John 10:10); and to become acquainted with the infinite potentialities which have been given to mankind through the incarnation and resurrection of Christ (Rom 8:17). Our participation in this life, in this glory, will reach its fulfillment in the *eschaton,* in the Second Coming. "When Christ who is our life appears, then you also will appear with him in glory" (Col 3:4). His glory radiates continually toward the whole world, to the whole of creation. The Ascended Christ is the One who "fills the universe." Thus the Kingdom of God, which already has begun within us and the fulfillment of which we are anticipating, is thus experienced with an astonishingly dynamic hope.

3. After the Ascension, the disciples "returned to Jerusalem with great joy" (Luke 24:52), full of certainty, strength, vision, and hope. "This Jesus," said the angels, "who was taken

up from you into heaven, will come in the same way as you saw him go into heaven" (Acts 1:11)—"this same Jesus" in His divine-human nature. There is a *deep joy that springs from a dynamic understanding of the coming of the Kingdom of God,* from the certainty that we know the most crucial message in human history.

There is a joy in the power that Christ has promised: "You shall receive power when the Holy Spirit has come upon you" (Acts 1:8). There is joy because of the decisive role that has been bestowed on us as "sons of the Kingdom" to work together "as co-workers of God" to spread this redemptive witness "to the end of the earth" (Acts 1:8).

Bringing the Kingdom to new frontiers is not a human activity. It is the Holy Spirit who continues the mission of Christ in time and in space with His "Christ-like" disciples making the Kingdom present "within us," and in every person in the Church. But primarily, this great joy is poured out into our lives as we view the tremendous potentialities which the Ascension of our Lord opened in the life of humanity and the whole world. Moreover, it is active even in our difficult hours: when we follow Christ on His way to the field of harvest, along the streets of the spiritual Jerusalem, to the mystical mountain of the Transfiguration, in His clash with the powerful religious or political leaders of His time, or on His way to Golgotha. We know that this road ends in the Resurrection, in the Ascension, "in the bosom of the Father." *This joy then is not closed*, not individualistic; it is developed within the Church, it is the doxology of the community of believers, the dynamic proclamation of the new potentialities of humanity.

In recent years, many proclamations have been heard about human rights. Considering humankind and our work in the light of the Ascension, we come to realize more and more that our Christian mission is a proclamation about and a *struggle for the highest human right*—to become that for which we are created; to become "Christ-like," by the grace of God; to realize our true nature. All other human rights are derived from this right.

In this they all find their fulfillment. Any thought that ignores the ultimate right of the human person results in disorientation, and makes one indifferent towards what is the essential element of human existence: one's divine origin and one's divine destination.

Our highest missionary obligation is summarized in proclaiming and in living the fact that every person has the right, and the obligation to activate the infinite potentialities which are offered to each human person in Christ through the Holy Spirit; so that we proceed to the fulfillment of human existence. In the theological language of the Eastern Church this is called "deification" (*theosis*), the "end" (*telos*) of which the Ascension of our Lord reveals to us in a daring, and joyful manner, one that transcends every static human thought.

8

EUCHARIST—SERVICE—WITNESS IN MUTUAL RECIPROCITY

(1983)

• Report to the 6th Assembly of the WCC in Vancouver, Canada.
• "Worship—Service—Martyria," Paper for the Sixth Assembly of the
World Council of Churches, *International Review of Mission* 72 (1983),
pp. 635–639. • «Εὐχαριστία, Διακονία, Μαρτυρία, σέ ἀλληλοπεριχώρηση»,
Πάντα τά Ἔθνη 2 (1983), vol. 13, pp. 6–8. • "Christlicher Zeugnis in einer
gespaltener welt. Leiturgia—Diakonia—Martyria," Hrsg. L. Coenen,
W. Tranmüller, Vancouver 1983. *Zeugnisse, Predigten, Ansprachen,
Vorträge, Initiativen* (Bzör 48), Frankfurt, a. m. 1984, pp. 124–128.
• *Ἱεραποστολή στά ἴχνη τοῦ Χριστοῦ. Θεολογικές μελέτες καί ὁμιλίες*, Ἀθήνα
2007.

The apostolic experience, upon which the Church developed, was not based upon the knowledge of a theoretical teaching, a new law, but, primarily, upon the knowledge of one Person and one power: the Person of Jesus Christ and the power of His Resurrection. The Lord chose the first members of the Church, His Apostles, "to be with him, and to be sent out to preach and have authority to cast out demons" (Mark 3:14–15).

A
WORSHIP

The primary objective of those who commit themselves to Christ is to "be with him" (Mark 3:14); to be constantly in a living relationship with Him. Shortly before His sacrifice on the Cross, the Lord entrusted to His apostles the sacrament of the Holy Eucharist in order to ensure this constant communion also in the future. Later, before sending them "to teach" the nations, He bestowed upon them the gift of the Holy Spirit.

It is precisely this apostolic experience of the knowledge of the person of Christ, and of "communion" with Him that remains the living experience within the Church. This experience is expressed and vigorously preserved in ecclesiastical worship. It is especially in the Holy Eucharistic which does not consist simply of the recapitulation of the mystery of the Incarnation, the Resurrection and Pentecost, but of the experience of Christ's redemptive event in the here and in the now. The liturgy is the vision that gazes towards the last things (*eschata*) when Pascha will be fulfilled "in the endless day of his Kingdom."[1] It is a way of participation in His life and glory.

Every Divine Liturgy renews the awareness of the Kingdom of God around and within us: (a) Revealing synoptically the meaning of history, which is the transformation of the cosmos within the divine love of the Logos of God and the energy of the Holy Spirit. (b) Inviting to a movement of liberation from every kind of conventionality, from all-encompassing impassioned thoughts and from the magnetism of egocentric tendencies. (c) Leading to a communion of love with the faithful of all the ages and all places in the world; strengthening the feeling of unity with all people. It brings together those people who are aware that they have within themselves the image of God and those who doubt it due to the influence of various religious or ideological systems.

Thus, the Eucharistic event of the Liturgy gives stability to the Christian experience and constitutes its culmination. It transfigures human existence and makes it a participant in the glory of God. Worship, and especially the Divine Liturgy, contributes to the uninterrupted reception of the Gospel of grace and salvation, not as abstract knowledge, but rather as power. The Divine Liturgy is a doxological announcement and manifestation of the Kingdom of heaven to a world that, even if it wants to ignore it, deep inside is seeking it.

As a "sign of the Kingdom," the Eucharistic gathering constitutes a challenge for the contemporary technocratic world, continually emphasizing the fact that there is yet another dimension of human existence. Furthermore, it is an invitation to a fellowship of love with the One who is Love, the Triune God. In this manner worship steadfastly preserves its "missionary character" for secular society, drawing it like a centripetal force

---

1. Hymn of Pentecost.

to the center of the universe, who is Christ, "to unite all things in Him" (Eph 1:10).

Through personal prayer this "communion" which is completed during the Liturgy extends into our daily activities and to our efforts that at first glance may appear neutral. The "Jesus Prayer" or the "prayer of the heart," constantly brings to mind and heart the presence of the risen Christ and radiates His presence into the environment.

B
SERVICE

The prayer of the Church culminates in the Eucharistic anaphora at the moment of the consecration of the Holy Gifts and by extension to the entire creation: "Let your Holy Spirit descend upon us and upon these gifts before us." It is in this way that Pentecost is constantly being experienced in the Church. But any community that receives the Spirit should be aware that it is not to be a possession or property of a few individuals, or for personal enjoyment and ecstasy, but *for a worldwide mission* (Acts 1:8). At Pentecost all the barriers and borders that divide human beings were destroyed by the mighty wind and the tongues of fire. Pentecost is the overcoming of the confusion of Babel; it inaugurates a new relationship of trust and love with God and human beings; a new decisive possibility for communion between God and humankind. The fruit of the Holy Spirit is not limited to ecstatic phenomena; rather, it refers to the transformation of personal relationships. "The fruit of the Spirit is love, joy, peace, patience, kindness, goodness, faithfulness, gentleness, self-control" (Gal 5:22–23).

The local Church, the diocese, the parish, but also every form of expression of ecclesial life, such as monasteries, religious organizations, missionary societies, various small informal missionary groups and communities constantly remain open and fulfill their duty within society to radiate the love and glory of Christ to the whole of humanity for the sake of the entire human race (*oikoumene*), always receiving and offering the Gospel. Any self-enclosure can result in the negation of their nature, and leads to suffocation. The continuous offering of what they have, of what they are, forms the mystery of their existence. When people give, their goods are multiplied—as it happens exactly when we share our joy. Whenever people hold their possessions exclusively for themselves they go to waste. This basic principle holds true for spiritual gifts, as well as material goods. This is true in all levels of existence from the simple to the complex. Whenever a church group, large or small, becomes self-enclosed, it loses itself, it self-destructs. You discover yourself essentially when you offer yourself. This is a Christian principle of universal application. Whenever people share, their possessions multiply. Thus selfless service within the broader human community is not merely an ethical "should," but the life, the very breath of the Church.

In our various international conferences and meetings we speak a lot about justice, unity, equality, and sharing in the problems of the poor. This is an easy thing! But afterwards, we fail to share and we prefer our own wealth, comfort, and security, that is, we finally prefer ourselves. The basic question is who can free us from this captivity to ourselves. According to the apostolic experience, only a living fellowship with Christ—as received in prayer and worship—can free us from our personal interests and continuously renew the spirit of sacrifice and courage, so that we may fight for justice and brotherhood even when situations appear hopeless. Without this inner power and freedom, all our attempts can degenerate into a boring verbiage.

Worship and service are connected like the two phases of one breath: inspiration and expiration. There cannot be a dynamic expiration in service, without a dynamic inspiration in worship, and vice versa. One cannot have the illusion of living "in Him," who was the "one who serves" (Luke 22:27), who "went about doing good" (Acts 10:38), unless one's life is a dynamic expression of this transfiguring power; that means, resistance against demonic powers that corrupt human existence through injustice, greed, distortion of the thought and meaning of life, and thus continuously polluting man's imagination. One cannot remain indifferent before the various forms of oppression of people just because they are poor, to unjust discriminations because of race, sex or age, or to human egotism, in its many forms, which is precisely in and of itself the sin, the rebellion against the love of the Triune God.

The participation, therefore, in any kind of dynamic movement to liberate human life from the domination of every demonic power, oppression and unjust construct is the direct result of the liturgical experience, the direct expression of the experience of salvation. At the Orthodox Conference at Etchmiadzin in 1977, we emphasized that, after the Divine Liturgy in the church, a new liturgy begins on the stone altar of everyday reality, a liturgy that every faithful must carry out. This became a codified phrase in the ecumenical movement: "the liturgy after the Liturgy (see end of Chapter 4). Whosoever wishes to live in Christ is obligated to follow Him, not only to the upper room and to the Mount of Transfiguration, but also in the dust of the apostolic way, uphill to Jerusalem and to Golgotha.

C
WITNESS

The apostolic experience is expressed in announcing the "Gospel of glory" continuously in new frontiers and areas considered unreachable, not only in the geographical sense, but also in social, scientific and structural terms. A modern sickness that threatens to paralyze Christian mission is the notion that since the whole earth is an area of mission, we are all "missionaries"; and, therefore, confine ourselves to our own circumstances, ignoring the more difficult areas thought unreachable by Christian witness. But in His final commandment, the Lord insists on a universal point: "And you shall be my witnesses in Jerusalem and in all Judea and Samaria and to the end of the earth" (Acts 1:8).

The apostolic experience and witness is crowned with martyrdom. "And you shall be my martyrs (witnesses)." In other words, "you must say something essential concerning 'My life' and 'My death' with your life and your death." It is indicative to point out that the Greek word "martyr" (*martus*) in the New Testament has a double meaning. One meaning is "I offer my testimony,"—to be a witness, and the other is to seal that witness with blood—with "martyrdom" (*martyrion*). The knowledge of the person of Christ will be completed through the existential knowledge of His death. "That I may know him [Christ] and the power of the resurrection, and may share his sufferings, becoming like him in his death" (Phil 3:10). This remains as a common calling for the members of the Church, a portion for all the faithful in her witness and her martyrdom. This kind of witness is bound up with martyrdom, transforming trials into deep joy, the external social failures to an inner maturity, into existential participation in the death and the life of Christ. Frequently that which one calls success is nothing more than a masked failure and that which society believes to be a failure hides sometimes an essential success. [. . .]

During the first centuries it was necessary for millions Christians to witness for Christ with their blood. In all of the critical eras, even until today—before the foundation of new local Churches or in the attempt to uproot ancient ones—martyrdom or the witness of blood has once again been required. We all know, more or less, some contemporary martyrs who paid with their lives for their faithfulness and devotion to the righteousness and truth of Christ.

There are also millions of other Christians "faithful unto death," who were not physically martyred, who lived their personal sacrifice, their love for the Crucified Savior in other ways. The Apostles lived the first phase of witness and martyrdom as they faced a thousand perils and difficulties in their missionary work, they even "despaired of life itself" (2 Cor 1:8; cf. 6:4–6; 11:26–27). Later, the monks and nuns lived the experience of martyrdom by their ascetic life in the desert, in their struggle against demonic forces, accepting freely and sharing the life of poverty and deprivation of the people, and by standing up to the transgressions of civil and ecclesiastical authorities.

In the Orthodox Church there is a continuous daily commemoration of the martyrs and saints, among whom are included equally, men, women, children, rich, poor, persons of both high and low rank; people "from every nation, from all tribes . . . and tongues" (Rev 7:9). In the life of worship there is accomplished a communion, a "festival," together with all those who loved Christ, without reservation and courageously, until death. The participation in this feast of the saints gives the faithful new courage, hope and inspiration to experience their personal martyrdom in whatever proportion or form presented in life.

Today participation in some kind of martyrdom takes on new and unexpected forms in the multifaceted struggles for social justice, equality, peace and unity, in order to experience the Gospel in personal life, in times of critical decisions, in conflicts with the powers of this world, within the challenges of the structures of contemporary society. In one way or another, all of us will know the martyrdom that God has given to each of us within the different circumstances of life: in the desert of the great cities, in the daily silent trial of cooperation or of responsible administration. We carry our personal Cross "daily" (Luke 9:23) always within the perspective of dynamic hope and mystical joy, ". . . in much affliction, with joy inspired by the Holy Spirit" (1 Thess 1:6).

***

In the contemporary spiritual quest, it is incumbent upon us to exert every effort to live the apostolic experience in its fullness. The exclusive emphasis on the particular leads to a heretical form of life and an essential weakening of all the other elements of life. Worship, service and witness find themselves in a state of mutual influence and interpenetration. Worship submits to a continuous "biological purification" of the various wastes of human egoism offering constantly the needed pure water to cleanse the diverse personal and combined energies. This purification and sanctification contributes to the renewal of human life and the life of the world.

9

THE DOXOLOGICAL UNDERSTANDING
OF LIFE AND MISSION

(1984)

• «Ἡ δοξολογική κατανόηση τῆς ζωῆς καί τῆς ἱεραποστολῆς», Ἐποπτεία, Ἀφιέρωμα στό Ἅγιον Ὄρος 96 (1984), pp. 1123–1232.
• Πάντα τά Ἔθνη 5 (1986), vol. 17, pp. 20–27, vol. 18, pp. 4–7.
• Ἱεραποστολή στά ἴχνη τοῦ Χριστοῦ. Θεολογικές μελέτες καί ὁμιλίες, Ἀθήνα 2007.

When we use expressions like the "glory of God," "doxological stance," "unto the glory of God," most people think of something being offered to God, an attitude of praise, or something being done for the glory of God. The parallel use of the word "glory" for matters pertaining to human life has contributed to altering its original biblical meaning. Some people even ask what need has the self-sufficient Lord of the universe for His creatures to offer Him glory? Nevertheless, the meaning, the message, and the timeliness of the truths related to the glory of God are far more broad and profound, and have multifaceted connections with life and mission.

A

A THEOLOGICAL AND BIBLICAL REVIEW

1. One of the fundamental truths of our faith underscores that God is incomprehensible and inaccessible as to His essence. But the biblical revelation overcomes the impasse of this initial position regarding the incomprehensibility of God by announcing clearly that, while the essence of God remains unknowable and incomprehensible, nevertheless, His presence becomes perceptible in the world, in the universe, with the *manifestation of His glory*. When God is revealed in the various *theophanies*, it is not His essence, but His glory that *becomes* perceivable. For man in his finite nature is in a position to understand and experience only the glory of God, which is the

fervency of the divine presence, inconceivable, inaccessible, but directly perceptible. This glory is the dynamic, creative, transfiguring energies of the divine supra-essence of the Holy Trinity. The glory of the Triune God embraces the universe, and brings "all things" into the range of His love and redemptive grace, and it remains in the vastness of eternity, even when time will be abolished.

This critical point of the incomprehensibility of God, revealed by His own initiative, is a subject which patristic thought attempted to shed light upon by using the *distinction between the essence and the energies of God*. From St. Basil the Great up to the more systematic development by St. Gregory Palamas, Eastern Christian thought distinguishes steadfastly between the created universe and the uncreated energies of God. The God who is "beyond all being" is not identified with any created conception or idea, as in the philosophical meaning of essence. That which man is able to receive, in the final analysis, is the glory of God. The distance between creature and Creator remains immeasurable. Any word about God, ultimately, can only be a word about the glory of God, which expresses both His immeasurable distance and His nearness.

Whatever we know about the mystery of God, about the evangelical message of the salvation of man, is related basically to the manifestation of the glory of God. And this is why the most authentic form of expressing this mystery is the one which deals with His glory. The most suitable reflection on the meaning and the manner by which this message is communicated is also doxological. It is not so much a matter of method, as it is a way of thinking, of disposition, of life before the unapproachable mystery of the eternal God. The true understanding of the glory of God, its proper experience and transmission, are of central interest in Orthodoxy, and is worthy of a more analytical approach to its biblical foundations.

2. The beginning of the Christian experience and the foundation of hope and optimism is the reality that *the glory of God is*

extended to the entire world. The more inaccessible and transcendent the essence of God, the more the energies of the divine essence, the glory of God, embraces the universe. "The heavens are telling the glory of God" (Ps 19:1). "Holy, holy, holy is the Lord of hosts; the whole earth is full of his glory" (Isa 6:3).

The tragedy of the world begins when, with the egotistical use of the freedom of rational beings—initially an order of the angelic world and later the first human couple—the glory of God was concealed. For after this explosion of selfishness and egotism, sin was interjected like a polluted mist between the reality of divine glory and the human conscience, the summit of creation. This disability weighs down human existence: "Since all have sinned and fall short of the glory of God" (Rom 3:23). The people, no longer able to enjoy the presence of God, ". . . did not honor (glorify) him as God or give thanks to him" (Rom 1:21). Victims of their illusions and their foolishness, the people "exchanged the glory of the immortal God" and replaced it with various idols of their imagination and their will (Rom 1:21–23).

A new decisive and definitive manifestation of the glory of God takes place with the revelation in Christ: "And the Word became flesh and dwelt among us, full of grace and truth; we beheld his glory, glory as of the only Son from the Father" (John 1:14). Knowledge of the Logos, communion with Him, according to the experience of St. John, is *the vision of his glory.* All the events in the life of Christ, through which the revelation of God and the renewal of the universe is accomplished, are expressions of the glory of God. His birth means: "Glory to God in the highest, and on earth peace among men with whom he is pleased" (Luke 2:14). The miracle at Cana, with which the "signs" of His Kingdom began, was an event by which Jesus "manifested his glory" (John 2:11). On the mount of Transfiguration—more directly and in a blinding way—"his glory," His divine and human nature, transfigured by the uncreated light of His divine glory, is revealed to the three disciples (Luke 9:32).

But it was particularly the Passion and the Crucifixion which manifested the glory of God, in its most inconceivable and original dimensions Christ Himself, in His final prayer to the Father, refers directly to this truth and connects organically and internally the themes of love, life, and glory which constitute expressions of the redemptive action (John 17:1–26). With His passion, which is followed directly by the Resurrection, Christ enters "into his glory" (Luke 24:26). Destroying decisively the power of death and receiving "all authority in heaven and on earth" (Matt. 28:18), the risen Christ "ascends in glory," unites "the things of earth to the things of heaven," raises human nature to the "right hand of the Father of glory," and returns human history to its rightful direction.

Since then, that which was accomplished ontologically for human nature in the person of Christ, the First-born of creation, is now being continued with the outpouring of the Holy Spirit. At Pentecost the glory of God is revealed and manifested in another dynamic manner, that of "the rush of a mighty wind" and "tongues as of fire" (Acts 2:2–3). The manifestation of the presence of the Triune God in the universe, in time and eternity, is accomplished with the constant energies of the Holy Spirit.

After Pentecost the apostles of the Church in every period of her history, invited the people "to lead a life worthy of God," who calls all of us "into his own kingdom and glory"(1 Thess 2:11–12). This invitation, "exhortation," and "encouragement" establishes "the purpose of Orthodox mission." The heart of the apostolic message is the proclamation, "how great among the Gentiles are the riches of the glory of this mystery, which is Christ in you, the hope of glory" (Col 1:27). The purpose of Christian life is determined to be participation in this glory of Christ.

The entire eschatological orientation of the Church reaches the summit where the glory of God will be manifested in all of its brilliance and fullness, when the Son of man comes "in his glory" and "sits upon the throne of his glory" for the final judgment and fulfillment of His Kingdom.

Those who have received the light of the glory of God with humility and faith, transforming it in their life into love, see indeed the glory of God as light. Those who rejected and pushed away the revelation of the glory of God in its humble form will encounter it, ultimately, as blinding and consuming fire. The radiance of the glory of God seals the course of history and exalts it into unimaginable dimensions.

The final pages of the New Testament, illuminating the eschatological vision of the Church, describe the "holy city of Jerusalem," which descends out of heaven from God and is illumined exclusively by "the glory of God" (Rev 21:11,23). All the powerful of the earth "shall bring their glory into it," and offer "the glory and honor of the nations" (Rev. 21:24–26). Every other glory of the world, of the civilizations of the people of the earth are laid at the feet of God and find its "end" and fulfillment in participation in the divine glory.

B

APPROPRIATING AND
RADIATING THE GLORY OF GOD

In the doxological perspective, mission is not understood as a method for proselytizing and attracting new members to a closed community living for itself. Rather, it is a polyphonic, multidimensional manifestation of the glory of God in the Church, with each believer glorifying God. The basic purpose of mission is the mobilization: (a) of the whole of humanity to appropriate and to radiate the glory of God; and (b) to a common journey within the realm that is illumined by the glory of God and to contribute to the return of all creation to the doxological rhythm.

1. Appropriating and radiating the glory of God are *two continuous movements of basically the same pulse.* The doxological proclamation of the Gospel comes as a response to the revela-

tion of the divine glory in the soul. And what follows is a new reason for receiving the glory of God.

Life in Christ does not mean a simple acceptance of some affirmations of faith, principles and rules of behavior. As often as the emphasis has been placed upon these, we have ended up with sterile and offensive external formalities, a legalistic spirit, and a dry moralistic mentality. The purpose of Christian life remains the appropriation of the glory of God in Christ through the Holy Spirit. This relationship is revealed as light, love, and joy even in this life. The radiance of the glory of God penetrates into human existence through the grace of the Sacraments.

The vision of the glory of God follows as a consequence of our living faith. The words of Christ are directed not only to Martha, but to each and every person. "If you would believe you would see the glory of God" (John 11:40).

Christ does not offer to us a legalistic type of deliverance from guilt, a static justification. "Calling" and "justification" are sequential stages. The end is still the glory, the journey, and participation in the glory of God. "And those whom he justified he also glorified" (Rom 8:30). Illumination and glory, faith and glory, praise and glory, glory and works advance together side by side.

All of the efforts and activities of the faithful must be offered to the glory of God. "So glorify God in your body and in your spirit, which are God's" (1 Cor 6:20). All of human existence, the bodily and spiritual functions and possibilities participate in the glory of God. The faithful receive it and they offer it up.

Participation in the glory of God, to which Christians have been called, means a general transformation of existence, a general transfiguration, within the breath and the fire of the Holy Spirit. It is a matter of a mingling of the human being with the energies of the Holy Spirit, seeking its total renewal. The moment that the believer becomes, with the presence of the Holy Spirit, a dwelling place of the glory of God, he or she begins to radiate the divine glory.

In the patristic sayings included in the *Gerontikon* there is recorded an excellent account about the life of an anonymous saint:

> Abba John Kolovos said that a spiritual elder became a recluse and became well-known in the city and had much glory. He was once informed, "One of the saints is dying; go to greet him before he falls asleep." And then he thought to himself: If I go out in the daytime, people will run after me to honor me and I shall lose my peace. So I will go at night, in the darkness, and avoid them all. So he went out of his cell with the darkness of night, because he did not want anyone to see him. But behold, from God two Angels were sent down with lamps to lighten his way. Thus, the whole city ran to him, seeing his glory. And the more he thought to avoid any glory, the more he was glorified. In this example we see fulfilled what was written: He who humbles himself shall be exalted.[1]

Those who become recipients of the divine glory consequently impart a transfiguring radiance within society as a whole. Only those glorified by divine grace are essentially able to glorify God, being themselves bearers of His glory. This is why the Saints remain the most significant "missionaries" of Christendom.

2. This expression of glory and way of life must not, nor can it, remain a personal act of faith or private communal experience of the Church. *It must be spread throughout the earth.* "Be exalted, O God, above the heavens and let thy glory be over all the earth!" (Ps 108:5). This biblical verse, which is recited at the end of the Divine Liturgy, is in fact a missionary message for the community of the faithful who will soon be dispersing to their daily lives. The hymn of doxology must be spread out to all of

---

1. Abba John Kolovos, *The Elder Said . . . The Gerontikon in Modern Greek,* eds. A. Astir and E. Papademetriou, Athens 1974, (in Greek) no. 28, p. 114.

humanity. "Declare his glory among the nations" (Ps 96:3). The experience of the divine light of the glory of the Triune God must not be permitted to remain the privilege of a few communities and peoples. It must come to pass that "all the peoples behold his glory" (Ps 97:6). Those who have been blessed to receive the glory of God, consequently, have an obligation to become vessels radiating the divine light, giving to others "the light of the knowledge of the glory of God in the face of Christ" (2 Cor 4:6).

The missionary effort within this perspective is clearly a doxological movement. "For this too is above all praise, this too is above all glory to God—when we seek to have many in the future enjoy His salvation."[2]

The missionary interest is extended to the renewal of all historical development and every form of cultural expression. We must put aside whatever tendencies toward platonic or neoplatonic dualism that exist, with the certainty that the revelation of the glory of God is not directed exclusively to the mind, to imagination, or to only a few of the functions of our immaterial inner self, but to the whole human person and to all of human nature. We are thus called to work for the renewal of all within this radiance of the glory of God.

"All things" participate in the process of transformation. Grace is given through matter, sanctifying all of creation with the bread and wine, which become the Body and Blood of Christ, "the Lord of glory." Through participation in the Eucharistic doxology, not only the human spirit, but also other material elements, such as fire, water, incense, and oil are sanctified.

The doxology of creation is harmonized with the free-willed doxology of free beings. The material universe partakes in the doxology of God. "The Lord is high above all nations, and his glory above the heavens!" (Ps 113:4). Through the unceasing activities of the Holy Spirit, the glory of God radiates over all the earth. "May his glory fill the whole earth!" (Ps 72:19). All those

____

2. St. John Chrysostom, Interpretation on *Psalm 145*, 1, PG 55:473.

who participate in the Church of Christ are called to contribute to this.

The manifestation of the glory, revealed to rational creation with the presence of Christ, with the proclamation of His authority over "all things," (τά πάντα) and then with the outpouring of the Holy Spirit "on all flesh" (Joel 2:28; Acts 2:17), must penetrate into history, into the social structures, and into the cultural expressions. All things are called to be transformed and recapitulated in Christ through the energies of the Holy Spirit. All the expressions of human creativity, "all things," are called to participate in this doxological movement. In the end, even "creation itself will be set free from its bondage to decay and obtain the glorious liberty of the children of God" (Rom 8:21).

The transformation of the world is being accomplished with the active participation of the faithful, who are living in the realm of the divine glory. The "logos," the reason and meaning of the world, is summed up in the glory of God. Mission, in the final analysis, means a global mobilization for a general doxology of the universe.

C

THE DOXOLOGICAL CHARACTER
OF THEOLOGICAL REFLECTION
AND THE LIFE OF WORSHIP

1. The doxology of the Church is a *portent and a prelude of the final hour*, during which the universe will be transformed within the ultimate manifestation of the glory of God. This perspective of glory and vision of the events of the history of salvation is summarized and preserved by the Church in her dogmatic definitions and expressions of worship, which determine doxologically even the rhythm of Christian life and mission.

Theological reflection, first of all, is in its more profound and essential expression doxological. "For even the one who in word of wisdom theologizes (θεολογῶν), brings glory to the

Lord,"[3] Origen has emphasized. The particular sensitivity of the Church regarding doctrinal definitions is not so much a theoretical philosophical preoccupation with the precise and true "opinion" and "doctrine," as it is vigilance for the correct orientation in the journey of humanity and the world to receive the glory of God. It is related directly with the decisive meaning of a true and proper doxology of God.

Every false and erroneous conception and belief about the Triune God and the meaning of human salvation alters and conceals the glory of God. It clouds the mind and the soul, it leads man astray in false directions, creating confusion in the way the glory of God is experienced and expressed by the Church. This is why in the Orthodox Tradition the anxiety and concern for the correct dogma goes hand in hand and is interwoven with the yearning for the proper glory of God.

Thus theology, and every particular expression of it, is not limited to being a "science." Rather, passing through the stages of preparatory scientific knowledge, philosophical or philological, it attempts a doxological leap into the realm of the infinite, approaching and receiving the divine glory in Christ; living and experiencing the limitless love and glory of God.

The attempt for an in-depth, theological penetration into the vision and the experience of the glory of God is particularly intense in the thought and life of the Fathers of the Church. The doxological stance directs them into the realm of essential religious experiences and offers an "understanding" which surpasses the boundaries and nature of empirical, analytical scientific knowledge. It leads to participation in, and to "communion" with, a divine and life-giving illumination.

2. The journey into the glory of God, to which we are referring, is not a personal matter. *It is accomplished in Christ, in the Church.* For this reason the direct and basic purpose of mission is the establishment of a local Church. It is within the celebration of the Sacraments, and within her entire doxological na-

---

3. Origen, *On the Psalms, Psalm 28, PG* 12:1289, 33-34.

ture, that she proclaims the glory of God and participates in the praise of the "one, holy, catholic and apostolic Church." The journey toward the glory, of deification by grace, *theosis*, unfolds within the Church and through the Church. "The Church is the reality of the mystery of the glory of God, where the creation of new life takes place in communion through participation in the glory." (N. Nissiotis)

The doxological life of the Church is cultivated and culminated in worship. In the worshipping assembly each believer, individually and corporately, as the "Body of Christ," stands existentially before the mystical glory of God. We live the mystery of the Kingdom of God, which has come and is to come, and proclaim doxologically her eschatological advent. It is especially in the Divine Liturgy, where the events of the divine Kenosis, of Agape, of the sacrifice on the Cross, of the Resurrection are repeated in the here and now, that we become partakers of the life and death of the risen and ascended Christ. We are being incorporated into His Body and into communion with divine glory.

The doxological stance was chosen from the beginning by the Church when it instituted the Eucharistic assembly to proclaim and celebrate the "Gospel of the glory of God." The Church chose this stance as the center of her life from which to live and express dynamically the reception and the appropriation of the divine glory, which was manifested in a unique and inconceivable manner in Christ.

This doxological attitude and stance created a centripetal missionary power of attraction for millions of people, even in the most difficult times of persecutions and martyrdom. It is in the worshipping assembly that the profound change takes place, repentance, the existential gazing at the humility in glory and the glory in the humility of Christ, who accepts to have His Body and Blood offered in our humble gifts and in the most humble and unworthy invocations.

With the doxological expression and lifting up, human existence is illumined by the mystical radiance of the glory of God;

charged with inexpressibly serene energy, resembling not so much mechanical energy, as nuclear energy.

This atmosphere of glory fills the Church of the East which preserves the tradition of the one, united Church. The doxological assemblies present here an exceptional variety of expressions, with the daily rhythm of Matins, Hours, Vespers, Vigils; feast days of Saints, within a succession of seasons in the ecclesiastical year. All of these assemblies steadily and uninterruptedly gather the faithful into a doxological rhythm which renews them in the certainty of faith.

Every act and every prayer in Orthodox worship is completed and crowned with an exaltation of glory, with the recurring announcement and proclamation of the glory of God. One of the most frequently repeated phrases is: "Glory to the Father and the Son and the Holy Spirit . . ." All of the exclamations in the Divine Liturgy return to and are crowned with the theme of glory. "For Yours is the dominion, the kingdom, the power and the glory. . ."; "For You are holy, our God, and to You we give glory. . . ." (We receive this glory, we accept it, and we offer it up again to its source). Here we must not see simply a reference to the divine glory, but a steadfast and ever recurring reorientation toward the reality of the glory of God; which beyond every other conventional "reality," penetrates the whole of life, the entire history of the world, and eternity itself.

At the center of the Divine Liturgy is the hymn, "Holy, holy, holy, Lord Sabaoth, heaven and earth are filled with Your glory . . ." In this way the cosmological principle which is that the glory of God fills the universe—space and time—is festively proclaimed. It is a faith that consequently fills the believer with optimism and joy; and with a certainty from which they also draw vitality and courage. The hymnological tradition and life of the Church, unites the faithful in a doxological body of praise, and offers them new power to carry forward the eternal life and hope in Christ into everyday life.

The monasteries in particular, as organized doxological communities of a continuous and intense life of worship, have preserved and continue to preserve, within the most varied historical conditions, a steady missionary radiance. In the West and in the East, in the cities and in the deserts, in developed and in primitive civilizations, their contribution in spreading and stabilizing the Christian faith, but also in revealing its spirit of resistance and endurance remains indisputable. It reminds us of the role of the monasteries in spreading Christianity to the regions of Northern Europe, to the vast lands of Northern Asia, and later in resisting the pressure of Islam in Asia Minor, in Egypt and the Balkans.

Influenced by the social categories and tendencies of our time, many limit themselves to seeing the contribution of the monasteries in their kerygmatic and social ministries only, but all of that work comes as a consequence—a breath of life. The primary work, that which makes the monasteries to be mainstays of evangelization and dynamic missionary centers, is the fact that they were and are steadfast communities of worship, living the mystery of the Kingdom and reflecting the radiance of its presence and eschatological advent.

Corroded by the usual mentality of practicality, we do not always have the sensitivity to evaluate true holiness which, by the very reason of its existence, radiates glory and transfigures. Nevertheless, in every age the Saints, who are the reflection of the mystical presence of the glory of God, are a perceptibly profound influence upon society.

But even those of us who are active in many ecclesiastical activities and missionary efforts, know from personal experience how we dangerously empty ourselves, distracted "about many things," and how renewed and liberated we become by returning to the doxological atmosphere of worship. This doxology offers inner spiritual strength, vision, and ascetic vigilance with direct and constant references to the purification and dedication of our daily service. This doxological stance of which we are speaking is consequently not static and passive. It is connected organically with the reception, the appropriation and the radiance of the divine glory.

Very often, in the classic expression "to the glory of God," the center of gravity falls on the fact that we do something which in turn we offer for the glory of God. However, the real meaning of this phrase is that all of our life is found in this journey and process "of being glorified with," of being transfigured, of being conformed to life in Christ. Prayer is a process of being conformed to the one "calling us to his kingdom and glory." Every creative attempt to participate in this ongoing transformation of the universe, which is being accomplished by the glorified Lord, whatever service is rendered within the Church, whatever expression of love—these are no more than a spark, a ray of the radiance of the glory, of the fervent love of God.

Prayer and love are the only things that will not come to an end in eternity; they are the language of the future age. When someone is planning to travel to a country and to live there, he must learn its language properly and have at his disposal the currency that is legal there. The same applies to the prayer of doxology, the language of the future age, and to love, which is the only currency in the "Kingdom of heaven."

D

LIVING IN HUMILITY THE CRUCIFIED LOVE "FROM GLORY TO GLORY"

The doxological stance, to which we have been referring, does not displace the other dimensions of Christian experience and life. It does not exclude them; on the contrary it includes them.

1. The doxology of God is not something which just happens, flowing autonomously out of the human mind and will. *It is accomplished in Christ, with the power and the breath of the Holy Spirit, within the Church.* Jesus was the only one of the human race who truly glorified the Father with His work and life.

The manifestation of the glory of God in Christ is accomplished primarily by self-emptying crucified love. This remains permanently as the revolutionary aspect of divine love, which causes it to differ definitively and decisively from common expressions of human glory.

With our thoughts polluted with the conventionalities of the world, we have a hard time reconciling humility with glory. Alienated by the thirst for publicity, self-aggrandizement and promotion, we forget that the authentic in the expression of the glory of God is the humble. Jesus Christ "emptied himself" to reveal the Glory of God (Phil 2:7). Whoever wishes to live in Him is obligated to partake without interruption in the humility of Christ. This is why in the East emphasis is given to the Jesus Prayer (to help keep His name and presence in the heart), to the constant request for divine mercy, and to the sense of our unworthiness and sinfulness. Only when we are inwardly emptied, does it become existentially possible to become vessels of the grace of God.

All of the other efforts to express the glory of God; the magnificent external organizations, the pompous and impressive creations of wealth and worldly powers, which imitate the human measures of glory, have been proven to be caricatures, weak and even dangerous for the proclamation of "the gospel of the glory of God."

Love for the glory of men stands in opposition to love for the glory of God (John 12:43); whoever desires human glory cannot work authentically in a missionary way to manifest the glory of God. The more one becomes familiar and receives the light of divine glory, the more he or she is liberated from the fascination of worldly recognition, money, fame, power, authority. This point is exemplified in a story we read in the *Gerontikon*: "There was an Abba by the name of Pambo who people say that for three years he beseeched God, saying the following prayer: 'Lord, do not give me any glory here on earth.' But God so glorified him that others could not gaze upon his face because of the glorious radiance that shone from his appearance."[4]

---

4. "On Abba Pambo," in *The Elder Said . . . . op.cit.* 1, p. 224.

The temptation to alter the meaning of divine glory with external displays of grandeur, spectacular demonstrations, and bold declarations has repeatedly wounded the Church and the missionary effort in its various forms. It has harmed Christianity in many regions of the world by identifying it with the thought of people with various self-interests and authorities of this world, thus giving the anti-Christian propaganda a handle for exploitation.

The hour *par excellence* for the glory of God is the hour of the free acceptance of the Passion. There is insistence in the words used by the Lord during the Mystical Supper, as a festive prelude and summary of what he would reveal about love, the way to the Father, the coming of the Spirit, the meaning of His martyrdom: "Now is the Son of man glorified, and in him God is glorified; if God is glorified in him, God will also glorify him in himself, and glorify him at once" (John 13:31–32).

The glory of God can be lived and revealed in no other context except in the context of crucified love. This is the profound conviction of the Saints. Here is how St. Symeon the New Theologian expressed it:

> We too must with diligence do these same things, so that through them we may glorify our heavenly Father who condescended to be called Father, and be glorified by Him with the glory of Jesus, which he had with the Father before the world was created. These things are the cross, that is, the death of everything worldly, sorrows, temptations, and whatever other sufferings of Christ. By enduring these with much patience, we imitate the sufferings of Christ and glorify through them our Father and God as his sons by grace and co-inheritors with Christ.[5]

The free and willing acceptance of suffering in the name of love and righteousness is not opposed to the life of doxology.

---

5. St. Symeon the New Theologian, "Theological and Practical Chapters," *Philokalia of the Neptic and Ascetic Fathers, Greek Fathers of the Church*, Thessaloniki, 1983, vol. 19A, pp. 524, 526 (in Greek).

On the contrary it supports it; offers it the true eschatological dimension (2 Cor 4:17).

Blessed are those who can see the radiance of the glory of God in the patient participation in the sufferings of humanity; in the poverty of the poor of this world, in the weakness of the weak, in the thirst for justice; in partaking freely in the pain and the sufferings of others with genuine selfless love. The decisively new in the love which Christ revealed is not to "love one another," but primarily what follows: "as I have loved you," that is, with selflessness, with fullness, with respect for human freedom, and with all the consequential dimensions of suffering. "The gospel of the glory of Christ" (2 Cor 4:4) constantly calls us back in line, placing us before the harsh and demanding form of the glory of the Cross.

Thus the doxological stance and way of life does not mean a hymnological escape into some closed idyllic environment. Rather, it means a universal openness, participation in the problems of the whole of humanity, particularly those of the humble and the wronged. It means to stand by in defense and support for all; it is an uninterrupted breath and radiance of the fire of the Holy Spirit. Directly connected with the meanings of "light" and "power," the "glory of God" expresses something particularly dynamic. The surprising and brilliantly shining lives of the Saints reflect such a living doxology of the humility and the love of Christ, preserving a missionary conviction that is timely for every person, every age, and every society.

2. The doxological movement of the believer and of the Church is an *uninterrupted dynamic development*. It is a continuous journey from "glory to glory." "And we all, with unveiled face, beholding the glory of the Lord, are being changed into his likeness from one degree of glory to another; for this comes from the Lord who is the Spirit" (2 Cor 3:18).

Therefore, as St. Gregory of Nyssa writes, "Let the believer be changed, in any case, for the better by being transformed from glory to glory through daily growth, by always improving and always advancing toward perfection, and yet without ever reaching the end of perfection. For true perfection is to never cease striving for perfection and to never reduce perfection to any limit."[6] In the final analysis it is a matter of the perpetual transformation of human capabilities and achievements, which lead to *theosis* (deification) by grace. Christian life is a continuous movement from purification to purification, from repentance to repentance, virtue to virtue, from knowledge to knowledge; it is indeed a dynamic movement of constant renewal in the Spirit.

The boundary remains steadfastly at the divine essence. This essence man will never reach. Man does not partake of the essence of God, but is exalted and deified with the illumination of the glory of God, the divine energies. What we call deification is participation in the energies, the glory, not the essence of God. At this point the human mind becomes aware of standing at a boundary, which cannot be transcended. For this reason he gives up on any attempt at description and abandons himself ecstatically, lovingly, with elation to the radiance of the glory of God, which recreates, transfigures and makes him full of light.

Every day in the life of the believer must be a journey toward the goal of being "glorified with" Christ. By living the mystery of inner transformation with prayer, with asceticism, with an intense vision of the beloved Person and the mystery of humility and co-crucifixion, we come to the entrance of communion with the glorified Lord. By living the effort to expand the glory of God into the hearts of other people, out of the silence of humility and their acceptance in love, the mystery of the Logos is revealed, and we discover the meaning and the infinite nature of our calling. Moreover, we are called to participate in the transformation and renewal of creation, of the world. And to do this with a positive, serene, creative effort within the realm to which each one of us is entrusted, regardless of whether the

---

6. St. Gregory of Nyssa, *To Olympios on Perfection*, 8, 1, *Greek Fathers of the Church*, Thessaloniki 1980, vol. 8, p. 422 (in Greek).

realm is scientific, practical, or administrative, or in any other area of social service.

***

Let us summarize: The doxological understanding of our life and mission and the clearest expression of this doxological disposition in our missionary reflections, studies and activities, does not mean expressive exclamations unto the glory of God, nor limitation of our activities to assemblies for celebration and praise. It does not mean the devaluation of other facets of the spiritual life, but rather their embrace and inclusion for articulation and synthesis. The glory of God has already been revealed in Christ, and we Christians are called to a continuous, vigorous experience and manifestation of this glory, which is identified in biblical terminology with the "Kingdom of God."

The theological thought, the life of worship, the daily movement and activity pass through this doxological vision and hope into another level; one that is far above any abstract analysis, sentimental exaltations, or self-willed expressions of duty. They become the heartbeat of life in Christ, a wellspring of light from the Holy Spirit, a hymn of joy.

10

"YOUR WILL BE DONE" MISSION IN CHRIST'S WAY

(A Theological Reflection on Mission)
(1987)

• Introduction for the Commission on World Mission and Evangelism, July, 1987 Geneva. • "Your Will Be Done—Mission in Christ's Way. A Meditative Introduction," *International Review of Mission 77* (1988), pp. 173–178. • "Your Will Be Done," in the commemorative volume for *Nicholas A. Nissiotis: Religion, Philosophy and Athleticism in Dialogue*, Athens 1987, pp. 93–105. • *Ἱεραποστολή στά ἴχνη τοῦ Χριστοῦ. Θεολογικές μελέτες καί ὁμιλίες, Ἀθήνα 2007.*

A

THE RELATIONSHIP OF CHRIST TO THE FATHER

When we ponder the prayer that our Lord gave us, as our continual petition, "Your will be done," then Christ's attitude toward the Father who sent Him comes automatically to mind. "For I have come down from heaven, not to do my own will, but the will of him who sent me" (John 6:38). This inner certainty, that He has come in obedience to God's will and the absolute identification of Himself with it, is what defines the self-awareness of the God-man, the new Adam, the "one sent," par excellence, by the Father.

Therefore, for all those who serve in the work of mission—faithful to the word of the risen Lord, "As the Father has sent me, even so I send you," (John 20:21)—there is no other alternative but to be continuously ready to do the will of the one who sends them. When we refer to "mission in Christ's way," we should first examine the content and the depth of our self-awareness, understanding what we are, what we want, what we are dreaming of, what we do, and to what extent we have harmonized ourselves to the will of Him who has sent us. Thus, we will find to what extent we have purified our own will from personal, egoistical criteria and motives, so that our will conforms, as much as possible, to the will of the One who has sent us.

Jesus Christ was in absolute accord and unity with His Father. Nevertheless, He emphasizes His firm resolution to obey the will of the Father. We, mere human beings—wounded as we are by the original sin of disobedience and seeing often "another law at war with the law of (our) mind and making (us) captive to the law of sin which dwells in (our) members" (Rom 7:23)—how are we able to free ourselves from our personal will and harmonize ourselves daily to the will of God? This effort calls for continuous vigilance and repentance, so that we will not "be conformed to this world but be transformed by the renewal of [our] mind, that [we] may prove what is the will of God, what is good and acceptable and perfect" (Rom 12:2).

In recent years, issues such as universal justice and "global community" have fascinated our hearts and dominated our discussions. But in our quest, other elements and prejudices may enter our preoccupations. The dreadful deviation of Israel is also a danger for the Church of Christ— the new Israel of grace. "They have a zeal for God, but it is not enlightened. For, being ignorant of the righteousness that comes from God, and seeking to establish their own, they did not submit to God's righteousness" (Rom 10:2–3). If we look at ourselves honestly and think of our behavior in some concrete instances, our dilemmas and decisions, we realize how often we have submitted to our own will.

The need to be more and more liberated from our will and readily accept the divine will is the first need for each of us in our spiritual life and the cornerstone for "mission in Christ's way." The danger of human egoism is encountered thousands of times in the history of the Church. The only outlet from our captivity within the labyrinth of egoism is to seek God's will continually in the here and the now. "And my judgment is just," said Jesus, "because I seek not my own will but the will of him who sent me" (John 5:30).

B

RESPONSE TO THE LOVE OF GOD

Very often we use the word obedience in a tone of "submission" to the will of God, as if it were a passive acceptance of a superior will. But this kind of emphasis is more reminiscent of Islam (meaning precisely, "submission") than of the Christian ethos. Christian obedience means *correspondence to the love of God and accepting the consequences of our love for God.* It is as in a loving relationship, whereby two wills achieve perfect harmony, in an absolute and spontaneous way. It is the kind of love that strengthens our whole existence and enables us to accomplish the most bold and unthinkable efforts and achievements. Every act, every thought, every word of Jesus is an expression of love for the Father. It is this sort of loving acceptance of God's will that has been the nerve of mission.

In theological thought, sometimes either "faith" has been stressed at the expense "works," or "obedience" to the commandments, thus contrasting antithetically with freedom and love. But separations of this kind have never proved fruitful to the spiritual life and work of the Church. The whole (*katholou*) conscience of the "one, holy, catholic, and apostolic Church" experiences all of them together as a harmonious unity. Commandments, love, vision and proclamation of the mystery of the person of Jesus, are all experienced together. "He who has my commandments and keeps them, he is the one who loves me; and he who loves me will be loved by my Father, and I will love him and manifest myself to him" (John 14:21). There exists no true love without wholehearted acceptance of the will of the Father, as it is expressed in His commandments. All these commandments define love. Every acceptance of that which the commandments define constitutes an expression of love. "And I will manifest myself to him." The vision of God, the loving relationship with and devotion to God are interwoven with the concrete, loving harmonization of one's will to God's will; to Him who is the God of love.

This inner faithfulness to the will of God offers to human existence a *serene* and *steadfast power.* The loving identification of our personal will with the will of God, who is love, gives crystalline clarity and a steely persistence to carry out the work of mission.

C
A SENSE OF POWERLESSNESS
AND OF POWER

Parallel to the inner certainty and power offered by the self-consciousness of those who serve in missionary work is the *internal problematic and sense of weakness.* In their narratives, the Evangelists do not conceal the doubts of many of those who are mighty and well-known regarding Jesus Christ Himself. They do not present all things bright, as for example in the descriptions in the texts related to Buddha. Very often indeed the New Testament presents the criticism and questioning of the theological and sociopolitical circles of Jesus' time; which reach the point of identifying Him with Satan—"He casts out demons by the prince of demons" (Matt 9:34). The dispute and denial culminates in the confrontation and rejection that is fulfilled in the Crucifixion outside the walls of the city.

These doubts came from various circles and continued during the apostolic age, not only from the pagan and Judaic side, but also from certain self-seeking ecclesiastical groups. St. Paul's letters are full of reports about disputes and defamations concerning even his apostolic status. He, who so intensively lived "mission in Christ's way," affirming that: "It is no longer I who live, but Christ who lives in me" (Gal 2:20), defined, in an astonishingly dramatic way, the identity of the apostolic life: "For I think that God has exhibited us apostles as last of all, like men sentenced to death; . . . We are fools for Christ's sake . . . We are weak . . . We (are) in disrepute . . ." (1 Cor 4:9–10).

One of the great gifts given by God to those who offer themselves to missionary work is a personal experience of such difficult hours and circumstances. Thanks to this gift the texts of the New Testament do not remain simply a historical narration, but they summarize new, existential, and revelatory experiences. This type of questioning, denial and weakness belongs to the nature of mission and, very often, underlines its genuineness. Love for Christ is related in one way or another to the Cross. The triple affirmation of Peter of his love for Christ was not answered by the promise of a life of comfort and honors, but the prediction that his love would culminate in sacrifice (John 21:15–19).

And yet, all external afflictions and sorrows are unable to shake the inner certainty and the enthusiasm of love, which animates and strengthens the one who has been sent by Jesus. "Who shall separate us from the love of Christ? Shall tribulation, or distress, or persecution, or famine, or nakedness, or peril, or sword?" (Rom 8:35). *The dual experience of personal powerlessness and at the same time of God's power* constitutes the two poles of the apostolic life: "We have this treasure in earthen vessels, to show that the transcendent power belongs to God and not to us . . ." (2 Cor 4:7–9; cf. 1 Cor 4:12–13).

Even a serious illness does not bring discouragement and despair; it becomes a hidden source of power. "When I am weak, then I am strong" (2 Cor 12:10). This is the most astonishing paradox of the Christian experience, an experience which defines the character, ethos and power of the Christian missionary to the end of the ages.

D

EXISTENTIAL EXPERIENCE
OF THE RESURRECTION

This dynamic attitude even in the depths of powerlessness is not merely the fruit of a simple theoretical certainty, but is first and foremost an existential experience of Christ's Resurrection. The theme of the Resurrection was so strong in the *kerygma* of St. Paul that the Athenians formed the impression that Jesus and the Resurrection (which is a feminine noun in Greek), which Paul proclaimed, were a couple, two new deities (Acts 17:18).

The promise of resurrection and eternal life is directly related to the will of God. Jesus repeats emphatically: "For this is the will of my Father, that everyone who sees the Son and believes in him should have eternal life; and I will raise him up at the last day" (John 6:40). The good news reaches its zenith in the proclamation of the resurrection of the dead, the ontological regeneration of human nature. Any concealment of this central truth leads to a dangerous and catastrophic distortion of the Christian message. The acceptance of the Resurrection remains always the presupposition for salvation (Rom 10:9). For this reason, in the Orthodox Church the whole spiritual life, all things, revolve around the axis of the Resurrection.

What transforms powerlessness into power is the final "authority" given to the risen Christ. "All authority in heaven and on earth has been given to me" (Matt 28:18). The correspondence and similarity of the second part of this phrase to: "on earth as it is in heaven" of the Lord's prayer is very important. Christian mission is essentially related to this "authority." In this verse, the word "therefore" *(οὖν)* that consequently connects the two sentences is often overlooked. Because "All authority in heaven and on earth has been given to me," therefore, for this reason, with this certainty, with this as the basis, "Go therefore and make disciples of all nations." The first and last word in history and in the world, "in heaven and on earth" belongs to the Resurrected One. Without fear or hesitation, bring this good news to the whole creation.

The opening to "all" the world—which means the whole of humankind and the so-called secular reality—is a consequence of the Resurrection and is clearly the will of God. The opening of the mission of Church to "all" is defined very distinctly and is proclaimed as the will of God. It is a new perspective embracing the whole of creation.

But to this horizon is related another aspect of the catholicity *(katholou)* of God's will. The first *"all"* (all nations) is followed by a second "all": ". . . teaching them to observe *all* that I have commanded you." It is inconceivable then to confine oneself selectively to only some of the commandments. The awareness of the fullness of the commandments must become stronger and stronger every time we proclaim that we belong to the "catholic and apostolic Church." The whole will of God must determine our life. One of the tragedies of Christian history and a reality in today's Church is the selection by Christians of some Christian principles and commandments, and the rejection—theoretically or practically—of others. We speak fluently for freedom, love, human community, but we stammer when speaking for self-control, humility, repentance, crucifying the old person, the "narrow gate" and self-sacrifice. We forget that the will of God constitutes one unity, one all-embracing reality. With this holistic understanding of mission, it is time to emphasize the need to understand the will of God as a whole.

E

A PROCESS WITH COSMIC DIMENSIONS

The same crucial word "all" (*ta panta*) appears again in the vision and perspective of the Apostle Paul when he gazes at the awaiting faces of Church of the future anticipating the final end of the cosmos. Through the pouring out of the Holy Spirit and the formation of the Church, through the continuous presence of the Spirit, a process of transformation of human life has begun which elevates humanity and transforms the world. In all this evolution there is a *mystery:* "the mystery of His will, according to his purpose which he set forth in Christ as a plan for the fullness of time" (Eph 1:9–10). Before this splendid vision human thought reels with vertigo. All things will find their own reason, their purpose, which is Christ. All "things in heaven and things on earth . . ."

It is in this "mystery of God" that we participate in mission. This perspective frees us from every individualistic piety, and tendency to marginalize the apostolic effort. *We take part in a divine process having cosmic dimensions.* Mission is—let us repeat it—God's mission, not ours. In His magnificent initiative, God calls us to be His co-workers and ambassadors. God's plan will certainly be realized. Our strength and endurance are based upon this truth. This is the source of our joy and optimism.

Christ is revealed as the center of creation, the *entelechy* (goal and purpose) of the world. The decisively new element that Christ offers is not a body of certain truths or principles such as that taught by a few wise men (as, for example, Gautama Buddha or Confucius), or by some "prophets" (such as Zoroaster or Mohammed). Jesus Christ, uniting divine and human nature in a unique and unrepeatable way, remolds human nature and communicates, I dare say, new *chromosomes*—spiritual chromosomes, which determine a mystic code of evolution: Moving from the human person to the Christ-like person, from the rational to union of the human person with the Logos, from human community to a fellowship *(koinonia)* of Love; and by extension, it constitutes a transformation of all creation.

Christ as love constitutes the *Omega* (ultimate) in the evolution of the world. We Christians continue the journey with this intuitive certainty, through all the adventures that humankind experiences in every era, with faith that all things, the entire universe and the whole creation, are in a process of transformation, evolving toward union with Christ who is the *Logos* of the universe. Incorporation in Christ constitutes the Christian proposal for a creative transcendence of the robot-like chaos which presages a cold technology, indifferent to human existence.

By the expression, "Your will be done—Mission in Christ's way," we usually focus our attention upon the earthly life of Christ, from the Incarnation to the Crucifixion. But Christ, in whom we believe, is also the resurrected one, the ascended one; He who will come again, the Lord, and *Logos* of the world. Upon this faith is based the solution to the problem of power and powerlessness. It is this faith that keeps our hope for the future alive.

The contemplation of the work of the *Logos*, before the Incarnation and after, especially after the Resurrection, is the center of liturgical experience and remains steadfast in the conscience of the catholic and apostolic Church.

Faith and confidence in the Lord determine the self-awareness of the Church, offering her an astonishing vitality and strength for giving witness, even under the most difficult persecutions. The certainty that, by accepting the will of the Lord of the universe, we undertake a clear and crucial role in the ecumene, now and until the end of the ages, fills our hearts with enthusiasm.

It is this confidence in the wisdom and power of God's will that fills us with the excitement to pray "Your will be done on earth as it is in heaven." Because we know in this will there is found life, freedom, hope, beauty and, most especially, love.

11

ORTHODOX MISSION
PAST, PRESENT AND FUTURE

(1989)

• «Ὀρθόδοξη Ἱεραποστολή. Παρελθόν—Παρόν—Μέλλον,» Γε-
νηθήτω τό θέλημά σου. Ἡ ἀποστολή τῆς Ὀρθοδοξίας σήμερα. ed. G.
Lemopoulos, Neapolis-Thessaloniki 1989, pp. 69–95. • "Orthodox
Mission, Past, Present, Future," *Your Will Be Done. Orthodoxy in Mis-
sion*, ed. G. Lemopoulos, Tertios-Katerini-Geneva 1989, pp. 63–92.
• German: "Orthodoxe Mission. Vergangenheit, Gegenwart, Zu-
kunft," *Die Orthodoxe Kirche*. Eine Standortbestimmung an der Jahr
Tausendwende. Festschrift für Anastasios Kalis, Hrsg. Eumenius von
Lefka, Athanasios Basdekis und Nikolaos Thom, Lembek, Frankfurt
am Main 1999, pp. 93–121. • "Orthodoxe Mission," *Leitfaden Oku-
menische Missionstheologie*, Hrsg. Chr. Tahlin-Sander, An Schultze, D.
Werner, H. Wrogemann, Chr. Kaiser, Güttersloch 2003, pp. 113–129.
• Ἱεραποστολή στά ἴχνη τοῦ Χριστοῦ. Θεολογικές μελέτες καί ὁμιλίες,
Ἀθήνα 2007.

Orthodox witness is interwoven with the longing to carry out God's will in a loving and heroic manner. To "live in Christ" and to "follow in his steps" has always been the ideal, the heart of Orthodox spirituality. This central longing of Orthodox worship is expressed in the petitions of the Liturgy of the Presanctified Gifts, when the faithful pray to the Father:

> So that by partaking of these divine gifts and receiving new life through them, we may be united unto thy Christ himself that with thy Word, O Lord, dwelling in us, and walking among us, we may become temples of thy Holy and ever venerated Spirit.

The transforming glory and power of the Trinitarian God must shine forth in time, in every manifestation of human life, and throughout creation through the mission of the Church.

Since the key word "mission," around which our discussions will revolve, is often used with different nuances, it is necessary to state that by this word we mean: witness to the living Trinitarian God, who calls all to salvation and binds together within the Church, people who otherwise do not belong to her or who have lost their connection to her. This characteristic distinguishes the Church from mere pastoral care, which is directed towards those already incorporated in the Church. The field of Christian mission today is not only the distant geographical regions of the so-called third world (more precisely, two-thirds of the total population of the world), and the rest of the inhabited world. It is henceforth a question of mission to the whole world.

For every local Church, mission is "domestic" or "internal" when it takes place within its geographical, linguistic and cultural boundaries, and "external" when it reaches beyond these boundaries to other peoples, and countries.

The Church, "the one, holy, catholic and apostolic Church," is obliged to witness to those near and afar, and to show interest in the whole human being, both on a personal and a societal level, for the progress of the whole world. Nothing relating to human existence is out of the scope of interest for Orthodox mission.

A

A QUICK GLANCE AT THE PAST:
BASIC PRINCIPLES OF ORTHODOX MISSION

When in 1958 there was a revival in contemporary Orthodoxy of the ideal of an external mission, we had to face two difficulties: The surprise of Westerners, who thought the Orthodox Church was introspective and uninterested in mission; and a passive internal opposition from Orthodox, who considered such an interest as something imported. For this reason, during the first decade, not only was external mission stressed as an Orthodox theological and ecclesiological necessity, but a special attempt was made to study its history.

From the relevant documents published during these last decades, it has become clear that the apostolic duty is a basic element of Orthodox self-awareness.[1] Even if, under certain con-

---

1. A. Schmemann, "The Missionary Imperative in the Orthodox Tradition," G. H. Anderson, ed., *The Theology of the Christian Mission*, New York, 1961, pp. 250–257. G. Khodre, "Church and Mission," *Porefthendes—Go Ye* 3 (1961), pp. 40–42, 56–58. N. Nissiotis, "The Ecclesiological Foundation of Mission," *The Greek Orthodox Theological Review*

crete historical circumstances, the evangelical activity of local Churches had slowed down and interest in various missions had become lethargic.

This year's (1989) anniversary of the millennium of the Baptism of Rus' sheds further light both on the missionary initiatives of the Byzantines and on the apostolic activities of their Russian disciples in later centuries.

1. Throughout the millennium of its existence, *Orthodox Byzantium* concerned itself with spreading the Christian faith, either to the heathen within its boundaries, or to the pagan tribes invading the Empire, as well as to neighboring countries. More particularly, we can distinguish two periods of intense missionary zeal: (a) from the fourth to the sixth century, culminating at the time of Justinian; and (b) during the ninth and eleventh centuries, under the Macedonian Dynasty. In the first period as well as the second, apostolic activity was combined with a deeper theological search and spiritual flowering.

During the first period, enlightened bishops labored in the mission field, such as St. John Chrysostom (†407), and holy monks, such as Saints Hilarion (†371), Euthymios (†473) and Sabbas (†532). The Byzantines took an interest in the evangeli-

---

8 (1962), pp. 22–52. A. Yannoulatos, "Orthodoxy and Mission," *St. Vladimir's Theological Quarterly* 8 (1964), pp. 139–148. *Idem, The Purpose and Motive of Mission (from a Theological Point of View)*, Athens 1966. Reprinted from *Theologia* 37 (1966) (in Greek). [See the republication in previous chapters of this volume]. *Idem*, "Initial Thoughts toward an Orthodox Foreign Mission," *Porefthendes—Go Ye* 10 (1968), pp. 19–23, 50–52, and *Ecclesia*, 55 (1968). *Idem, Indifference for Mission Means Denial of Orthodoxy*, Athens 1971 (in Greek). J. Meyendorff, "The Orthodox Church and Mission: Past and Present Perspectives," in *St. Vladimir's Theological Quarterly* 16 (1972), pp. 59–71. E. Voulgarakis, "Orthodoxe Mission," in *Lexikon Missionstheologischer Grundbegriffe*, eds. K. Müller and Th. Sundermeier, Berlin 1987. *Martyria—Mission. The Witness of the Orthodox Churches Today*, ed. I. Bria, Geneva 1980. For a broader presentation of the subject and a detailed bibliography see J. Stamoolis, *Eastern Orthodox Mission Theology Today*, New York, 1986. (See also note 10 below.)

zation of peoples bordering on the Empire, such as the Goths, the Huns, the Iberians and certain tribes of Colchis and the Caucasus. Moreover in the South, following the Christianization of the Ethiopians, they took an interest in the evangelization of Nubian tribes, and to the northern regions of what is today Tunisia. Little is known about this first period because this missionary activity took place in areas where later there would be a great mingling of populations.

The second period, linked to the conversion of the Slavic world, has been investigated more thoroughly; especially during the last few years worldwide interest has focused on the celebration of the 1100th anniversary of the missions of Saints Cyril and Methodios, as well as the aforementioned millennium.

The Byzantine mission was based on a few clear-cut, basic principles. Let us remember, at the forefront of which was a desire to create an authentic local Eucharistic community. Thus, precedence was given to translating the Holy Scriptures, the liturgical texts and the writings of the Fathers, as well as to the building of beautiful churches which would proclaim, with the eloquent silence of beauty, that God had come to dwell amongst humanity. The importance attached by Byzantine theology to a life of worship and "deification" (*theosis*) did not hinder Orthodoxy from taking a direct interest in the social and cultural dimensions of life. Together with the Gospel, the Byzantines transfused into the peoples being Christianized, the whole of their experience—political, artistic, economic, and cultural—permeated by evangelical principles and the Christian vision of life. They contributed to this work so that the young nations could formulate their own self-awareness and develop their own culture.

By the power of the Gospel, which it infused into the waves of uncivilized peoples invading Europe, Christian Byzantium brought to them a completely new life; spiritually, socially, and politically. The flexibility and understanding with which the Greek missionaries adapted the Byzantine liturgy and tradition to local circumstances gave them an ecumenical character and made them a bond connecting the various Orthodox peoples. At the same time, the development of the vernacular and of a national temperament among these peoples, for which many Byzantine missionaries toiled with such reverence and tenderness, helped preserve the personality of the converted peoples. Far from indulging in an administrative centralization and a monolithic conception of the Church, the Byzantine missionaries saw the unity of the extended Church in its common doxology—albeit with many voices, but in "one spirit"—and in their sacramental participation in the cup of life, "Because there is one bread, we who are many are one body" (1 Cor 10:17).

Finally, missionary work in Byzantium was not carried out by a handful of "specialists." Bishops, priests, monks, emperors—whether of great or of medium stature—princesses, diplomats, officers, soldiers, merchants, mariners, emigrants, travelers, and captives[2] were all involved. The modest and patient heroism shown in this direction by thousands of known and unknown Byzantines during the centuries-long life of the Empire, forces the student of history to agree with what Charles Diehl wrote concerning the conversion of the Slavs: "Missionary work was one of the glories of Byzantium."[3]

---

2. See also A. Yannoulatos, "Byzantium, Work of Evangelization," *Encyclopaedia of Religion and Ethics*, (in Greek) vol. 4 (1964), col. 19–59. *Idem, Κύριλλος καί Μεθόδιος, δεῖκται πορείας,* reprinted from *Ecclesia* 53 (1966) (in Greek). *Idem,* "Monks and Mission in the Eastern Church during the Fourth Century," in *International Review of Mission* 58 (1969), pp. 208–226. For specific aspects of Byzantine mission see: F. Dvornik, *Les Slaves, Byzance et Rome au IXe siècle,* Paris, 1929. M. Lacko, *Saints Cyril and Methodius,* Rome, 1963. M. Spinka, *A History of Christianity in the Balkans,* Hamden, CT, 1968. D. Gonis, "Life and Work of St. Methodios," *Πάντα τά Ἔθνη* 4 (1985) vol. 15, pp. 6–9 (in Greek). See other articles in the same commemorative volume.

3. C. Diehl, *Les grands problèmes de l'histoire byzantine,* Paris, 1943, p. 17.

2. *Russian missionary activity* also exhibits very broad interests and extraordinary variety. During the first period, which extends from the baptism of the inhabitants of Kiev to the Mongol conquest (988–1240), monasteries and convents were created and became missionary bases. Enlightened bishops, priests, and monks worked heroically for the evangelization of the Slavic tribes of the North.

In the second period, from the Mongol invasion to roughly the end of the fiftteenth century, a great number of monks retreated to the forests and made their hermitages centers of missionary and cultural activity. Prisoners of war became the first apostles to the Tartars. Apart from the various anonymous evangelists, this period is famous for its great missionary personalities, such as Stephen of Perm (†1396).

During the third period, from the sixteenth to the eighteenth centuries, hundreds of thousands of Moslems from the local population around Kazan converted to Orthodoxy. As the Empire extended into Siberia, where Christianity was until then unknown, churches and monasteries mushroomed, and yet their numbers were insufficient to cover the local needs. During this time, state policy was often hostile to mission. Nevertheless, great missionary figures, such as St. Tryphon of Novgorod (†1583), who brought the Gospel to the Lapps, Bishop Philotheos of Tobolsk (†1727) and others, through their missionary zeal drew thousands to Christ.

The fourth period, lasting from the nineteenth century to the Russian Revolution (1917), presents a more ecclesial character and is distinguished by its fruitfulness. The missionaries were numerous: distinguished bishops, priests, monks, and laypeople: Such as, the monk Macarios Gloukharev (†1847), apostle to the warlike tribes of the forbidding Altai mountain range; Bishop Innocent Veniaminov (†1879), (later Metropolitan of Moscow), who worked among the Aleutians, the Eskimos and other Alaskan tribes; St. Herman, also in Alaska; the merchant Sidenikoff among the Samoyeds; the linguist and theologian, Nicholas Ilminsky, who introduced new methods of translation and missionary work among the Tartars. The Russian missionary efforts were directed towards many tribes and the Gospel was translated into many languages.

In all this missionary effort, a great contribution was made by the Orthodox Missionary Society, which was founded in Moscow in 1870; and which undertook the economic support of the Russian missions. Another great contribution was made by the Kazan Academy, which became a center for missionary studies. Their department of translations published books in dozens of languages for the regions of the Volga, Siberia, and the Caucasus and many others.

Russian missionaries were active as well outside the boundaries of the Empire, in China, Korea and Japan, with such champions, and enlightened personalities as Bishop Innokentiy Figurovsky in China and Archbishop Nikolai Kasatkin (1836–1912) in Japan.[4]

The Russian missionaries were inspired by the Orthodox principles of Byzantium, and they developed them with originality and daring. They created an alphabet for unwritten languages. The Bible and liturgical texts were translated into new

---

4. For more on the Russian missions see: E. Smirnoff; *A Short Account of the Historical Development and Present Position of Russian Orthodox Missions*, London 1903. Otis Cary, *Roman Catholic and Greek Orthodox Missions, Vol. 1: A History of Christianity in Japan*, New York, 1909. S. Bolshakoff, *The Foreign Missions of the Russian Orthodox Church*, London, 1943. J. Glazik, *Die russisch-orthodox Heidenmission seit Peter dem Grosse*, Münster 1954. *Idem, Die Islammission der russisch-orthodoxen Kirche*, Münster 1959. A. Yannoulatos, "Orthodoxy in China," *Porefthendes — Go Ye* 4 (1962), pp. 26–30, 36–39, 52–55. *Idem,* "Orthodoxy in Alaska," *Porefthendes — Go Ye* 5 (1963), pp. 14–22, 44–47. *Idem,* "Orthodoxy in the Land of the Rising Sun," *Orthodoxy 1964. A Pan-Orthodox Symposium*, Athens 1964, pp. 300–319, 338–340. E. Voulgarakis, *Mission according to the Greek Texts from 1821 to 1917*, Athens 1971. E. Widmer, *The Russian Ecclesiastical Mission in Peking During the Eighteenth Century*, Cambridge, MA, 1976. P. D. Garrett, *St. Innocent, Apostle to America*, Crestwood, NY, 1979. J. J. Oleksa, "Orthodoxy in Alaska. The Spiritual History of the Kodiak Aleut People," *St. Vladimir's Theological Quarterly* 25 (1981), pp. 3–19.

tongues. The Liturgy was celebrated in various local dialects, and they carried out systematic linguistic efforts. They prepared and promoted native clergy as quickly as possible and encouraged the joint participation of clergy and laity, with an emphasis on the mobilization of all the faithful. They provided for education in agriculture, technological development, and generally, the sociocultural evolution of the tribes and peoples attracted to Orthodoxy. Continuing the Orthodox tradition, they gave a central position to liturgical life, to the harmonious architecture of the churches, to the beauty of worship and to the social consequences of life in Christ. Certain fundamental principles, which have only recently been adopted by Western missionaries, were from the beginning the unquestioned foundations of the Orthodox missionary efforts.

3. Many Orthodox Churches, forced to live under Islamic regimes—four centuries of Turkish occupation in the Balkans and thirteen centuries of Arab domination in Egypt—were, of course, not in a position to organize missions abroad. On the contrary, in order to confront the terrible danger of the conversion of the Christian population to Islam, they were obliged to fight hard to keep control of their flock and to win back, from time to time, those who had strayed. This lengthy missionary effort, which amounted to a heroic resistance to varied and powerful pressures from another religion, added thousands of new martyrs to the Church.

Even in the twentieth century, in countries ruled by fanatical antireligious regimes, the Orthodox Church has lived her *mission as resistance*, in a steadfast manner, peacefully, in accordance with the ethos of the early Christians. It has provided some of the most heroic and authentic chapters of church history, which await a systematic study.[5]

------

5. For the neo-martyrs see: Nicodemos of the Holy Mountain, *New Martyrologion*, Athens, 1961 3rd ed. (in Greek). Chrysostomos Papadopoulos, *The Neomartyrs*, Athens, 1934, 2nd ed. (in Greek). I. Perantonis, *Lexicon of Neomartyrs, from the Fall of Constantinople to the Liberation of*

4. We should look, however, at another aspect of the past. When we Orthodox find ourselves in a Western setting, we automatically tend to describe how excellent everything is in our Church. Often we also have a tendency to compare our own achievements with the shortcomings of others. It is now time, when analyzing the past, to become more objective. This is, moreover, imposed by the Orthodox ethos, which is guided by the light of the Holy Spirit: "For the fruit of light is found in all that is good and right and true" (Eph 5:9).

Studying the historical facts with such an "Orthodox" spirit, we need to *pay attention* not only to the high-water marks of Orthodox mission, but also *to periods of bleakness and lethargy*. The former led to new creations, such as the Christianization of numerous peoples, and especially the Slavic peoples. While the hours of lethargy and omission provoked historical evolutions and socio-religious upheavals that were unbelievably costly for Orthodoxy. The weakening of interest in Byzantium for a proper, consistent, and perpetual external mission contributed to the evolution of a spiritual vacuum that propelled Islam in the Arabic world, and finally to the collapse of the Byzantine Empire. If, in the fourth, fifth and sixth centuries, the Byzantine Church had made a systematic and essential effort for the proper translation of the Holy Scriptures into Arabic, in order to foster a cultural identity among the Arabic tribes, as it did later in the ninth and tenth centuries for the Slavic tribes and the Russian peoples of the North, the evolution in the South, and its own journey, would have been quite different.

Later on, too, the lukewarm "internal mission" in the vast regions of Russia, the lack of sensitivity to social developments

---

the Enslaved Nation, 3 vols., Athens 1927 (in Greek). A. Vakalopoulos, *History of Modern Hellenism,* vol. 2, Thessaloniki 1976 (in Greek) (especially pp. 236–242). I. Menounos, *Biography and Teachings of Kosmas Aitolos,* Athens 1976 (in Greek). D. Constantelos, "The 'Neomartyrs' as Evidence for Methods and Motives Leading to Conversion and Martyrdom in the Ottoman Empire," *The Greek Orthodox Theological Review* 23 (1978), pp. 216–234 (in Greek).

and to the application of Christian ideals in the social and political realms, contributed to the development of Marxism-Leninism, which took hold of most of the Orthodox countries in the twentieth century. Both of these so very different sociopolitical realities, Islam and Communism, sprang up in the geographical, and also frequently cultural, areas in which Orthodoxy had developed and flourished; each of them eclectically absorbing some of her particular elements. One could even be so bold as to see in the initial formation of these two systems radical "heresies" of the Orthodox East. Islam adopted, fragmentally, elements of Orthodox Christianity, altering and distorting them; while the socialist ideology of Lenin reshaped other characteristics of the Russian Orthodox mentality, such as the heroic ideal of struggle and the eschatological vision of a brotherhood of humankind.

B

THE CONTEMPORARY PERIOD

Sociopolitical conditions, such as those which have developed in many local Orthodox Churches, and the danger of deviation on the part of the people, have in the twentieth century brought about a particular emphasis on "internal mission." We can distinguish three separate settings in which the local Orthodox Churches have been obliged to live and give their witness today (1989): (a) The Moslem setting, in which move chiefly the dioceses belonging to the ancient Orthodox Patriarchates. (b) The socialist-Marxist setting, in which many Churches continue to develop in Eastern Europe (1989). (c) The new, secularized, pluralistic and technocratic setting, with its swollen agnostic current, in which the Orthodox Churches of the *Diaspora* find themselves in Western Europe, America and recently in Greece.

All these settings exercise a multifaceted dynamic, often with disruptive influences, in certain local Churches. I shall restrict myself here to mentioning a few facts relative to the new

Churches formed in the twentieth century in Africa and Asia, and the centers responsible for supporting external missions.[6] The missionary Orthodox Churches of Africa and Asia, even though they still remain limited in number, have opened up a serious chapter in the history of Orthodoxy. They are contributing to transplanting Orthodoxy into new regions, although their numbers are not impressive. Compared to other Churches, the results are poor, but in comparison with the past, they show serious growth, and are a hopeful nursery for the future.

1. We shall start with the mission being carried out under the immediate *ecclesiastical jurisdiction of the Ecumenical Patriarchate of Constantinople*. The Orthodox Church in Korea today (1989) has four church buildings and parishes in relatively large cities, two Korean priests and about 2,000 members. They are supported by two missionary priests, two laymen and three nuns, all from Greece. To prepare native leaders, a seminary functions three afternoons a week. In recent years, many Orthodox books have been translated into the Korean language; both liturgical or of a more general, historical or edifying nature. Orthodox nuclei have also been developed in Hong Kong and Singapore. In India recently two Orthodox parishes in Arabachi, 100 km from Calcutta, have been created. Two Indian priests have been ordained, and one missionary is working there.

2. More extended is the missionary effort undertaken under the *jurisdiction of the Patriarchate of Alexandria and All Africa*. The first Orthodox groups have been formed in East Africa through the initiative of the Africans themselves. Today (1989) there are roughly 210 Orthodox parishes and small communities, served

---

6. For the recent development of the missionary Churches see (in Greek) the reports and chronicles in the periodicals: *Porefthendes — Go Ye* 1 (1959) to 10 (1968); *Φῶς Ἐθνῶν*, Patras; *Ἐξωτερικλη Ἱεραποστολή*, Thessaloniki; *Πάντα τά Ἔθνη*, Athens; and *Mission—Ἱεραποστολή*, St. Augustine, FL.

by seventy-five African clergy and fifty reader-catechists. The main body of Orthodox Christians is in Kenya, where there are eighty-five parishes and sixty-seven smaller communities. They run ten nursery schools, five primary schools, one secondary school and three dispensaries. The number of faithful exceeds 60,000. The missionary team consists of the bishop, a priest, two nuns and eight laypeople, sent and financed by the Churches of Greece, Finland, America and Cyprus. This inter-Orthodox collaboration is a new characteristic in the history of Orthodox missions.

The Orthodox Church in Uganda has twenty-nine parishes, served by an African auxiliary bishop and fourteen African priests. The number of faithful is roughly estimated to be 10,000. A number of Ugandans have studied in theological schools and other universities abroad. The mission runs two secondary schools, ten primary schools and a medical clinic. There are also four dispensaries. The country has suffered from civil war, and many plans for rebuilding churches and other centers have been delayed.

The Orthodox Church in Tanzania, which has taken shape in the last eight years, has nine parishes, twenty-one small communities and nine church buildings. The number of faithful is estimated at 8,000. Recently three dispensaries were built and equipped. The African clergy totals four priests and two deacons.

In Nairobi, the Macarios III, Archbishop of Cyprus, Orthodox Patriarchal School has been functioning since 1982 for the education of native clergy. In 1988 it had twelve professors and forty-seven students.

The Orthodox Christians of East Africa belong to different tribes. To meet liturgical needs, the Divine Liturgy of St. John Chrysostom has been published in Swahili, Kikuyu, Luya and Luganda; other liturgical translations have also been made into these languages, as well as into Haya and Lwo, and translations with a view to publication are systematically being developed into Nandi and Lango.

In Central Africa, two big missionary centers have been established, one in Kanaga and the other in Kolwezi, Zaire. There are forty-nine parishes and roughly 9,000 Orthodox in the country, served by twenty-two Zairian clergy. The local Church is assisted by two Greek archimandrites and twelve laypeople. There is also a secondary school, a primary school, a small seminary for future priests, a hostel for young people, and a dispensary. For purposes of worship and catechism, French, Swahili and local dialects are used.

In West Africa we have the following information: In Cameroon, there is one Orthodox community with two native priests. In Ghana (since 1977) there are twelve Orthodox parishes, with nine church buildings served by five native priests and two deacons. The Divine Liturgy, a summary of Church history, and the Baptism, Marriage and Burial services have all been translated into Fanti. In Nigeria there are sixteen parishes, served by one missionary priest and nine native priests, with twelve church buildings, four primary schools and a number of nursery schools.

The Orthodox missionary efforts in Africa continue with intensive rhythm. Orthodox Churches are also developing in the countries of Madagascar, Mozambique, Congo, South Africa, Zambia, and Zimbabwe. For more information see the official periodical of the Patriarchate of Alexandria and All-Africa: *Pantainos* (in Greek), also see the publication, *Orthodox Christian Mission Center*, St. Augustine, FL.

The prayer and vision of us all is for the establishment of truly local African Churches, capable of assuming by themselves the proclamation of the Gospel, self-governed and self-supported. However, in order for these Churches to develop and consolidate during the coming decades, serious and continuous assistance needs to be given by the older Orthodox Churches, together with theological and pastoral guidance.

3. *Other Orthodox missionary hearths.* Since 1991 a specific missionary effort has been developed in Albania, for the evan-

gelization of the people and the restoration from ruins of the Orthodox Autocephalous Church, which during twenty-three years of absolute religious persecution had been completely destroyed.[7]

The spectrum of missionary work is very broad, and it grows ever broader, for example, when we consider the responsibility of the local Church for supporting people in matters of health, education and culture. All the expressions of human life need to be transformed by the grace of the Triune God.

In our time, the Churches of *Alaska, Japan and China* still remain special cases. The Church in Alaska now belongs to the United States of America. It mainly confronts mission as "internal," stabilizing the populations there (Aleutians, Eskimos and others) in the Orthodox faith, and resisting the technological current of American society, which is undermining their racial traditions, and with it their Orthodoxy. The Church there is served by twenty-six native priests under a Russian bishop. The training of native clergy is carried out by the St. Herman Theological Seminary, which has been functioning on Kodiak Island since 1972, and has close ties with St. Vladimir's Orthodox Theological Seminary in New York.

The Church of Japan is already one hundred years old. The leadership and all the activities are in Japanese hands. Like a tiny islet amid the archipelago of a dynamic Japanese society, hastening dizzily towards the new era of electronics, it also has to face the great technological challenges upsetting the Western world. At the moment, the Japanese Orthodox Church has in its bosom some 30,000 Japanese Orthodox, who attend to the

---

7. See A. Yannoulatos, "The Restoration of the Orthodox Church of Albania (1991–2000), pp. 495–506 in *2000 Years of Church Art and Culture in Albania*, Papers of the International Symposium, Tirana, 16–28 November 2000, Tirana 2005. Jim Forrest, *The Resurrection of the Orthodox Church of Albania. Voices of Orthodox Christians*, Geneva 2002; Lynette Hoppe, *Resurrection—1991–2003. The Orthodox Autocephalous Church of Albania*, Tirana 2003. L. Veronis, *Go Forth, Stories of Mission and Resurrection in Albania*, Ben Lomond, 2009. (See also pp. 289–290 in the present book.)

upkeep of 150 churches, and are served by an Archbishop-Metropolitan and thirty-five Japanese priests. Certainly cooperation with the older, larger Orthodox Churches would contribute to her development, but the form of spiritual assistance required will need to be determined and decided on by the Church herself.

The case of the Church of China is more complicated. All that remains of the earlier Russian Orthodox missionary effort is a flickering candle flame. Most of the Orthodox Church buildings have been pulled down (Beijing, Tianjin, and Harbin). In 1983 a church building was inaugurated in Harbin, and it is now served by a Chinese Orthodox priest. Recently there have been rumors of another Orthodox community in Urumchi. The most immediate problem is the preparation and ordination of new Chinese clergymen to hold on to the "small remnant" of Orthodox in this vast country, given that foreign missionaries are strictly forbidden to establish themselves. It may be that the new candle of Orthodoxy that was lit in Hong Kong will prove valuable for preserving the flame of Orthodoxy in China.

4. In many local Orthodox Churches, alongside a growing interest in biblical studies, patristic texts and liturgy, we are still living a dual flowering: First, a longing for monasticism, with, at its peak, the renewal taking place on Mount Athos; and, second, a revival of missionary zeal. This latter began first as an expression of "internal mission," and during the last few years it has been complemented by the revival of "external mission."

The resurgence of monasticism, with its emphasis on personal repentance (*metanoia*) as a way of life, expresses the need for a more consistent experience of the Gospel; it certainly contributes to the coming of the Kingdom of God and the realization of His will, both in personal life and in the world as a whole. The missionary revival, with its accent on the apostolicity and catholicity of the Church, is a reminder that the gift of repentance and salvation should by no means be turned into a private, individual affair. Our duty is to live it "ecclesiastically," within the Church and with a view to the "fullness" (*katholou*) of the ecclesiastical horizon which is ecumenical. It is a gift destined for the whole world, given to transform all things. Christ was crucified for the sake of the whole world. And whoever is crucified with Him is co-crucified for the sake of the whole world. They are set apart from the world, but his prayer, attuned to the prayer of Christ, embraces the suffering and the hopes of all humanity and all creation. "Blessed is the monk who is separated from all and joined (*synermosmenos*) with all," maintain the first books of the *Philokalia*.[8]

I believe that from those two currents, and especially the combination of the monastic rebirth and the revival of the Orthodox missionary awareness, excellent fruits may come to ripen to maturity and be of significance to contemporary Orthodoxy. The whole world is secretly longing for an authentic expression of the Gospel of freedom, of love, and of the new life in Christ. It yearns for holiness.

More particularly, during the past decades, great strides have been made *in the development and support of external mission.* Centers and groups have been created for the exclusive purpose of supporting and promoting foreign missions. The oldest, *Porefthendes,* in order to collect funds for this purpose was incorporated as a legal entity in Greece in 1961, and yet, never lost its inter-Orthodox approach to matters. Later its example was followed, on a local level, by "The Friends of Uganda," in Thessaloniki (1963), which later changed the name to "Greek Brotherhood of Orthodox External Mission," and by "The First-Called," in Patras (1974). In the decade of the 1980's, other smaller groups were formed in various Greek cities.

From its inception, *Porefthendes* declared that the intent was not to found a particular "movement," but to put all its efforts, projects, programs, research, publications and personnel at the Church's disposal for the creation of a wider ecclesias-

---

8. St. Neilos the Ascetic, *On Prayer*, 124, *Philokalia of the Holy Neptic Fathers*, Athens 1957, vol. 1, p. 187 (in Greek).

tical missionary activity. So, with members of *Porefthendes* as the pioneers, the "Bureau of External Mission" was founded in 1968 within the framework of the *Apostoliki Diakonia,* a ministry organization of the Synod of the Church of Greece. Soon after, a "Week of External Mission" was adopted by all the Metropolises of Greece. In 1969 its director was invited to assist in the creation of the "Desk for Research and Relations with Orthodox Churches" at the World Council of Churches. In 1971, the "Center for Missionary Studies" was organized, with the collaboration of the Holy Synod and the Theological Faculty of the University of Athens, and functioned up until 1976. In 1972, the first women's monastic group was founded, which later developed into the Convent of St. John the Forerunner, Karea, with the aim of serving mission. In 1976, at Athens University, a Chair of Missiology was created. Since 1981, *Porefthendes* has taken on the editing of the official missionary magazine of the Church of Greece, Πάντα τά ᾽Εθνη.

At the beginning of the 1960s, efforts were made to extend the organization of *Porefthendes* to other Orthodox Churches as well, and similar groups of *Syndesmos* were created in Finland, America, and other countries with Orthodox youth movements. However, the well-known autonomy of the ecclesiastical jurisdictions did not favor this effort at coordination and, finally, in each local Church there developed other structures, in accordance with local conditions. In Finland, a "Mission Desk of the Finnish Orthodox Church" (*Ortodoksinen Lähetysry*) is functioning (1981). In the Americas there is the "Mission Center of the Greek Orthodox Archdiocese of North and South America." (Ed. note: Now the Orthodox Christian Mission Center). The latter was organized on a permanent basis in 1985, systematically extending the work of the old "Commission for Mission," which had begun in 1963.

In the realm of theoretical investigation into mission in the Orthodox tradition, a significant contribution has been made by the "Desk for Research and Relations with Orthodox Churches," of the World Council of Churches, which has organized a series of consultations on specific themes.[9] Thus an opportunity has been given both to Orthodox circles to make a systematic study of mission and to ecumenical missionary environments to be enriched from the Orthodox perspectives.

5. In spite of the facts mentioned thus far, we have to admit that the *missionary work* of the Orthodox Church on new frontiers in non-Christian regions *remains very limited*. Of course, we have never stopped confessing our faith in the "one, holy, catholic and apostolic Church." Yet, it would not be an exaggeration to say that, in many cases, the Orthodox self-awareness and faithfulness to the catholic and apostolic dimensions of the Church appears to be rather weak. The excessive nationalism of the local Churches has contributed considerably to this situation.

Certainly, every nation that has become Orthodox owes a lot to Orthodoxy, which has strengthened not only the personal dignity, but also the value of its entity as a people. But this national gratitude and self-consciousness has often led to a turning inward, to a dangerous deviation theologically, and

---

9. A. Yannoulatos, "Confessing Christ Today," Cernica, Romania, June 4–8, 1974, *International Review of Mission* 64 (1975), pp. 64–94. *Idem*, "Confessing Christ Through the Liturgical Life of the Church Today," Etchmiadzin, Armenia, Sept. 12–21, 1975, *International Review of Mission* 64 (1975), pp. 417–423. *Idem*, "The Role and Place of the Bible in the Liturgical and Spiritual Life of the Orthodox Church," Prague, Czechoslovakia, September 12–18, 1977, *International Review of Mission* 66 (1977), pp. 385–388. Contribution to the theme: "Your Kingdom Come," Paris, France, September 25–28, 1978, *International Review of Mission* 68 (1979), pp. 139–147. "The Place of the Monastic Life within the Witness of the Church Today," Al Anba Bishoy Monastery, Egypt, April 30—May 5, 1979, *International Review of Mission* 68 (1979), pp. 448–451. "Preaching and Teaching the Christian Faith Today," Zica Monastery, Yugoslavia, September 20-25, 1980, *International Review of Mission* 70 (1981), pp. 48–59. For a summary of the theological positions emphasized in these consultations, see *Go Forth in Peace: Orthodox Perspectives on Mission*, ed. Ion Bria, Geneva 1986.

to a nationalistic, psychological imperviousness. There is thus a syndrome that often inhibits Orthodox mission: the idea that our own responsibility is restricted to our own area, and that the problems of others are "not our problems." But on this planet, no one people or social unit can live in isolation. There is a reciprocal influence, and in our times, interdependence is increasing with geometric progression.

The lack of continuity in Orthodox missionary endeavors has been and remains another of our basic weaknesses. Frequently the call to mission appears as the sudden spiritual excitement of an era, as an exception, which does not leave in its wake pan-Orthodox structures and institutions that ensure an Orthodox presence on difficult fronts. It is time we asked ourselves why the Orthodox mission to China, after centuries of hard struggle, has had such poor results. As the snows of persecution are melting in China in our days, and as hundreds of Protestant and Roman Catholic communities are sprouting like wheat, the Orthodox communities are limited to only two. Was the Orthodox mission perhaps tainted with too much nationalism?

Why, in these twentieth century trials, were not other Orthodox called in to help and to continue the race? For example, such continuity happened when the German Lutherans in East Africa turned over the responsibility for continuing their mission to the Scandinavians. Also why, while the Orthodox mission began almost simultaneously with the Protestant mission in Korea, do the Protestants in that country today number five and one-half million and the Orthodox a mere two thousand? Still other painful questions need to be asked when we review sixty years of Orthodox Church presence in Uganda. Can its development be considered satisfactory in comparison with the progress of the other Churches? We should stop generalizing, simplifying and beautifying the facts. Sobriety is needed, and an unbiased study of the past. Not, of course, in order to judge or to condemn others, but to set out aright on the path to planning the future, with a sense of responsibility, with sufficient seriousness of purpose, and in accordance with our possibilities.

Finally, there is the danger of thinking that the missionary obligation is fulfilled when the faithful indulge in simple mutual assistance. Mission, however, is not accomplished by just attending to the care of "our own." It is not synonymous with pastoral care,[10] even though it is closely linked to it. It is not right to call every spiritual effort "mission," and to be content and at ease with ourselves that we have fulfilled our missionary duty by a few pastoral activities.

Mission is principally the binding of "nonbelievers" to the Church; those who have become indifferent or hostile to the faith; those who deny, in theory or in practice, the teachings and principles of that faith. The type of sensitivity needed is one that leads the bishops, priests and frequent churchgoers to another attitude towards those outside the faith. Not an attitude of antipathy or conflict, but an effort to understand their language, problems, reservations, temptations, doubts, sins, even their hostility. It leads, finally, to an attempt to overcome existing barriers through the power of truth, prayer and love.

C

TOWARD THE DEVELOPMENT
OF ORTHODOX MISSION IN THE FUTURE

For the steady growth and fruitfulness of Orthodox mission in the future, I consider two things to be of fundamental importance: First, the development of missionary theological thought and the awareness, if possible, by all members of the Church that mission is a basic expression of our ecclesiastical self-awareness and self-consciousness, and then to transfer this certainty to our ecclesiastical infrastructures and institutions. Second, simultaneously, a sober study of the modern world, the new, electronic, global civilization which is emerging with the setting of the second millennium and the understanding of its pluralistic character is necessary.

---

10. See Chapter 4 of the present volume.

1. *The theological understanding of mission* is *a necessity* not only for theologians. It is of decisive importance for the whole Church. For this reason, I consider it necessary to underline briefly some fundamental theological truths.[11]

(a) The firm basis of every missionary effort is *the vision of mission within the light* of the Revelation and especially of *the mystery of the Holy Trinity.* The starting point of any apostolic activity on our behalf is the promise and commandment of the risen Lord in its Trinitarian perspective: "As the Father has sent me, even so I send you . . . 'Receive the Holy Spirit'" (John 20:21–22).

The love of the Father has been expressed through the sending of the Son. "For God so loved the world that he gave his only Son . . ." (John 3:16). The Son then sends His disciples, with the power of the Holy Spirit, to call all the children of God, those who have been scattered, into His Kingdom. All of humanity created in the likeness of God, must return to the freedom of love, and share in the life of love of the three persons of the Holy Trinity. God's glory, which illuminates and gives life to all creation, must transform all things, and "be exalted over all the earth and above the heavens."

The sending of the Son forms the beginning, and defines more especially Christian mission. The work of Christ is not simply an announcement it is an event, the event *par excellence* of world history, which opens the way for the ultimate end, for the completion of the upward evolution of the world. It is a matter

---

11. Other theological aspects of the same subject have been developed in my previous studies, such as: "A la redécouverte de l'ethos Missionnaire de l'Eglise Orthodoxe," in *Aspects de l'Orthodoxie*, Strasbourg 1978, pp. 78–96. "Eucharist, Service, Witness in Mutual Reciprocity," Πάντα τά Ἔθνη 4 (1985) vol. 13, pp. 6–8. "The Doxological Understanding of Life and Mission," Πάντα τά Ἔθνη 5 (1986) vol. 17, pp. 20–32; 18 (1986), pp. 4–7. (Ed. note: These studies have been re-edited and published in previous chapters of this volume.) "Culture and Gospel: Some Observations from the Orthodox Tradition and Experience," *International Review of Mission* 74 (1985), pp. 185–198; "Remembering Some Basic Facts in Today's Mission," *International Review of Mission* 77 (1988), pp. 4–11. (See also footnote 1 of this study.)

of the assumption of human nature, for its regeneration within the life of the Holy Trinity. This assuming in love, the continuous transfer of the life of love, the recreation of all things in the light of God's glory is being continued in space and time through the mission of the Church, the body of Christ.

The conjunction "as," which is found in John 20:21, "As the Father has sent me," remains very decisive. Christ stresses, *it is I who always remains your prototype. You must walk in the way that I have walked, and follow my example.* The Christological dogma defines the way by which the faithful will continue the mission of the Trinitarian God. The most crucial point in mission is not what one announces, but how one actually lives, what one is. Humankind "becomes" what he or she is by remaining in Christ. "Being in Christ" forms the heart of mission. "He who abides in me, and I in him, he it is that bears much fruit, for apart from me you can do nothing" (John 15:5).

From the very beginning, the Holy Spirit participates in the sending of the Son. The incarnation is realized "by the Holy Spirit and the Virgin Mary." The Spirit cooperates with what is the best in the human race: the All-holy Virgin, who without reservation and with much joy submits herself to the will of God, for the realization of the mission of the Son. It is the Spirit in the form of a dove, who at the Jordan River seals the beginning of the public ministry of the Son. In the form of tongues of fire and "like the rush of a mighty wind," the Spirit creates the Church, transforming the scared disciples into heroic Apostles, full of divine light, knowledge and power. It is the Spirit that unceasingly gives life to the Church, transforming each member into a living cell of the mystical body of Christ, enabling them to share in the safeguarding of Christ's mission for the salvation of the whole world. The energies of the Trinitarian God are always personal: from the Father through the Son in the Spirit. This Trinitarian faith and thought must be found in the depth of our considerations and activities.

(b) The strengthening of the Orthodox missionary conscience contributes also to a *deeper understanding of Orthodox ecclesiology*. In a time when there were so many terms to define the different religious communities, groups and societies, the first faithful, in order to define and express their self-understanding chose the word *ecclesia*: a word that means the assembly or gathering of the people of the whole community. In the new reality, in the new eschatological "city," which was erected upon the Cross and the empty tomb of the risen Lord, God is the one calling and the community being called is the whole *oikoumene*, the entire inhabited earth. This is the catholic "Church of God." In an age of empires and kingdoms, the new community gathered by the Triune God, in choosing the term *ecclesia* to identify herself, wanted also, through it, to underscore the responsible participation of all its members.

We cannot forget that we belong to the "catholic" Church, which embraces all things, the whole of humanity, all of life. We Orthodox stress the tradition of the ancient Church, according to which, when speaking about the "catholic" Church of a concrete city, is meant the Church which is constituted and held in unity in each Eucharistic local gathering. Just as Christ is fully present in the sacrament of the Holy Eucharist, in the same way the Church, His mystical body, keeps its fullness in the local "catholic" Church.

This basic thesis does not abolish the other great truth. Which is, that the perspective of the Apostles, from the beginning, had been to spread the Gospel "to the end of the earth," to invite all nations to enter the Church. "Go therefore and make disciples of all nations" (Matt 28:19). No one is excluded. No local Church has the right to individually enjoy the Christian tradition and keep it exclusively as her own treasure. The basic duty of every local "catholic" Church remains to live the whole tradition and offer it in its fullness, peacefully, but decisively, in a universal perspective. The word *Orthodox* was first used as an adjective: "Orthodox Catholic Church"; that is, a truly "catholic" Church, having a true faith and a true worship, with the two meanings previously mentioned. The understanding of these two aspects of the "catholicity" of our Church must be studied and emphasized more.

It is time for us to live this apostolicity of the Church in a more consistent way, not only placing emphasis on the apostolic succession, but by living the apostolic dynamic and self-awareness of the Church and by strengthening the apostolic mentality and the apostolic responsibility of all the faithful. When we confess our belief in the "one, holy, catholic and apostolic Church," we simultaneously declare our duty to share in her mission.

Since the Church is "Christ extended into the ages," we have the obligation to continue His salutary work for the reformation of all humanity. Orthodox mission cannot become individualistic; it is personal and "ecclesiastical." It is in organic communion with the Body of Christ, the Church, with the others who are communicants, the others who yearn for the love of this Body, and ultimately, with all people who are created in the image of God.

The center of Orthodox spiritual and missionary life is the Holy Eucharist by which we become one body in Christ. By sharing in His life, we share in His mission. "Being" in Christ is not expressed through a mystical or emotional escape, rather in continuously walking in the same way He walked. "He who says he abides in him ought to walk in the same way in which he walked" (1 John 2:6).

(c) By participating in mission *we share in a divine plan, which is still in evolution and has cosmic dimensions.* We are already moving within the eschatological era. Through the outpouring of the Holy Spirit and the founding of the Church, and through His abiding presence in the Church, a process of transformation of human life has already begun which raises humanity and transforms the universe. Mission is a presupposition of the coming of the Kingdom. "And this gospel of the kingdom will be preached throughout the whole world, as a testimony to all nations; and then the end will come" (Matt 24:14).

But the final judgment is a universal event. "Before him will be gathered all nations . . ." (Matt 25:32). All things within the eschatological era have universal dimensions. The basic element which remains is surprise, the breaking down of things conventionally accepted. Neither those who have done well, nor those who have done evil had ever thought that the criteria of the Last Judgment would be whether they had been able to recognize Christ in the humble and poor of the earth, with which He identifies himself. "As you did it to one of the least of these my brethren, you did it to me" (Matt 25:40). The participation in the suffering of the poor is essentially an encounter with the Lord who suffered for us. This view makes Christian eschatology always revolutionary, missionary and opportune in every age.

According to Orthodox thought and tradition, the whole world is being led toward transformation. The whole universe has been invited to enter the Church, to become the Church of Christ, in order to be transformed at the end of time into the heavenly Kingdom of God. "The Church is the center of the universe, the sphere in which her destiny is decisively determined."[12]

The idea, developed mainly by the Greek Fathers, that the human person must include the whole world in the ascent to the personal God, defines and develops the specific Orthodox respect, not only for every human person, but also for creation. All things will be recapitulated in Christ (Eph 1:10). All things will find their own logos, reason, and purpose, which is Christ Himself. This includes "all things in heaven and things on earth." It is this mystery of the will of God that we participate in when we work for mission. This perspective frees us from any individualistic piety, any tendency to marginalize the ap-

---

12. Cf. V. Lossky, *Théologie mystique de l'Eglise d'Orient*, Paris 1944, p. 175. According to O. Clément, "The Church, as a mystery of thanksgiving, grants us the knowledge of a universe created with the purpose of becoming, as a whole, thanksgiving." *Theology after the 'Death of God,'* Athens 1973, p. 118 (in Greek).

ostolic effort and gives to mission a universal eschatological perspective.

2. In the Gospel of Mark, mission is connected more intensively with "the whole world" and "the whole creation." "Go into all the world and preach the gospel to the whole creation" (Mark 16:15). It is *"this world" that the Church must take seriously into consideration and continuously study and observe its evolution,* and its multiformed dynamic.

(a) Many Orthodox are often absorbed by the marked historical consciousness that characterizes our Church, and frequently orient their selves towards the past. Nevertheless, the eschatological dimension, which we have already spoken about, remains a basic aspect of the Orthodox theological inheritance. We constantly refer to Him "who is who was and who is to come, the Almighty" (Rev 1:8). Consequently, the future must also be for us a basic field of vision.

Within this perspective, it is imperative to conduct a serious theological study of the new emerging civilization and new means of communication, which connect humanity and contributes to interpenetration of thoughts, insights and customs. It is incumbent on us to study seriously the tremendous revolution which is pushing humanity from the old industrial era to a universal electronic culture, to a world society of interdependence.

In a former time, the passage from the "oral word" to the "written" one, created tremendous possibilities for humankind for storing knowledge and experience, and decisively accelerated human progress and evolution. The current passage from the "written word" to the "electronic word" has opened infinite possibilities for accumulating new universal knowledge and for the creation of a new human intelligence. The Gospel must also play a crucial role in the forthcoming new culture.

Closely related to this is the new way of life experienced in the great urban centers or megacities. Today, city dwellers comprise about one half of the world's population (1987). There are about 3,050 cities having a population of more than 100,000, and approximately 296 "megacities," each with over one million in population.[13]

However at the same time, together with the search for the ways to spread the Gospel of hope within these new situations and new languages is the need for an understanding of the new existential problems that are created by modern atheism, agnosticism, and absorption by daily earthly activities, which push every spiritual interest into the shadows of indifference. Our basic obligation is for a responsible and serious dialogue with the contemporary currents of thought which shape the achievements of science.

In many instances, the leadership of the Orthodox Church has been limited to a liturgical and regional role and has been indifferent to approaching the intellectuals and artists, who are more receptive to the vibrations of modern thoughts and ideas, and thus grasp, transmit and create new ideas through their art. This is a difficult area, one which needs special sensitivity, cultivation, patience and labor. In any case, the Church cannot be indifferent to this area of concern. The word of life, freedom, justice and hope, which it continues to transfer through the centuries, has to reach, in a dynamic way, the thought and heart of even the most troubled of her children.

(b) As our planet is becoming a megalopolis of which Christians constitute a minority of the world population, less than one third, the need for Christian unity and dialogue with people of other religious convictions are taking on new dimensions and a new intensity.

More direct and imperative, indeed, is the obligation of Christians to achieve a more essential *rapprochement*.[14] We Chris-

---

13. D. Barrett, "Annual Statistical Table on Global Mission: 1987," in *International Bulletin of Missionary Research* 11 (1987), p. 24.

14. E. Voulgarakis, "Mission and Unity from a Theological Perspective," *Porefthendes—Go Ye* 7 (1965), pp. 4–7, 31–32, 45–47. A. Yannoulatos, "Réflexions d'un Orthodoxe sur la coopération inter-confession-

tians are now aware that we cannot offer our witness in a convincing manner as long as we are divided. Reconciliation and unity of Christians has direct missionary dimensions and repercussions. For the Orthodox, priority has to be given to closer collaboration with the ancient Churches of Africa and Asia, which have lived throughout history being faithful only to the first three Ecumenical Councils. These are Churches of heroism and martyrdom. Miraculously they have survived, despite the terrible conditions they have had to confront for centuries; and yet today, they are vibrant lungs able to breathe out the Gospel to Asia and Africa.

The recent decades have shown that we Orthodox have the possibility, and also the obligation, to contribute in a decisive way to the ecumenical quest, using the richness of twenty centuries of theological experience from various historical and social circumstances. Moreover, our participation in the relative conferences and consultations of the World Council of Churches has proved fruitful, not only for others, but also for ourselves; due to the new insights into our own theological problems, and new themes provoked by the experiences and the successes or mistakes of others.

Finally, in the new interreligious dialogue, which has already begun, we have been given the opportunity to practice another kind of "Orthodox witness"; through a positive and essential unfolding of the theology and experience of our Church. This has often helped to transcend the one-sided trends that have developed in the thought and the ethos of other Churches. A serious study in the science of religion is to the general missionary effort what mathematics is for the development of the physical sciences. In addition, we Orthodox, with our experience of the weaknesses and trials of the past, can counterbalance the accusation by the followers of other religions expressed against Christianity, that it has been aggressive and colonial. We

---

nelle dans la Mission," *40e semaine de Missiologie de Louvain*, Louvain 1970, pp. 101–110. J. Meyendorff, "Unity and Mission," *Worldmission* 26 (1975), Vol. 3, pp. 39–42.

Christians of the Orthodox Churches have to give, as a counter-weight to the pressure and the mistakes of Western Christianity, the weight of our own experience and our own martyrdom in the long history of sufferings of and pressures by Moslem countries and majority populations (Middle East, Balkans, Egypt, and Syria).

Concerning the theological understanding of non-Christian religious beliefs from an Orthodox point of view, I will limit myself to the reminder [15] that: According to biblical history, several "covenants" between God and humankind have been made at different times and still keep their importance and validity. The first was made with Adam and Eve, that is, with the representatives of the whole of humankind (Gen 2). The second was with Noah and the new humanity who were saved from the flood (Gen 8). The third covenant was made with Abraham (Gen 12), the father of a nation of people who were to play a basic role within God's plan for the salvation of the whole human race. The final and definitive new covenant of the "New Testament" was in the person of Jesus Christ, the new Adam. All human beings, created in the likeness of God, are in a relationship with God through some covenant.

Acknowledging the presence of serious values existing in the religious convictions of others, even the "seeds of reason"

---

15. See more on this subject in L. Philippides, *Religionsgeschichte als Heilsgeschichte in der Weltgeschichte*, Athens 1953. N. Arseniev, *Revelation of Life Eternal: An Introduction to the Christian Message*, Crestwood, NY, 1965. G. Khodre, "Christianity in a Pluralistic World—The Economy of the Holy Spirit," *The Ecumenical Review* 23 (1971), pp. 118–128. A. Yannoulatos, *Various Christian Approaches to the Other Religions: A Historical Outline*, Athens 1971. *Idem*, "Emerging Perspectives on the Relationship of Christians to People of Other Faiths: An Eastern Orthodox Contribution," *International Review of Mission* 77 (1988), pp. 332–346. See in Greek: *Idem, Globalization and Orthodoxy*, Athens 2004. I. Karmiris, "The Universality of Salvation in Christ," *Minutes of the Academy of Athens for 1980* 55 (1981), pp. 261–289. *Idem*, "The Salvation of the People of God Outside the Church," *Minutes of the Academy of Athens for 1981* 56 (1982), pp. 391–434.

(*spermaticos logos*), we also admit that they possess the possibilities for a new flowering from within. Justin Martyr concluded his brief reference to the *logos spermaticos* with a basic principle which, strangely enough, is not stressed sufficiently by those referring to his position. He emphasizes the difference between "seed" (*sperma*) and the realization of the fullness of the life inherent in it; and he also differentiates between inherent "force" (*dynamis*) and "grace" (*charis*). "Because a seed of something, a type given according to the inherent force, is not the same with this, through the grace of which the transformation and copying (of it) is realized."[16] [. . .]

***

Let us summarize by repeating some of our basic points: In today's existential quest by the entire human race, the Orthodox Christian experience and ethos bring together a unique richness for humanity. Our mission is to assimilate it, to live it, and to develop it creatively within the new conditions which are taking form. Always keeping our antennas sensitive to the messages given to us by the world—or better yet, by God through His people and creation—investigating them seriously and realistically, we are called to re-evaluate our position and life within an Orthodox Trinitarian, ecclesiological and eschatological perspective.

Mission, like everything else in Orthodox life, is not only realized "in the name of the Father, and of the Son, and of the Holy Spirit," but mainly, it is a participation in the life of the Holy Trinity, "with all (our) hearts, and with all (our) souls, and with all (our) minds." It forms a cry for action, for the fulfillment of God's will "on earth as it is in heaven." Allow me to repeat again a basic point that we have been emphasizing for the past twenty-five years; that indifference to mission is a denial of Orthodoxy.

Orthodox mission—internal or external—is by nature "ecclesiastical." It cannot be understood as an individual or a

---

16. Justin Martyr, *Second Apology*, 13, *PG* 6:1-3. (See more on this subject in Chapter 12 of this volume.)

group activity, disconnected from the Body of Christ. For those who work for it, it is the Church that they serve, the Church that they represent; it is the life of the Church that they transplant. No one is saved alone; no one offers Christ's salvation alone. One is saved within the Church, one acts within the Church, and what one lives and offers to others is done in the name of the Church.

All that the Church possesses is for the sake of the whole world. The Church radiates it and offers it, transforming "all things." "The whole world," "the whole creation," not only humanity, but the whole universe participates in the restoration, which has been realized by the redeeming work of Christ, and finds again its destination in glorifying God.

Mission is the extension of the love of the Trinitarian God, for the transformation in love of the whole world.

12

DIALOGUES AND MISSION

(1991)

• Last section of the study: "Dialogue and Mission—An Eastern Orthodox View with Special Reference to Islam," *Bulletin, Pontificium Concilium pro Dialogo inter-Religiones* 26 (1991), pp. 61–76. • Published as the third part in the study, "Relations of Orthodoxy with Other Religions," in *Living Orthodoxy in the Contemporary World*, eds. A. Walker, K. Karras, Athens 2001. (The first two parts were republished in Greek in my recent book, Ἴχνη ἀπό τήν ἀναζήτηση τοῦ Ὑπερβατικοῦ. Συλλογή θρησκειολογικῶν μελετημάτων. Ἀθήνα 2006, 3rd ed.)
• Ἱεραποστολή στά ἴχνη τοῦ Χριστοῦ. Θεολογικές μελέτες καί ὁμιλίες, Ἀθήνα 2007.

A
INTER-RELIGIOUS DIALOGUE

The Orthodox stance may be critical of other religions as systems and organic units, but towards the people who live in the climate of other religions and Confessions the stance is always one of respect and love according to the example of Christ. For man continues to bear within himself the "image" of God and the possibility of "likeness" by virtue of the innate components of his existence—free will, a mind capable of reason, the disposition and the possibility of love.

1. From the beginning Christians were obliged to be in dialogue with people of other religious convictions, offering their witness of faith, their self-consciousness and their hopes. Some of the main theological principles were formulated within the processes of dialogue. Dialogue belongs to the tradition of the Church and served as a motivating factor for the development of Christian theology. The greater part of patristic theology is the fruit of either a direct or indirect dialogue with the ancient Hellenic world, with its religious currents, as well as the purely philosophical systems that were sometimes in opposition, and other times in synthesis.

With the spread of Islam, the Byzantines sought a dialogue with the Moslems, but did not always receive an analogous response.[1]

---

1. Emperor John VI Kantakouzenos (1383) notes characteristically: "The Moslems opposed some of their own from having a dialogue

Today, in the vast megalopolis which we call earth, in a new emerging culture, religious and ideological fermentations, the *dialogue* presents itself as a *new possibility and challenge*.[2] Living together and sharing the common human adventure and looking forward to a global community of peace, justice and brotherhood, each person and each tradition has an obligation to offer the best that they have inherited from the past and, in light of the experience and criticism of others, to cultivate the healthiest seeds of truth that they possess.

The dialogue can contribute to the transplanting of new seeds from one civilization to another, to the sprouting of seeds that have been dormant in the fields of other religions, and to their development. As we have noted,[3] religions remain organic wholes and, as they are experienced by living persons, they become "living organisms" evolving and developing. They have their own inner dynamism and their own *entelechy* (purpose and goal). They are influenced by and assimilate new ideas coming from their environment, and adapt themselves to new challenges.

Various religious leaders and intellectuals introduce or discover in their traditions elements that correspond to the new needs of society. Through this dynamic, Christian ideals penetrate and develop during the various religious quests through-

---

with the Christians, as expected, lest perhaps in the course of such discussions among themselves they come to know clearly the truth. The Christians on the other hand, encouraged by their pure faith and the correct and true doctrines that they adhere to, in no way prevent any of their own, but with every permission and authority, each of them discuss with all that are interested and willing," *Against Islam, PG* 154:380BC.

2. See more on this in A. Yannoulatos, "Problems and Prospects of Inter-religious Dialogue," *It is no longer I who live, but Christ who lives in me*. Dedicated to Archbishop Demetrios, eds. S. Damaskenos, F. Doris, B. Kyrkos, E. Moutsoulas, G. Babiniotis, K. Beis, Th. Pelegkrines, A. N. Sakkoulas, Athens 2002, pp. 1–8.

3. A. Yannoulatos, *Facing the World, Orthodox Christian Essays on Global Concerns*, New York, 2003.

out the world by means of different channels. At this point the contribution of dialogue can be decisive.

In such a perspective, the new questions arising from the recent revolution in technology, electronics, and the new challenges shaking global society could become more edifying; for example: the appeal for world peace, justice, and human dignity; the significance of human life and history; the protection of the physical environment, bioethics, human rights.[4] While at first sight these may appear too "external," a closer look from a religious point of view could possibly offer to these related concerns new ideas and new horizons. The teaching about the Incarnation, bridging the gap between transcendence and imminence in the Person of Christ, gives a unique value to humanity that is inconceivable to any other non-Christian anthropology.

2. Orthodoxy, as it proceeds (1991) into the third millennium with confidence in her self-consciousness and identity, is neither uneasy nor fearful; it does not attack, nor despise people of other religious persuasions. Orthodoxy is *open to dialogue.* Her word is a positive word. The primates of the Orthodox Churches, in their festal Message during the first co-celebration in Bethlehem on January 7, 2000, emphasized without reservation: "We look to the other great religions, particularly the monotheistic ones of Judaism and Islam, and we are prepared to build up even further the presuppositions for

---

4. Characteristically, the French original thinker, Rene Girard, Professor at Stanford University in California, in an interview with Christos Makarian (*L'Express*, and reprinted in the Greek newspaper *Kathimerini*, January 20, 2002, p. 50) observed: "The system of values created [by Christianity] in the past two thousand years will not cease to be of value, independent of whether or not more people will espouse this religion. . . . Finally, all people are partaking of the Christian system of values. What other meaning does human rights have than the protection of innocent victims? Christianity in its secular form has become so predominant that it is no longer recognized as just one religion among others. The real globalization is Christianity!"

dialogue with them, looking to achieve a peaceful coexistence of all peoples. . . . The Orthodox Church rejects religious intolerance and condemns religious fanaticism wherever these phenomena may appear."[5] In general, the Orthodox Church supports the harmonious co-existence of religious communities and minorities and the freedom of conscience of each person and each nation.

We have an obligation to proceed into interreligious dialogue with respect, with discretion, with love and hope, seeking to understand the vital points of others, and avoiding tendencies to confine ourselves to a sterile array of opposing points of view. The followers of other religions have a right to explain for themselves how, in the light of the new challenges of our time; they are reinterpreting their religious convictions under these new conditions. From this sincere dialogue new understandings arise for all religions.

At the same time, we do not have the right to under estimate the significance of difficult problems in order to appear polite. No one desires a superficial type of religious dialogue. In the final analysis, the essence of the religious problem remains the quest for the highest Truth. And no one has the right or the interest to castrate this power of human existence in order to achieve a naive consent in the name of a conventional agreement, which might contribute to some ideological compromise.

In this perspective, the essential contribution of the Orthodox is not to keep silent, but to reveal their particularities and their own more profound spiritual experiences and beliefs. And here we come to the sensitive subject of Orthodox mission, or—as I proposed thirty years ago—the "Orthodox witness."

---

5. "A Message of love without discrimination is sent by the primates of the Orthodox Churches from Jerusalem," newspaper *Kathimerini*, January 8, 2000; cf. newspaper *Eleftherotypia*, January 8, 2000, pp. 8, 18, 47 and other newspapers of that day.

B
RIGHT AND OBLIGATION
OF ORTHODOX WITNESS

1. In every authentic spiritual communication there is always a critical moment, when we touch the real problem that makes a difference. During his encounter with the Athenians on the Areopagus, the Apostle Paul, after the dialogue (Acts 17:17), proceeds to a direct witness (17:22–31). In his preaching, having referred to a common religious foundation, he proceeded on to the critical core of the Gospel: the significance of the Person and the work of Christ. This message was completely outside the ancient Greek world view and in opposition not only with the popular and complex polytheism, but also with the more refined atheism of the Epicurean philosophers and the pantheism of the Stoics.

In unsettling the understanding of a closed, self-contained cosmic system that was autonomous and impersonal, the Apostle Paul was bringing a message of the actions of the one, personal God; who created the universe from nothing, who provided for the world and intervened decisively in history. In contrast to the concept of an individual functioning autonomously, the emphasis was now placed upon freedom and love, which are activated in the communion of God and man. With this paradox, which for the Athenians approached the boundaries of the irrational, Paul introduced a new type of thought. He proposed a radical revision of Hellenic wisdom, by accepting Christ as the center of creation and the *entelechy*—the goal and purpose of the world.[6]

Up until then, Greek thought had based itself and was enthralled in the concept that man is a thinking being who becomes conscious of himself and his environment through the

______

6. A. Yannoulatos, «Ἀθήνα, πόλη συνεχοῦς θεολογικῆς καί πολιτιστικῆς συμβολῆς». Lecture for the Symposium (with the same name) of the Theological School of the University of Athens, Ἐπίσημοι Λόγοι, vol. 28, Ἀθήνα 1988, pp. 361–369.

development of his logic. For Paul, "repentance," the basic turning of humankind, must take place in the direction of that which is the inaccessible for the mind of man, that is, the love of God, which was revealed by the Crucified and risen Christ.

Here we have a clear example of understanding and respecting the old religious concepts and, at the same time, their transcendence with the truth and the power of the Christian revelation. Orthodox "witness" (or mission) means precisely the *deposit of experience* and conviction. We confess our faith, not as our own intellectual discovery, but as a gift of the grace of God. Underestimating or putting off this obligation of personal witness would mean the denial of the Gospel.

The personal experience of "the love of Christ which surpasses knowledge" (Eph 3:19) remains the most profound Christian experience and is related absolutely with the authentic Christian mission and evangelization. Love liberates inner strengths and opens to life new horizons, which the mind is helpless to imagine. The believer's sense of being united with all of humanity, and his love for each human being, motivates him to be interested, at every instance in informing his neighbor about the great good which he has discovered. The gifts of God cannot be held tightly, selfishly. They must be placed at the disposal of all. The particular energies of God, even if referring to one people, or one person, have to do with all of humankind. If we are convinced that the highest human right is the right to transcend the simple biological and intellectual human existence by participation in the relationship of the love of the Triune God, then we cannot keep this conviction to ourselves. This would be the worst injustice.

This obligation does not mean an offering to others out of compulsion, and even more so, not as a cover-up for other goals, political or economic. It is not a matter of imposition, but an offering of a conviction, a personal experience. It is definitive that during the first centuries the Christians spoke about "witness" (*martyria*) and "martyrdom" (*martyrion*), which meant the testimony of an eye- and ear-witness, which was often made at the cost of life itself, with martyrdom. The most profound spiritual stirrings that kindle within the human being cannot be ignored. Everything that the human race possesses must be utilized, and each person must remain absolutely free as to the final choice. The respect for the freedom of each person will always remain a basic principle of Orthodoxy.

2. The Church, being the "sign," the mystery of the Kingdom of God, the first-fruits of the new humanity transfigured by the Holy Spirit, must be offered to the whole world. She cannot be a closed community. Everything she has and everything she lives are destined for the entire human race.

The Orthodox "witness" starting out in silence, and participating in the pain and suffering of others, advances with joy to the proclamation of the Gospel and to its summit in worship. Her goal remains the creation of Eucharistic communities in new places, where the people will celebrate the mysteries of the Kingdom of God in their own particular cultural environment, and radiate His presence and glory in a specific area. Orthodox witness constitutes a personal *participation in the process of the transformation of the world*, which has already begun "in Christ" and will be fulfilled at the end of the eschatological age.[7]

For the re-evangelization of the world, the Orthodox Church does not need to rely upon authoritative and insincere methods, which from time to time have traumatized the integrity of various "Christian missions." She respects the particularity of the person and of his or her culture, but works with her own means; her liturgical life, the offering of her Holy Sacraments and her unfeigned love. Orthodox mission cannot be limited to

---

7. For the Orthodox view of mission see Chapters 3 and 14 of the present volume, as well as A. Yannoulatos, "All of Us Are in a Missionary Situation," *International Review of Mission* 71 (1982), pp. 452–454. Idem, "Understanding and Witnessing to Christ in a Pluralistic World, from an Orthodox Perspective," *From Baar I to Baar II, Current Dialogue*, Geneva, No. 26, June, 1994, pp. 43–49. *Idem*, "Understanding Mission," *Orthodox Christian Mission Center* 18 (2002), No. 1, pp. 5–7.

the offering of education, health care and other means of external development. She is bound to offer to each person, particularly to the poor and oppressed, the faith that each person has
a unique personal worth; that because each person is created
in the "image and likeness" of God, he or she is destined for
the highest possible achievement: to become "Christ-like," to
partake of the divine glory, to attain, by grace, deification (*theosis*). This is the basis for every other expression of human dignity. The Christian faith offers the most dignified anthropology,
one that transcends every type of merely humanistic theories. If
people in the end accept it or not is a matter of their own freedom and choice.

The followers of other religions practice a harsh criticism
against certain Christian missions, when they see them associated with arrogance, with egotism, with state power and other
nonreligious interests. Nevertheless, it is not right to identify
Christian mission with the mistakes of Western Christendom in
a specific period of history, such as that of colonization.

The austere criticism is directed to the "Christians," but not
to Christ. The great change will come in the world when the
Christians will live, will practice, will respond to our mission,
walking in Christ's way. The power of God is often expressed in
the paradox of the absence of worldly power and can be lived
only within the mystery of love with external simplicity.

We need a constant, sincere self-criticism and repentance.
This does not mean a limitation of the Orthodox witness to
achieve some colorless dialogue, but free acceptance of the logic
of love, the ever revolutionary logic of Christ, who "emptied
himself" in order to enter and to dwell within the specific reality of humanity. It also means acceptance of His way of life
and His death, in an ongoing personal transfiguration "from
one degree of glory to another" (2 Cor 3:18). The quest for the
Orthodox is not to limit or to reduce our "witness," but to live
out our mission in Christ's way.

13

THE GLOBAL VISION
OF PROCLAIMING THE GOSPEL

(1995)

• The keynote address at the International Conference on Mission and Evangelism, Brookline, MA, August 6–11, 1995. • "The Global Vision of Proclaiming the Gospel," *The Greek Orthodox Theological Review* 42 (1997), pp. 401–417. • *Ἱεραποστολή στά ἴχνη τοῦ Χριστοῦ. Θεολογικές μελέτες καί ὁμιλίες,* Ἀθήνα 2007.

"May God be gracious to us and bless us and make his face to shine upon us" (Ps 67:1). This verse from the Psalms is repeated by Orthodox Christians in the daily services of the Church; it summarizes our yearnings and our petitions. This biblical verse continues and is followed by two other critical verses whose meaning usually remains unknown. Indeed, we absolutely need God to show pity towards us, to bless us and to have mercy upon us; we long for Him to reveal His face to us. And yet, all these things do not end with "us." These blessings must not be confined to our own circle, as large as it may be. There exists a clear goal which must be fulfilled and follows as a natural consequence of our having been blessed by God. And this something is that the way of salvation must be made known to the whole earth so that all peoples may share in the glorification of God: "That thy ways may be known upon earth, thy saving power among all nations. Let the peoples praise thee, O God; let all the peoples praise thee" (Ps 67:2–3).

This hidden side of universality, which must accompany every demand for personal or collective blessings and salvation, is illuminated and revealed in the Resurrection Vigils of Pascha and is repeated throughout Bright Week. In the second Antiphon of the Paschal Liturgy, Psalm 67, in its entirety, is interwoven with the prayer, "Save us, O Son of God, who are risen from the dead." It is within the light of the Resurrection especially, that the universal perspective and meaning of the Gospel of salvation is manifested.

The global vision is not something complementary, it is not an appendix to Orthodox thought and consciousness—something to consider, if you want, and if you do not, to set it aside. This dimension forms a most basic element of: (a) Orthodox teaching, (b) of Orthodox worship; and (c) the decisive factors that must determine our ecclesiastical action and life.

A
STEADFAST FRAMEWORK AND CLEAR PERSPECTIVE OF THE GOSPEL

1. As we have stressed in another context, the universal vision appears in biblical thought from the very first verse of *the Old Testament* ("In the beginning God created the heavens and the earth . . ." Gen 1:1); it penetrates and is interwoven in the Scriptures and seals the last chapters of the New Testament with the vision of the new heaven and the new earth (Rev 21:1). The Sacred Scripture refers to the adventure of all humanity, to universal salvation. It is preoccupied with the entanglement of human freedom and existence in the process of the death and corruption of the entire world; and it is especially concerned with the transcendence of this process through the saving intervention of the God-man and His Second Coming. The Bible maintains a steadfast universal perspective and dimension, even within the pages which extensively refer to specific issues, peoples or persons. For example, Israel's adventure, which is referred to in the books of the Old Testament and extends through the ages, foretells the coming of the Messiah and leads to the salvation of all nations. Israel's story contains the way for the realization of God's plan for the whole world.

Especially in the prophetic books of the Old Testament and in the Psalms of David, the ecumenical vision repeatedly occurs. Besides the verses of the Psalm with which we began, let us be mindful of other often repeated verses. "The earth is the Lord's and all that is in it" (Ps 24:1). "All the ends of the earth shall remember and turn to the Lord; and all the families of the nations shall worship before him. For dominion belongs to the Lord, and he rules over the nations" (Ps 22:27–28), "Praise the Lord, all nations! Extol him, all you peoples!" (Ps 117:1).[1]

2. From the beginning of the *New Testament* and onwards, there is a global meaning and message. The incarnation of the Word of God takes place in a specific place and time, and among a specific people. Nevertheless, it embraces all of humanity. Without exception, Jesus Christ invites all people to His Kingdom, showing a special affection towards the least, toward those that are suffering and being persecuted. This great joy must be transmitted to give new life to all people without discrimination of race, language, and origin. The elder Simeon, receiving in his arms the forty-day old Jesus, blessed God because his eyes had seen the Savior whom God prepared "in the presence of all peoples, a light for revelation to the Gentiles . . ." (Luke 2:31–32). The Logos of God, through His Incarnation, assumes all of humanity, the depth of human nature, and not just something of its external shell. By assuming human nature, the inaccessible God granted special value to the human person, including the human body—His masterpiece of creation—as well as to the whole of creation, in which man participates organically. The world does not form something that exists outside, parallel or independent of the Creator. Finally, the universality of the Gospel of Jesus Christ transcends the meaning of "all of humanity," it extends to the whole creation.

The teaching of Christ unfolded at a specific place and time, but it always had a steadfast universal and eschatological character. With complete clarity, the Lord declares that "this gospel

---

1. See also the following: "Clap your hands all you peoples! Shout to God with loud songs of joy. For the Lord, the Most High, is awesome, a great king over all the earth" (Ps 47:1–2). In the New Testament some of the verses of the Psalms take on an added apostolic nuance: "Their voice goes out through all the earth and their words to the ends of the world" (Ps 19:4; cf. Rom 10:18).

of the kingdom will be proclaimed throughout the whole world, as a testimony to all nations; and then the end will come" (Matt 24:14). And when referring to the final judgment of humankind, He points to its universal framework: "When the Son of man comes in his glory, and all the angels with him, then he will sit on his glorious throne. Before him will be gathered all the nations..." (Matt 25:31–32).

Jesus Christ, the spiritual Sun, illumines and gives life to the whole world: "The true light that enlightens every man was coming into the world" (John 1:9). John the Evangelist repeatedly proclaims that Jesus came in order "that the world might be saved through him" (John 3:17). "And we know that this is indeed the Savior of the world" (John 4:42). His sacrifice on the Cross, although it takes place at a specific place and time, is offered for the salvation of the entire human race, for the salvation of the whole world. His Resurrection brings a definite liberation to the entire human race from the bonds of sin and death. The essential message of the Church is not only that Christ rose from the dead, but that His victory has an overall importance for the whole of humanity, for human nature, which He assumed as a second Adam. Inasmuch as disobedience, the sin of the first Adam led to death all of humanity, in the same way the obedience through love unto sacrifice on the Cross, leads all of humanity to the Resurrection. "Christ has been raised from the dead, the first fruits of those who have fallen asleep . . . For as in Adam all die, so also in Christ shall all be made alive (1 Cor 15:20, 22). Consequently this light, which is emitted by the risen Savior, is not intended exclusively for a few chosen people or nations; or is it confined only to them. But, this light must embrace all, without discrimination of nation, race, color, language, and origin.

He who was resurrected from the dead transforms all things, every form of life, relationship, and development. Through His Resurrection, "Christ lifted up from the depths of Hades all of humanity and raised it to the heights of Heaven." All human beings, all peoples have the right to participate in the victory, love, and joy of the Resurrection. Through Christ's resurrection "the whole visible and invisible world" is renewed and Christ receives "all authority in heaven and on earth . . ." (Matt 28:18). After the Resurrection, the horizon became the whole world.

The setting for the sending of the disciples is defined with absolute clarity before the Ascension of the Lord (Acts 1:8). The witness must be given "both in" the specific places where the Apostles were born and had lived until then, "and to" the end of the earth. In order to make this enormous jump from the local to the universal, the Apostles needed to receive "power" from above. The coming of the Holy Spirit, who now upholds the Church into the future, empowers the disciples, abolishes barriers that divide people, such as language and race, and opens before the apostles the worldwide horizon for the transmission of the Gospel of salvation "to the end of the earth." The Apostles each turn towards different and concrete directions, however, the apostolic vision remains firmly universal.

Within the providence of God, for the writing and first phase of the transmission of the Gospel into the world, the Greek language and culture were used, of which one of its main characteristics was ecumenicity (*οἰκουμενικότης*).[2]

In the Letters of the Apostle Paul the ecumenical dimension and universality are repeatedly emphasized in relation to the mystery of the Church. God "has put all things under his (the Son's) feet and has made him the head over all things for the Church, which is his body" (Eph 1:22–23; cf. Col 2:10: ". . . the head of all rule and authority," and Col 1:18, ". . . the head of the body, the church"). Christ rules over all the universe,

---

2. The ecumenicity of Greek culture was cultivated in many ways through Greek philosophy, science, art and language, and with the use of reason, argument, and dialogue, giving birth to dialectical thought; also with the constant seeking, the extraordinary blossoming of creativity and innovation in all areas, as well as through a dynamic communication among individuals and peoples.

inasmuch as, "in him all things were created . . . He is before all things, and in him all things hold together" (Col 1:16–17). The words "all things," (*ta panta*) "everyone," and "all" are repeatedly used in the Letters of Paul, especially those written during his imprisonment. It is within this sense that the Gospel embraces "everything" and has been destined to be preached "to every creature under heaven" (Col 1:23) that the life and work of the Apostle moves. St. Paul preaches Christ "the head of the body, the church; he is the beginning, the first-born from the dead, that in everything he might be pre-eminent" (Col 1:18). And in the "proclaiming," of Him, St. Paul exhorts and teaches "every man" to present themselves "mature in Christ Jesus" (Col 1:28). "The grace" given to Paul is "to preach to the Gentiles the unsearchable riches of Christ and to make all men see what is the plan of the mystery hidden for ages in God who created all things" (Eph 3:8–9). Thus, the work of the apostles is this spreading of the "mystery," of this salvation to all of humanity, within the Church, of which Christ is the head.

3. *Orthodox ecclesiology* firmly moves *toward this perspective of universality*. Our Church, being "the Church of God," rooted in the life of the Holy Trinity, embraces with her prayer and concern all that He has created and for which He provides; her care enfolds "all things." Each local Church, being the gathering of all those who believe in Christ in a concrete place, witnesses and manifests the catholicity of the Church in that place and forms an eschatological "sign of the Kingdom of God" which dominates the universe and will be completed in the *eschata*.

According to St. Cyril of Jerusalem, "The church is given the name *ecclesia*, because she calls all people to gather in the same place for a common cause."[3] Within the meaning of the catholicity of the Church, St. Cyril includes the *ecumenical*, as well as the *qualitative* dimensions. He writes,

---

3. *Catechesis* 18, 24 *PG* 33:1048B.

The Church is called catholic: (a) because she exists within the world, from one end of the earth to the other; (b) because she integrally and completely teaches all dogmas which must be made known to all people; (c) because she subjects every race of men to piety, [and he adds] independent of their social rank and education (rulers and those being ruled, the scholars and the illiterate); (d) because she heals and cures every kind of sin . . .; and (e) because she possesses within herself all that is called virtue, in words and deeds, and spiritual gifts.[4]

The global apostolic vision reaches its culmination in Paul's reference to the secret will of God, to "the mystery of his will" which is to be realized "as a plan for the fullness of time, to unite all things in him, things in heaven and things on earth" (Eph 1:9–10). "All things" must be recreated, transformed in Christ. Nothing remains outside of His radiance and influence.

All these aspects illumine particular characteristics of the global vision concerning the proclamation of the Gospel to the modern world. In our approach to the mystery of the Church as "communion" (*koinonia*), being guided by Trinitarian theology, Christology, Pneumatology, and also by the steadfast relationship to Eschatology, we always have before us the indisputable global vision of universality. The Church was, is and will remain the "body (of Christ), the fullness of him who fills all in all" (Eph 1:23).

---

4. "It is called Catholic then because it extends over all the world, from one end of the earth to the other; and because it teaches universally and completely one and all the doctrines which ought to come to men's knowledge, concerning things both visible and invisible, heavenly and earthly; and because it brings into subjection to godliness the whole race of mankind, governors and governed, learned and unlearned; and because it universally treats and heals the whole class of sins, which are committed by soul or body, and possesses in itself every form of virtue which is named, both in deeds and words, and in every kind of spiritual gifts." *Catechesis* 18, 23, *PG* 33:1044B.

B
THE GLOBAL VISION IN THE
LITURGICAL EXPERIENCE OF THE GOSPEL

All of Orthodox liturgical life steadily moves within this universal vision, which embraces all Christian teaching.

1. *The Orthodox rhythm of the daily and weekly life of worship*, together with personal *ascesis*, vibrates with the spirit of the universality of salvation. First of all, this spirit is found most vibrantly at the heart of the Orthodox prayer and spirituality given to us by the Lord—the Lord's Prayer. We beseech and reiterate daily: "Your kingdom come, your will be done, on earth as it is in heaven." It is not simply that His will be done "in me" or "in us," but "on earth." The heart of the Christian, before praying for daily problems, for daily bread, must first focus upon the steadfast universal horizon. Immediate and personal concerns do not prevent the believers from seeing the global view, nor does the global vision prevent them from dealing with daily realities.

In every Divine Liturgy, which sums up the mystery of salvation, we begin our supplication: "Let us pray for peace in the whole world," and the Anaphora culminates with the offering of the Holy Gifts "in all and for all." This reasonable and spiritual worship is offered "for the whole world, for the catholic and apostolic Church" (Liturgy of St. John Chrysostom) which extends, "from one end of the inhabited world to the other" (Divine Liturgy of St. Basil the Great). After Holy Communion, the priest offers incense, and expresses the Church's universal longing with the verse: "Be exalted, O God, above the heavens, and let Your glory be over all the earth." The Divine Liturgy, while liberating us from absorption in the cares of our small egos, opens the horizon for us, helping us to live existentially the universality of salvation in Christ. The liturgical revival that has appeared in many local Orthodox Churches in the twentieth century, has contributed a great deal to regaining the awareness of this global vision. But this will need to be even more vividly illumined during our Eucharistic assemblies and be experienced with greater consistency as well in our daily life after the Liturgy. So that the Orthodox witness and mission may be extended and developed *in a liturgy after the Liturgy.*

The daily cycle of prayer (Midnight prayers, Matins, Hours, Vespers, and Compline), parallel with ancient tradition, is based especially on the Psalter in which, as we have already mentioned, the global vision is obvious. But also in the *Parakletike,* the basic hymnological text of our Church, the subject of the global vision of salvation in Christ is repeated often in several troparia, in order for it to be firmly fixed in the conscience of the believers. So it is in the troparia of the Crucifixion on Wednesday and Friday, as well as in the apostolic troparia of Thursday, but particularly in the troparia for Pascha, Saturday Vespers and Sunday Matins, the emphasis is unmistakable: "Your life-bearing Resurrection, O Lord, has illumined the whole world . . . and the light of Your Resurrection has brought joy to all." "Rejoice, O heavens, be glad, O earth . . ." (Tone Three, Saturday Vespers). "Your Resurrection, O Christ the Savior, has given light to all humanity . . ." (Tone Two, Saturday Vespers).[5]

---

5. This theme recurs often in the hymns of the *Parakletike*. Phrases are repeated frequently referring to the whole world, such as: "Providing great mercy to the world," "granting life to the world," "that You, O Christ, might redeem our race from death," "through the Holy Spirit all creation is renewed" (Tone One, Sunday Matins). "Out of Your good will and love, O Lord God, You have brought all things into being through Your Logos and Your Spirit" (Tone One, Sunday Vespers). More particularly, the Crucifixion hymns remind us: "O merciful One, having spread Your arms upon the Cross, You have gathered the nations that were far from You to glorify Your great goodness" (Tone One, Wednesday Matins). "At Your Resurrection You have filled all things with joy" (Tone Four, Sunday Matins). "Come, all nations, know the awesome power of the mystery; for Christ our Savior, the Logos in the beginning, was crucified for us, and willingly was buried; and He rose from the dead to save us all, let us therefore worship Him." "All things are filled with joy, when they receive the experience of Your Resurrection." "For You rose from the dead, granting life to

All the great Orthodox feasts, celebrated throughout the year, provide an opportunity for us to remember the ecumenicity and the universality of the Gospel. First of all, the biblical texts which are read on those occasions, underline the truths we referred to in the first part of this study. The related hymnology that comments on and develops the meaning of the great Orthodox festal cycles steadily points to the universal meaning of each feast. For example, in the Feast of the Transfiguration, we characteristically sing: "Today on Tabor in the manifestation of Thy Light, O Word, Thou unaltered Light from the Light of the unbegotten Father, we have seen the Father as Light and the Spirit as Light, guiding with Light the whole creation" (*Exapostilarion*).[6]

2. The universal perspective is emphatic in the troparia of the *Triodion,* and is particularly illumined in the *Pentecostarion* (in which many of the hymns of the *Parakletike* are included). The global importance of the Cross and the Resurrection is interwoven with Orthodox hymnology. "Come, all ye faithful, let us worship Christ's Holy Resurrection; for behold, through the Cross, joy has come to the whole world" (Hymn of Resurrection). The Paschal hymns steadfastly refer to the global vision of the Gospel. The Church, in ecstasy before the universal dimensions of the event of the Resurrection, sings: "Today the whole creation, heaven and earth and the underworld are filled with joy. Let the whole creation celebrate the Resurrection by which

---

all mankind, that all creation may glorify You" (Tone Three, Sunday Matins). "Angels and humans, O Savior, praise Your Resurrection on the third day, through which all places of the inhabited earth were granted a new dawn of light" (Tone Four, Saturday Vespers).

6. Cf. "Thou hast put Adam on entire, O Christ, changing the nature grown dark in past times, thou hast filled it with glory and made it god-like by the transfiguration of your face" (*Kontakion,* Hymn of the Transfiguration). "In the divine Transfiguration today, all of human nature receives the first light of deification" (pre-feast *Kontakion,* Hymn of the Transfiguration).

it was strengthened" (Easter Canon, Ode 3). The whole creation receives new light.

Through your Resurrection, O Lord, the universe was illuminated and Paradise was opened again; thus, the whole creation praising Thee, offers you daily hymns" (Tone 3, Bright Monday evening).[7] The tradition, according to which the hymn "Christ is Risen" is sung in different languages, proclaims the great truth, that the Gospel of Christ is intended for all people, races and languages, and that the Church has the duty to proclaim it everywhere. It is this that bridges disputes and contradictions, and brings people together in brotherhood, peace, mutual respect and solidarity to the world community.

The ecumenicity of the Church also appears in the Feast of Pentecost in a most joyful way. The disciples receive the Holy Spirit in order to fulfill the commandment of Christ, that is to be witnesses of Him "to the end of the earth," "to attract the ecumene" (Apolytikion hymn).[8] The Holy Spirit will remain forever He who is "ever present and fills all things." Nothing can remain outside His enlightening, purifying and sanctifying grace. "And thus through Him all Creation is illumined and guided to worship the Holy Trinity" (*Exapostilarion*).[9] The Holy Spirit, who "gathers the whole in-

---

7. Cf. also: "Having illumined the world in Your Resurrection on the third day, O Lord, deliver Your people from the hand of Your enemies, O Lover of mankind" (Tone Three, Saturday Vespers). "O light-giving Lord, You have shown the light of the Resurrection to the nations" (Tone Five, Saturday Vespers).

8. Since then the old prophecy of the Prophet Joel is being fulfilled without interruption. "And it shall come to pass afterward, that I will pour out my spirit on all flesh..." (Joel 2:28 [LXX:3:1]). The hymn writer comments: "As you promised, Lord, You did pour out Your Spirit abundantly on all flesh and it was all filled with Your knowledge" (Sunday of Pentecost, Canon, Ode 6). "The light of the *Paraclete* has come to illumine the world" (*Kathisma* hymn, Matins of Pentecost).

9. With the coming of the Holy Spirit, the tragedy of confusion which began with the tower of Babel, finds its solution and the centrifugal tendency of mankind toward separation is corrected: "When God distributed the tongues of fire, He called all to unity" (Kontaki-

stitute of the Church," uninterruptedly grants all things, so that the mystery of salvation is preached in all the world. For that reason, the believers praise Him: "O, You, the Renovator of the universe, blessed are You" (Iambic Canon, Ode 7). "Let us praise the Holy Spirit who sanctifies the universe" (Thursday of Pentecost, Vespers).[10]

Finally, the feast of All Saints proclaims that those who receive the Holy Spirit and become sanctified belong to the whole ecumene. Their witness and martyrdom adorn the Church. "Adored in the blood of Thy Martyrs throughout all the world as in purple and fine linen" (Vespers of Sunday of All Saints). "As the creation's Planter, all the world doth offers unto Thee as nature's first-fruits the God-bearing martyrs . . ." (*Kontakion*). From the first apostolic generation, the Gospel was preached in every direction. "Speaking with the Spirit's words, the Savior's blessed disciples, who by faith became as well the Spirit's true instrument, sowed and cast abroad to the earth's farthest ends

---

on Hymn of Pentecost). In the *Antiphons* and the *Prokeimenon* of the Epistle readings, the verse from the Psalms, with its new significance, is prominent: "Their word has gone out into all the earth, and their message has reached the ends of the earth." The Holy Spirit "has now filled the Apostles with wisdom to preach throughout the world" (Tuesday Matins after Pentecost). "All the ends of the earth have been filled with heavenly power through the Apostles and the good will of God" (Thursday Vespers after Pentecost). Through the Holy Spirit "all things are brought into being and preserved, while life is affected to live, to abide and to be saved" (Thursday Vespers after Pentecost).

10. This universal vision of the action of the Super-essential Holy Trinity is also presupposed in the Prayers of Pentecost, which are recited on bent knees: "Who didst create heavens and the earth and the sea and all that was fashioned therein." (First Prayer) Then the tongues of fire are mentioned, with which the lips of the Apostles were endowed, so that ". . . we, even every race of men, receiving divine knowledge by the hearing of the ear, each in his own tongue" (Second Prayer). The Father, the Holy God, "created all things through the Son with the synergy of the Holy Spirit." "And all creation that was made doth bless the only Savior and creator of all, as their benefactor" (Iambic Canon of Pentecost, Ode 8).

their most holy preaching in a manner wholly Orthodox" (Vespers of Sunday for All Saints).

The immediate conclusion from this short review is that the apostolic pulse vibrates the Orthodox liturgical worship and the global vision remains its dynamic perspective.

C

THE GLOBAL VISION IN
ECCLESIASTICAL ACTION AND LIFE

While the global vision dominates so intensely the teaching and the worship of the Orthodox Church, this vision does not have a corresponding influence upon her everyday spirituality. If we want to be sincere in our self-criticism, we must accept that among the immediate ecclesiastical Orthodox interests, the national issues of the different autocephalous Churches prevail, while the global vision of the proclamation of the Gospel still remains dim and weak. Indeed, the historical reasons which led us to this situation were quite important, but we will not refer to them now. Nevertheless, today's reality imposes upon us the need to evaluate again what Orthodox theology and worship has already revealed to us.

1. *"Globalization"—New worldwide problems.* The older generation experienced the "hot war" (1940–45), as well as the "cold war," due to the competition of the two superpowers (1945–1990). With the collapse of the socialist regimes, the second war also came to an end, and great expectations were created for humanity for a new period of peace in the world. Unfortunately, instead of the "New Order" that we were expecting, we find ourselves confronted with a "New Disorder," with many new problems prevailing on humanity and, in many instances, creating chaos: with the new wars in various regions of our planet; with the transfer of great masses of populations; with the new proliferation of nuclear weapons; and with the newly established regimes which need guidance and assistance in the process of establish-

ing a stable democracy. In a parallel way, the chasm between "North and South," between rich and poor countries continues to deepen; terrorism, the spread of drugs, and the damage to the environment all constitute new threats for humanity. However, the basic characteristic of our time is the fact that these problems have become the problems of all of humanity.

We continually hear that we are proceeding towards a global community. Science, technology, mass media, arts, commerce, and finance are moving today within universal frames and are shaping a new, international economic culture. Moreover, a defining role is being played by the 2,000 multi-ethnic local and international news media organizations on the world stage. The mutual influence among national traditions and local cultures, which, of course, were not absent in the past, are more intense today. New problems have also appeared which have presented global economic dimensions from the first moment of their creation; such as: the ecological issue, with the immediacy of its many critical aspects for our planet; the issues arising from the developing bioethics and eugenics; the situations created by the invasion of a multiplicity of electronic computer products and their application with the worldwide internet and in our social and private life. These new issues tend to alter not only human relations, but the very essence of human life.

At the same time, old problems, such as social exploitation, injustice, and crime are acquiring new forms and dimensions on multinational and intercultural levels. The globalization of these issues demands that a new, global approach be undertaken by the national leaders, as well as by "public opinion." But as a rule, the multidimensional size of the problems has not yet been realized by either party and they remain absorbed in "their own" internal affairs. The great problems of today demand a new holistic approach. They form new challenges for theology and the ecclesiastical conscience and actions. They constitute the new, global, "multiform" culture, within which we are called to proclaim the Christian message, a culture the Gospel must oriented and transform.

The believers are not surprised by these new global situations. The teaching and worship of the Church have already opened our visual field and our heart's perception to the dimensions of the *ecumene*. Especially now we have new possibilities to face, in common, these global issues with people from other cultures, based on different religious beliefs. These possibilities give us the opportunity for witnessing the Gospel in new situations, in new ways, penetrating into environments and influencing mentalities which have been previously closed to Christianity. Thus, the Gospel of Jesus Christ is not proclaimed only by classical "didactical" preaching; it may also be proclaimed as a proposal, as a display of its principles and of the "logic" of the Word of God. So, the new problems can be confronted by transmitting its content as the personal experience of all those who have wholeheartedly received the Gospel and live in Christ. But here the need becomes intensely obvious for the creation of new codes of communication within the global environment and the obligation of clergy and laypeople to think and act from a perspective that is both "catholic" and eschatological.

2. *Toward new codes of communication.* In the process of communicating the Gospel to the modern world, it is necessary to study carefully, and to synchronize the relationship between the sender and the receiver, as well as the relationship between the message and code of communication. Each culture has its own ways and "codes of communication" that are based upon and are mainly defined by the one who receives, the situations of life, the structures of thought, the new problematics of each society; which in our case is the formation of a new global community. These codes of communication must not be confronted as enigmas or threats, but as new languages for transmission of the eternal message of the Gospel.

In order to confront these theme correctly, it will be necessary for us to realize more intensely that the centre of our message is He "who is and who was and who is to come, the Almighty" (Rev 1:8). In many instances, our Orthodox orientation concerning the proclamation of the evangelical message looks to the past; to the description of the marvelous things that God has done for the sake of humankind. At the same time, however, the Gospel unceasingly refers both to the present moment and to that which is to come, to the *eschaton*. Without this clear, eschatological vision, the preaching of the Gospel loses its warmth, its resonance, and its truth. The Kingdom of God, which has already come, is coming, and is expected definitely to come, remains the center of the Christian message.

For a correct understanding and acceptable approach to the contemporary realities which will form the new codes of communication, initially, the role of conscientious lay members of the Church is of basic and primary importance because they are directly involved in modern scientific, economic, and social problematics. It is a special blessing of God that laypeople can be found leading a deep and genuine religious life in the frontiers of the modern world. Their experience, thoughts, methods, and intuitions constitute precious material for the formation of the new code of communication with the modern world. The same applies also to persons with artistic sensitivities, politicians, journalists, and the mass media. All these people, men and women, who find themselves at the very heart of this quest and articulation of the new problems, are precious collaborators for the transmission of the Gospel. They must be seriously invited to participate in this work. Surely their contribution to forming new codes of communication in the new global culture and their proper use will be decisive and invaluable.

The Gospel of salvation, which is addressed to all peoples and transforms all things, cannot be proclaimed only by the ordained clergy. All the members of the Eucharistic community, those who through baptism and the Holy Eucharist participate in the cross and the Resurrection of Christ, are invited to and must participate in the communication of the message of the Gospel to the modern world. What takes place at the Vigil of Pascha constitutes the basic symbolism of the transmission of the Christian message. First, the bishop or the priest sings:

"Come, receive the light from the unwaning light." Immediately, all people come to receive and then to give to another the light of the Resurrection— men and women of all ages, of every educational or spiritual level. Ultimately, this contemporary world, which is often tormented by the madness and odor of death, is waiting to hear and learn how the certainty of the Resurrection can penetrate their darkness and anguish and give meaning to human existence, hope, the abundance of love, the power for life.

Missionary activity is closely connected with the new problematic. In the past, when the Gospel entered a new cultural reality and a local Church was created, this same Church, during the process of her formation, adopted certain cultural elements, rejected others, and transformed others.[11] In a similar way, even within the new contemporary culture, the process of forming the Church will have to move towards the world in a similar way: sometimes in "communion," sometimes in confrontation, and at other times, by attempting to give the world a new orientation.

3. *Harmonizing local and global obligations.* What has already been said is easily accepted by the Orthodox world today. As a rule, however, our interests are confined within the local, ethnic field. Thus, an astonishing depression emerges when we are called to live with this global vision in new environments, transcending the classic frontiers of traditionally Orthodox countries and peoples.

During the past decades, serious attempts have been undertaken and significant progress has been accomplished in raising awareness of the ecumenical dimension, and apostolic responsibility of the Orthodox Church. The title of the first missionary manifesto: "Indifference for mission means denial of Orthodoxy," no longer sounds strange and heretical. The duty for an Orthodox world mission has, by now, been theo-

---

11. A. Yannoulatos, *Παγκοσμιότητα καὶ Ὀρθοδοξία*, Ἀκρίτας, Ἀθήνα 2004, pp. 109–136.

logically justified. Nevertheless, that granite-like "but"—the absorption by our immediate local, "our own," needs—will often check and suspend the Orthodox worldwide activity. One of the most dangerous checks to outreach to the contemporary ecumene for Orthodox apostolic responsibility seems to come each time from the popular proverb: "When your own garden is thirsty, do not pour the water outside." Thus, all the energy is absorbed by "our garden," which, as a rule, is determined by national or local criteria. Only a few drops—and these by mere evaporation—irrigate other "gardens." This secular logic is one of the secret weaknesses and sins of modern Orthodoxy. It seems to dominate on various levels: in the parish, in the monastery, in the diocese, in the autocephalous local Church. On other occasions we have repeatedly attempted to confront this argument, which like an invincible "virus" sickens the Body of the Church with chronic infections of localism that lead a large part of the Church to suffer respiratory insufficiency and inertia.[12]

The correct understanding and implementation of our apostolic duty in the local, as well as in the global framework is a primary demand of Orthodox life today. Every form of polarization between local and universal, I believe, leads to a false spirituality which finally denies the Orthodox mentality and ethos (*phronema*). This does not mean that we must all hurry towards new missionary frontiers. But it does demand that more and more young people and adults make such resolutions. Primarily, what we must ask is how the global vision of proclaiming the Gospel will inspire us towards the fulfillment of our missionary duty, in the place where the will of God has led us. And how we will actively participate, in thought, in prayer, and in our practical contributions to make this global vision a conscientious and living reality in our Churches.

Even in the absolute quietness of the ascetic life in the desert, one of the saints of our century, Saint Silouan, used to pray:

---

12. See chapter two of the present volume.

"O Lord, make all the peoples of the earth to know Your love and the sweetness of the Holy Spirit, so that they forget the pains of the earth, abandon every evil thing, adhere to You with love and live peacefully doing Your will for Your glory." And on other occasions, he prayed: "Lord, make me worthy to weep for myself and for the whole world. May all the peoples come to know You and live eternally with You." [. . .]

In every local Orthodox Church there needs to be an organization for the cooperation, support and assistance of the weaker Orthodox Churches. The gifts possessed by each Church, ought to be utilized to help one another. The Ecumenical Patriarchate and the Patriarchate of Alexandria have included mission in their activities. Similarly in the Churches of Greece and of Finland, several considerable initiatives for external mission have developed. The Mission Center of the Greek Orthodox Archdiocese of North and South America, which was reorganized with an inter-Orthodox character as the Orthodox Christian Mission Center, forms a special blessing in the realization of the vision and purpose that was communicated and developed, for the first time, in the framework of the youth initiatives of *Syndesmos* and *Porefthendes* in the beginning of the 1960s. Something analogous should form a basic section of every Orthodox Church for the help of Orthodox Churches who are in greater need.

At first glance this proposal appears to be quite modern, but it belongs to a very old patristic command. According to St. John Chrysostom: "The leader of the Church ought to care not only for the Church that has been entrusted to Him by the Spirit, but also for the entire Church existing throughout the ecumene. . . . If he must pray for the *catholic* Church which extends to the ends of ecumene, he must all the more show care for the entire Church, concern for all Churches."[13] [. . .]

And now, please allow me a personal note. The experience of these last years in Albania has revealed to me what kind of surprises God reserves for us in our effort to live the global vi-

13. St. John Chrysostom, *Eulogy for our Father among the Saints, Eustathios, Archbishop of Antioch, PG* 50:602, 26-35.

sion of spreading the Gospel. During the first phase of my missionary search and diaconia, the words "to the end of the earth" were rather colored by geographical meaning—the depths of Africa or Asia. I had never thought that "the end of the earth" could be so near geographically. That it could be in Albania, where for decades the breath of Hades reigned; where they had crucified and buried Christ again. Where, during the second half of the twentieth century, the Albanian government proclaimed, definitively, with statements from conferences and with articles in the country's Constitution, that God had died; there, where they had also killed, together with God, the human person by distorting and deviating human conscience and by dissolving finally human freedom and society.

Albania today, I believe, is a microcosm within the broader macrocosm of the modern ecumene. The majority of the population belonged traditionally—before the Communist regime—to Moslem families. This fact causes the situation to present similarities with those faced by the ancient Orthodox Patriarchates. The majority of the people, including the new generation, are still imbued with the theories of atheism, which for almost fifty years dominated the country; a fact that makes them resemble the other regions that were influenced by a-religious socialism. Due to the recent democratic and economic changes, a fast-paced secularization is taking place, creating problems and conditions similar to those that are faced by the Orthodox Churches living in western cultural regions, with the exception that the economic situation is so low that it is creating phenomena primarily found only in the Third World.

The activities of different religious communities concerning Albania, highlights the weakness of Orthodoxy throughout the world to come to the support, as she should, of a needy Church which had been completely dissolved and is only now being reconstituted from the ashes of a fifty year persecution. Let me say, as an indication only, that the Roman Catholic Church (representing about 10% of the population and less than half the number of Orthodox) is being helped in her reorganization by 300 foreign priests, monks, nuns, and hundreds of laypeople. The Protestants (which comprise less than one percent of the population) are being helped by 450 foreign missionaries. The Moslems are being assisted by thousands of foreigners. In all of this, the only foreign assistance the Orthodox Church has is six priests, three nuns, three laymen and three lay women, all foreigners. I have noted these numbers because they symbolically reflect how other religious communities hasten to one region that has urgent needs and how big appears the inertia of many local Orthodox Churches. Of course, Divine grace which "heals the weak and fulfills the lacking," has given other solutions. So our Lord is granting us blessings in the ongoing restoration of the Orthodox Autocephalous Church of Albania from ruins.

***

Let us summarize: The global vision is the correct Orthodox framework for everything that we do or transmit on the local, parish level. No correct understanding of the living Orthodox tradition can exist when this perspective of universality is missing. This is not a vision we observe as spectators, but an area of existence, of thought, of activity within which we live. Whoever looks with a sense of doxology at the mystery of the Holy Trinity, the Almighty God, the "Creator and keeper of all things," is concerned with "all things." Whoever has become one body with Christ tries to think, feel and acts like Him. Whoever receives the Holy Spirit becomes inspired from the universality of His activities. We address ourselves to the All-holy Spirit in the beginning of each Orthodox prayer service and ask Him to come and to live "in us." But this finally means that we are ready to be coordinated with His realm, His presence and activity. A person bearing the Spirit (*pneumatophoron*) thinks, feels and acts with a universal perspective. His reflection, his prayer, his interests and efforts acquire a global horizon. The Holy Spirit, like the rush of a "mighty wind," carrying away the small airtight self, opens our soul to the ecumene (the inhabited world). All of the Spirit-bearing people, men and women, beginning with the Apostles, lived in this manner the presence of the Spirit in their life. The Holy Spirit is not offered for individual possession or enjoyment. The direct and immediate result of a Spirit-filled life is missionary witness.

The Psalm with which we began may form a summary of our subject and a constant remembrance of it. We beseech with intensity in our daily prayers, that "God may be gracious to us and bless us and make His face to shine upon us" (Ps 67:1). However, a genuine Orthodox spiritual life is realized and completed within the wider global context, which determines as our goal what follows in this Psalm: "That your way may be known upon the earth, your saving power among all nations. Let the peoples praise you, O God; let all the peoples praise you." (Ps 67:2–3) Let us add these verses to the end of our daily prayers and understand them in the light given to them by the event of the Resurrection Christ and the descent of the Holy Spirit on Pentecost, as well as by twenty centuries of the witness of the saints who lived the Gospel. "Let the peoples praise you, O God; let all the peoples praise you."

14

REDISCOVERING OUR APOSTOLIC IDENTITY IN THE 21st CENTURY

(2003)

• A paper given at the Symposium on Missions, St. Vladimir's Seminary, February, 2003. • "Rediscovering Our Apostolic Identity in the 21st Century," *St. Vladimir's Theological Quarterly* 48:1 (2004), pp. 3–20. • *Ἱεραποστολή στά ἴχνη τοῦ Χριστοῦ. Θεολογικές μελέτες καί ὁμιλίες,* Ἀθήνα 2007.

No one questions it in theory. On the contrary, we confess it solemnly and repeat it nearly every time we gather to worship. We profess our belief in the "one, holy, catholic and apostolic Church" and proclaim our membership in it. In practice, however, it would seem that many Orthodox believers, and even many local Churches, commonly embrace a rather limited definition of apostolicity. As a rule, most of the handbooks on dogmatic theology, with which generations of clergy of the Orthodox Church are educated, emphasize primarily three main points: (a) The Church is apostolic in that it was instituted by Christ and its foundations laid by the Apostles. (b) The Church preserves intact and unchanged the teaching of the Apostles, the apostolic faith and tradition. (c) The Church is erected firmly upon the unbroken succession of Bishops from the Apostles.

These are incontrovertible truths which have already been vividly described, and yet, there is another fundamental dimension, essential shading, to this colorful portrait of apostolicity that I would like us to focus on. Our guide to a deeper understanding of this theme will be the New Testament.

A

THE WORDS "*ΑΠΟΣΤΕΛΛΩ*," "*ΑΠΟΣΤΟΛΗ*,"
AND "*ΑΠΟΣΤΟΛΟΣ*" IN THE NEW TESTAMENT

1. The idea of a divine mission appears in other religions (for example, Zoroaster, Mohammed, Nanak, and in the Greek

world: Epictetus and Hermetism). In biblical revelation, however, this idea is directly related to the salvation of the whole world and is expressed in language that draws especially from the basic verb ἀποστέλλω (I send out), and its related forms.

Christ's awareness that He *has been sent* by the Father is vividly portrayed in the Gospels. He is the one "whom the Father consecrated and sent into the world" (John 10:36; cf. 5:36 "The Father has sent me" 5:38; 6:29; 6:57; "I have not come of my own accord; he who sent me is true . . . and he sent me" John 7:28-29; cf. John 8:42).

In the Gospel of John, in particular, we encounter this truth forty times, like an impressive refrain. The absolute unity of the Father and Son is such that the attitude one takes towards Jesus is directly referred to the Father (John 5:233, 12:44 ff.).

This witness constitutes the basic point of the preaching of the Apostles: "And we have seen and testify that the Father has sent his Son as the Savior of the world" (1 John 4:14). "In this the love was made manifest among us, that God sent his only Son into the world, so that we might live through him . . . he loved us and sent his Son to be the expiation for our sins" 1 John 4:9–10; Gal 4:4). "Therefore, holy brethren, who share in a heavenly call, consider Jesus, the apostle and high priest of our confession" (Heb 3:1).

From the beginning, others were also called to participate in the work of announcing the salvation that was completed in Christ. At the time of Jesus, there were various understandings about perfection in man, as well as different groups of pious seekers. The well-known Essene community comes to mind, as does the circle of disciples that gathered around John the Baptist. Such groups usually were localized geographically. The characteristic of the new group that gathered around Jesus was the fact that from the first year of their discipleship, He sent them on a mission: "And he appointed twelve, to be with him, and to be sent out to preach and have authority to cast out demons" (Mark 3:14–15). Christ Himself gave His disciples the name of apostles (ἀπόστολος). "He called his disciples, and chose from them twelve, whom he named apostles" (Luke 6:13). Jesus did not found a static community that withdrew from the world. Nor did He attach Himself to one particular place. He traveled from town to town, village to village, and was constantly on the move. He sent out His disciples, still imperfect beings with weaknesses and shortcomings, who were at once His "disciples" and His "apostles." The community which He had gathered around Himself had mission (ἀποστολή) as its inner dynamic. Their work had a centrifugal energy, moving outward from the Lord, the Teacher, to the others; and at the same time, a centripetal attraction back to the one person, the Person of Christ.

As His earthly deeds drew to a close, Christ associated His own mission with that of His apostles. The theme is pronounced in His high priestly prayer: "As thou didst send me into the world, so I have sent them into the world" (John 17:18). When Christ completed His salvific work, through His Crucifixion and Resurrection, the mission of His disciples was made explicitly clear. The risen Lord appeared to them while they were still terrified and shaken by the tragic events, and entrusted to them the continuation of His work. "As the Father has sent me, even so I sent you. And when he had said this, he breathed on them, and said to them, 'Receive the Holy Spirit'" (John 20:21–22). He clearly indicated to them that their mission would be accomplished through the power of the Holy Spirit. At Christ's Ascension, He again reassured them, ". . . you shall receive power when the Holy Spirit has come upon you" (Acts 1:8).

2. The opinion has been formulated that the apostolic identity was limited exclusively to the Twelve who were eye- and ear-witnesses to the life, death and resurrection of Jesus Christ. Naturally, the Twelve hold a unique position in the life of the Church. They are the bedrock of the New Israel and will be its judges at the end of time (Matt 19:28). The election of a twelfth disciple, in the place of Judas, was made in order to maintain

the symbolic type of the New Israel that had come into being (Acts 1:15–26). At the same time, however, the election of Matthias demonstrated the recognition that others too possessed the attributes of eye- and ear-witnesses to the sacrifice and resurrection of Christ. The Twelve will always be the foundation of the Church. "And the wall of the city had twelve foundations, and on them the twelve names of the twelve apostles of the Lamb" (Rev 21:14). Nevertheless, the apostolic obligation is not limited to the activities of the Twelve; they in turn passed on to others the exercise of their apostolic work.

Already in the Gospel of Luke we find the tradition according to which Jesus "appointed seventy others, and sent them on ahead of him, two by two" (Luke 10:1). The purpose expressed here, to send them out into the world, was the same as that assigned to the Twelve; both have the same formal character: "He who hears you hears me, and he who rejects you rejects me, and he who rejects me rejects him who sent me" (Luke 10:16; cf. Matt 10:40). Consequently, the work of those who are sent out, the apostolic work, is not limited to the apostleship given to the Twelve.

Besides the Twelve and the Seventy, the risen Lord also sent out Paul, with a special calling from heaven. Paul's vocation widened the apostolic circle and the nature of apostolic work. Paul insists again and again that he is "a servant of Jesus Christ, called to be an apostle, set apart for the Gospel of God (Rom 1:1; cf. Eph 1:1; 1 Tim 1:1; Titus 1:1; "I am an apostle to the Gentiles" Rom 11:13). The manner in which Paul himself understood his apostleship reveals that it is possible for the Lord to entrust a particular mission to new persons. In the New Testament, the name apostle is given to other less prominent personalities: Barnabas, Sosthenes, Epaphroditus, Timotheus, Titus. The Churches of Antioch and Rome already existed when the leaders of the Church arrived there.[1] Broadly speaking, apostolic ac-

---

1. See Xavier Léon-Dufour et al., eds. *Vocabulaire de théologie biblique*, Paris 1974, 3rd ed., s.v. *"apôtres."*

tivity is the work of every disciple who is "the salt of the earth" and "the light of the world" (Matt 5:13–14).

Of course, apostolic tradition is based on the witness of the original Apostles, *par excellence*. But the apostolic work was not completed with the generation of the first Twelve, *it is continued in time.* The Lord's final commandment to the Eleven (Judas had by then definitively cut himself off from their circle) did not concern only those particular disciples. In the same way, Christ's teaching and the other commandments given in a broader or narrower circle of disciples, did not exclusively concern those particular audiences, but were of relevance to the entire Church.

Let us consider how absurd it would be to interpret in such an exclusive fashion the Lord's words at the Last Supper, when He said to His disciples "Do this in remembrance of me" (Luke 22:19). Would it be possible to support the proposition that this commandment was of concern only to His circle of Twelve? If that were the case, there would be no Church. Instead, this commandment concerns the entire lifespan of the Church. Likewise, the final commandment given to the Eleven is determinative not only for those eleven, but for all who believe in the Gospel message, for the entire Body of the Church that would come into being from the seeds of the first Apostles' words and deeds. Apostleship is a basic element—permit me the term—in the genetic code of the Church.

3. The Lord's last commandment, as it is preserved in the Gospel of Matthew, defines the Church's scope and character. From the stirring words with which the risen Christ directs His apostles emerge all the propositions that constitute the seamless, organic whole (Matt 28:18–20). [. . .]

Many people prefer to focus their attention on the last sentence, "And lo, I am with you always, to the close of the age," (Matt 28:20) which reinforces intellectually and emotionally, the certainty of Christ's presence in our everyday life.

No doubts have been expressed as to whether the first, as well as the last verses refer to the fullness of the Church, that is to say, to all believers, without exception. Still it is peculiar and inconsistent to consider that the middle link, the verse "Go therefore and make disciples of all nations," refers exclusively to the Twelve. If we take away the conjunctions *therefore* (οὖν), *and lo* (ἰδού), the logical connections are lost. The revelation that, "All authority in heaven and on earth has been given" to Christ implies a specific obligation on the part of the Apostles and their successors. This obligation is the consequence of the great truth described in the first verse. Upon the fulfillment of their apostolic duty, they will have the guarantee of Christ's presence. Without the "and" (*kai*), connecting the last phrase to the preceding ones, the promise of Christ's constant presence is cut off and remains in suspension.

The obligation belongs to the *whole Body* of the Church. The Church, as the Eucharistic community of the Resurrection, shoulders the responsibility to proclaim the mystery of the Tri-une God, the divine Economy (*Oikonomia*) in Christ through the Holy Spirit.

A basic characteristic of apostolicity is that the disciples must *"go."* Their lives will unfold on an open horizon, with challenges, dangers, successes and failures; forever in motion. They must not be limited or obstructed by any boundaries whatsoever. Their duty is to go out and teach "all nations," without exception. From the very start, the universal character of the Church's mission is clearly defined.

The advent of the Holy Spirit at Pentecost dynamically constitutes the new community of disciples and empowers her for her mission "to all nations." The commandment is firmly bound up with the promise of the Holy Spirit's advent that was given by Christ. The Holy Spirit comes for the inauguration of a global mission. The gift of tongues was not given, of course, to demonstrate linguistic prowess, but as a tool for their mission and work among foreign peoples with different means of communication.

Christ completed His salvific work, but the transmission of His message to the whole world was not to be done by Him. He entrusted the responsibility to His Apostles (the Church He founded). The Apostles in turn entrusted the continuation of their work to their successors; this spiritual relay race is continued by the Church as a whole "until He comes." This characteristic of apostleship is indelibly wrought in the very nature of the Church and should be lived in every age. Apostolicity is an innate element of the Church. Mission is part of the Church's genetic material, a fixed element in its DNA. It is a gift of grace organically ordered in the Church, nourished by the Eucharistic community, which it constantly renews. And it will continue to be so constituted with the uninterrupted presence and energy of the Holy Spirit, within an eschatological perspective. Apostolicity is a process that has both historical and eschatological dimensions.

I believe that the perpetuation of the apostolic dynamic in historical time, in other words, the preservation of the apostles' flame and spirit, is a distinguishing feature of the Church in its entirety. An awareness of the magnitude of apostleship is utterly essential for our understanding of the very nature of the Church.

B

LIVING THE APOSTOLICITY
OF THE CHURCH TODAY

Circumstances in the world at the dawn of the third millennium after Christ are certainly not the same as those of the first or second. So many events have intervened; so many different conditions have been formulated and consolidated. *How then will the Church's apostolic identity be lived out in our age?*

1. To begin with, it is necessary to stimulate our slumbering awareness that we belong to a Church that is "apostolic," in the sense that we have elaborated above, and that this "apostolic"

vocation belongs to the entire Church. Each one of us personally, bears his or her share of responsibility, as a living cell of
this organic whole. Interest in apostleship, in mission, is not the
specialty of particular groups or individuals, but a definitive
characteristic of the Church herself. It is designated as the occupation of the Church. It is the *sine qua non* of its life.

Through the grace of God significant progress has been
made in this direction during the last decades. [. . .]

Many Orthodox believe that the local Church to which
they belong fulfills her obligation to the final commandments
of Christ through pastoral care of her flock, or, at the most,
through reaching out to those sheep that have strayed in order
to bring them back into the fold to which they were born. This
activity has been called "domestic mission" (without most people suspecting that this term has been adopted from pietistic
Protestant terminology). The consequence of taking onboard
what is immediately at hand has been an indifference to that
part of the Church's obligation that extends beyond the local
to the universal. Let us make here a short parenthesis in order
to consider a working hypothesis. If humanity had waited for
Orthodox Christians to make a move toward the mission "to all
nations," innumerable areas, Africa, for example, would have
been lost to Christianity and the great victor would have been
Islam.

Many local Orthodox Churches, with thousands of clerics
and monks, are circumscribed within their ethnic boundaries.
They do not even dare to think of sending even a few properly
prepared missionaries—with an appropriate ecclesiastical understanding—to work in other places, to strengthen the already
existing, often small, cells of Orthodox believers. This exclusive,
turning-inward to one land or one people simply does not correspond to the meaning of apostleship, of mission, as it is defined in the New Testament.

In North America especially, the Orthodox witness is offered within a dynamic society with universal interests. In such
a society Orthodoxy is in a state of mission—and she cannot,

certainly, be content with a museum-like preservation of the glorious Orthodox past of far away homelands. Something substantially new and important ought to arise from this situation. We live in an age of extraordinary human creativity, the fruits of which are especially apparent in the realm of scientific achievement. I believe that a basic characteristic of our human nature, of being created in the image of God, together with freedom, reason, and love is *creativity*. In each new generation, with its unique challenges, we are called to offer the eternal treasure contained in the Church, thinking and acting creatively, and in organic continuity with the original, the apostolic tradition.

Of course, what we do not need are a few isolated missionary activities in distant lands. Let me repeat: It would be a great mistake to restrict the apostolic reawakening in our generation to the exotic escapades of a handful of zealots and others, as the peculiar, marginal activity of a few romantic types with a craving for adventure. Nor do we need to propagate the rumor that missionary work represents Protestant influences on Orthodoxy, whereas the true Orthodox spirit is expressed through asceticism and monasticism. Instead, firm foundations must be laid: (a) through serious theological study; (b) through probing deeply into the dynamic meaning of the Church's apostolic identity; (c) through educating the ecclesiastical congregation, both clarifying and invigorating the apostolic awareness of the faithful; (d) through honest self-criticism regarding the direction Orthodoxy is taking and should take, while disposing ourselves toward repentance. (e) Moreover, we must always be sensitive to the contemporary world, to its new challenges and inclinations.

The world "outside" the Church—that mission field *par excellence*—is inconceivably complex. One must be constantly drawing new maps and staying alert to new developments. Such mission also demands creative thinking about how best to execute and make viable the apostolic idea within each context.

2. It is enough to mention just a few *characteristics of our time*: The amazing speed with which information circulates around the globe. The electronic revolution and continuous advances that hasten further the spread of information with the speed of light. We have the pursuit and, at the same time, the undermining of Christian unity. On a day-to-day basis, we have a political, social, and educational co-existence with people of different faiths, or no faith at all. One could also mention the penetration of the Western world by ideas from the religious traditions of India. The return to, and airtight isolation of various religious communities, whose proprietors appeal to the need for security, the preservation of ethnic self-consciousness and cultural identity. One could include the multifaceted revival of Islam whose dynamic presence is assuming a central place on the world stage. A basic feature of this revival is the growing attempt, using intensive proselytism and the mobilization of violent means, to resist the so-called Christian world. Finally, people everywhere are waking up to the tragedy wreaked across most of the planet by poverty and illness at epidemic levels, as in the case of AIDS.

Amidst this constant flux, these endless shifts in the landscape of the inhabited world, how can we discern the path toward "all nations"? Clearly, not on the basis of the old geographical representations of the nineteenth and twentieth centuries, that assumes the existence of a "Christian *oikoumene*," from which heralds of the Gospel can be sent out to other nations. Frontiers are no longer defined geographically—between the Christian and the non-Christian worlds. Just as the boundaries between good and evil do not lie outside us, but are drawn across each of our hearts—and these are shifting boundaries—so we must realize that in the same way the boundaries between Christian and non-Christian should be sought within those countless people who are Christian in name. Among many people with a Christian tradition, vast swathes of the population are either totally ignorant about or indifferent to religion. These people are found "outside" the Church. Amidst peoples whose majority embraces other religions; islets of Christianity still rise above sea level and need encouragement and reinforcement.

The mission of the Church must keep a clear horizon to "all nations," without exception. In geographical terms, those who lie "outside" the Church may be close at hand, or far away, but neither can be ignored for reasons of ease. Apostleship is the obligation of the "whole" Church and there is no justification for focusing solely on those who belong to our nation or resemble ourselves. The field of responsibility and action is the whole world and that cannot change. The Lord's commandment is: "Go into all the world and preach the gospel to the whole creation" (Mark 16:15).

We also must realize that responsibility for those "outside" is incumbent upon *all of us.* It is not a matter of disinterest for the faithful. Rather, it *is of direct concern* to the apostolic Church, of which we are members. The Church ought to be "present" constantly through its emissaries.

3. Apostolicity requires that the Church—and I stress the whole Church—not limit herself to pastoral care of those within; to cultivating what comes easily, what is beautiful and spiritually inspiring for the benefit of those who are "within the Church." The Church is called constantly to dare to make an *exodus,* to *reach out.* [. . .]

We are called to go out from the confines of our closed, entrenched communities, to transcend our prejudices, misgivings, and fears and to bear witness together—to the best of our abilities—to the risen Lord. We are called to meet our contemporaries where they are grappling with the most pressing problems. We must do this "not to be conformed to this world" (Rom 12:2), but to help in its orientation toward the sacramental grace of the Church and the power of her truth. We must do this with earnest respect for the distinctiveness of every people and culture, for the freedom and dignity of each human being and with unfeigned love for the whole person. It is a matter of personal spiritual concern and not a political matter.

The issue is not for the Church to conquer "all nations," but for the Church to teach "all nations"; to share with "all nations" the knowledge, salvation and experience she possesses. Every individual, every people are free to accept or reject the Gospel message. They have the right, however, to be informed responsibly—not catch it in bits and pieces, or from dubious sources, but from the apostolic Church.

4. I would like to underscore just two essential elements of our contemporary apostolic responsibility.

(a) *We must be present* as persons, conscientious members of the Church, and where possible, as a Eucharistic community proclaiming in peace the Kingdom of God. We must present in the countryside and in cities, and in the gatherings of those who are "outside." We must present as living members of the Church, at conferences, at meetings, both intra-Christian and interfaith; but also even at scholarly, scientific, political, and economic occasions; offering calmly and humbly the Orthodox view and witness, helping to find worthy solutions to vexing problems. In our day, divine providence has opened for the Orthodox doors into areas that were previously hermetically sealed. The Orthodox witness should by all means be proclaimed in these areas as well.

(b) *We have to share* with others whatever we have, whatever goods God has granted us, both material and spiritual; knowledge, sacred and profane, means, capabilities, joys and hopes, the experience and power of love, the peace of God "which passes all understanding" (Phil. 4:7). To such "sharing" belong the innovative ideas and programs for the development of areas dominated by grinding poverty.

The presence of every living member of the Church radiates not simply thoughts and ideas, but also something of the grace of God. The apostolic service remains the duty of the Eucharistic community. It must be assumed by that community and experience by it. The Church, as a whole, in order to remain faithful to her apostolic self-awareness has no right to be absorbed in her internal problems. In each generation, the right people must be sought and sent out to those "outside"—both geographically and socially.

Those who will dedicate themselves to this mission in the modern context should be prepared to avoid simplifications or naive romanticism. As soon as possible, they must become accustomed to being "strangers in a strange land." It will be their lot to be the "other," to live as minorities, sometimes enveloped in a cloud of suspicion and circumspection. We must all also free ourselves from the concern for immediate and large-scale results.

Throughout history, the attempt to establish the Christian ideal has produced two solutions: "the flight to the desert and the creation of the Christian empire." As Fr. Georges Florovsky pointed out, "We are well aware that these two solutions were shown to be unsuccessful because it was never possible for everyone to escape to the desert, and the Christianity of the empires was never anything but nominal."[2] Nonetheless, the Church continues to impart the Gospel message of salvation and the grace of the mysteries to all nations; she continues to give meaning to life and death and to the history of the world. Her mission preserves both its historical and eschatological dimensions. "And this gospel of the kingdom will be preached throughout the whole world, as a testimony to all nations; and then the end will come" (Matt 24:14). "The failure of all utopian hopes cannot overshadow the Christian message and the Christian hope. The King came, the Lord Jesus, and His Kingdom shall come."[3]

---

2. G. Florovsky, "The Body of the Living Christ, An Orthodox Interpretation of the Church," in *Three Theological Essays*, trans. I. K. Papadopoulos, Thessaloniki 1972, (in Greek) pp. 92–93. Cf. Idem, "Antinomies of Christian History: Empire and Desert," in *Christianity and Culture. The Collected Works of Georges Florovsky*, vol. 2, Belmont, MA, 1974, pp. 67–100.

3. *Ibid*, p. 94

The Orthodox Church is called to be an apostolic people, the light and salt of the world, offering an ongoing, living witness to the living God.

C

RENEWING THE APOSTOLIC CONSCIENCE

A revival of the Church's apostolic consciousness means also a rediscovery and the living-out by the Orthodox clergy and peoples: (a) of the apostolic vision, (b) of the apostolic zeal, and (c) of the apostolic ethos.

1. *The apostolic vision* embraces all the world's peoples, as the risen Lord had directed in His last commandment. This vision had nothing to do with today's globalization of the economic market. The sending of Christ's disciples "to all nations" had in view the *universalization* of the love that elevates the human being toward the *theanthropos*, recreating him anew. That vision lives on as the goal of the Eucharistic community, made up of those joined by the Holy Spirit in each and every place. Their mission is to create a community of solidarity, a community of free persons filled with love for one another. The Apostle Paul refers to the honor, glory and power granted to the risen Lord and emphasizes that "all things" are under His authority (Col 1:16–21; Eph 1:21–22). This vision extends not only to the entire inhabited world, but reaches even unto the last things, preparing the way for the fullness of time, "to unite all things in him" (Eph 1:10). The teaching and the worship of the catholic and apostolic Orthodox Church broadens our optical view and the range of our heart to the dimensions of the whole *ecumene*, and ultimately, to the end of time.

2. *The apostolic zeal* that typifies the dynamic work of the Apostles is not something external, a straightforward task, a formal execution of one's duty. Their work sprang forth unceasingly from the depths of their beings. It was an inner neces-

sity. "For if I preach the gospel, that gives me no ground for boasting," states the Apostle Paul. "For necessity is laid upon me. Woe to me if I do not preach the gospel" (1 Cor 9:16). This need applies to the Church as a whole. The love burning in their hearts for Christ and for humanity needs to be expressed. One searches for ways to share with others the divine gifts that have been received, not to impose them on others. It is the gift of the grace of God, which was given "by the working of his power" to St. Paul "to preach to the Gentiles the unsearchable riches of Christ, and to make all men see what is the plan of the mystery hidden for ages in God who created all things" (Eph 3:7–9). This love is a flame that is nourished by the fire of Pentecost and must be passed on to other souls (cf. 2 Tim 2:2).

3. *The apostolic ethos* is described in amazing terms and preserved in the Letters of St. Paul. It is an ethos of self-renunciation, filled with unfeigned love, spontaneous joy, and vigorous hope.

The apostolic service is sustained and upheld by the unique treasure given to the Apostles by grace, and not thanks to any particular worth or strength of their own. "But we have this treasure in earthen vessels," writes Paul, "to show that the transcendent power belongs to God and not to us" (2 Cor 4:7). St. Paul even approaches boldly the rather sensitive matter of underestimating the Apostles by those with authority in his time. "We are fools for Christ's sake, but you are wise in Christ. We are weak, but you are strong. You are held in honor, but we in disrepute . . . When reviled, we bless; when persecuted, we endure; when slandered, we try to conciliate" (1 Cor 4:10–13).

An apostle's worth and power does not derive from his personal virtue or knowledge. "But by the grace of God I am what I am, and his grace toward me was not in vain. On the contrary, I worked harder than any of them, though it was not I, but the grace of God which is with me" (1 Cor 15:10). This grace is experienced, rather, in the sense of personal sinfulness, even in a state of utter powerlessness.

It is toward such apostolic spirituality that St. Paul directs the members of the Eucharistic community of Corinth—a spirituality which preserves a crystalline inner purity, even under the most difficult external conditions. He summarizes the apostolic ethos in an extraordinary manner in the Second Letter to the Corinthians:

> Working together with him, then, we entreat you not to accept the grace of God in vain . . . but as servants of God we commend ourselves in every way; through great endurance . . . by purity, knowledge, forbearance, kindness, the Holy Spirit, genuine love, truthful speech, and the power of God . . . as sorrowful, yet always rejoicing; as poor, yet making many rich; as having nothing, and yet possessing everything (2 Cor 6:1–10).

Finally, throughout the entire course of the apostolic work there prevails a distinct awareness of Christ's continuous presence. "And lo, I am with you always" (Matt 28:20). (I prefer the translation, "all the days"—*pasas tas imeras*—which we can understand as *in all sorts of days*.) This presence enlightens their existence, whatever difficulties each day may bring. Everything is done with the power of the Lord through the Holy Spirit. This awareness has emboldened the apostles across the ages to confront even the most painful moments. It brings them comfort and peace along the most tortuous paths they must walk, at times of sorrow and suffering. It fills them with constant rejoicing and the light of tranquility. This is not something graspable by the mind, something belonging to the realm of abstract thought. Rather, we are confronted with the radiance of grace pouring out from the Holy Spirit that penetrates and enlightens all existence. This is what it means to live and work in Christ (cf. Gal 2:20).

***

Summarizing the views about the Church's apostolicity we discern these main features. Our Church is apostolic because:

(1) She was established by the One sent by God, His Son, Jesus Christ, and its foundations were laid by the Apostles; (2) She understands herself as being directly identified with the apostolic community as it was described in the New Testament and in Holy Tradition; the womb from which was born also the Canon of the New Testament; (3) She preserves intact and unchanged the teaching of the Apostles with an unswerving consciousness of its uninterrupted continuation throughout history and its faithfulness to the Word of God; as it was understood in the apostolic age and was preserved across the course of time, guided by the Holy Spirit; (4) She has rooted her life in the celebration of the Sacraments, as Christ ordained and as was passed down by the Apostles; (5) She is unshakable, erected on the unbroken apostolic succession of bishops and the clergy they themselves have consecrated.

There is, however, yet another aspect of this apostolic identity which I have tried to bring out by the points emphasized above. (6) Our Church is apostolic because: (a) She is in a state of constantly being sent out to do mission; (b) It is necessary, in that case, that the whole Church, following the example of the Apostles, continue to proclaim the Gospel to the whole of humanity, until the end of the world; (c) Our local Churches, but also each and every one of us, should, as members of the "one, holy, catholic and apostolic Church," take up our corresponding share of the apostolic calling. We should do this with consistency and with the use of our creativity, in both thought and deed. And finally, (d) we ought then to carry on the *diaconia of the logos* (the service of the word), of the sacraments, and of reconciliation with apostolic vision, zeal and ethos. The whole world is our stage, throughout the course of history that remains until the "coming of the Lord."

15

INSTEAD OF AN EPILOGUE

«Καί ἰδού ἐγώ μεθ' ὑμῶν εἰμί . . . »
"And lo I am with you . . ."

(Matthew 28:20)

(2002)

• Lecture given in French at the celebration of the 75th anniversary of the inter-Christian theological movement, "Faith and Order," Lausanne, France August 25, 2002. • «Καί ἰδού ἐγώ μεθ' ὑμῶν εἰμι πάσας τάς ἡμέρας ἕως τῆς συντελείας τοῦ αἰῶνος» (Matt. 28:20), *Synaxis of Thanksgiving*, honoring the Elder Aimilianos, Indictos, Athens, 2003, pp. 111–118. • *Ἱεραποστολή στά ἴχνη τοῦ Χριστοῦ. Θεολογικές μελέτες καί ὁμιλίες, Ἀθήνα 2007.*

There are three major themes in the risen Christ's final words to His disciples. They form an indivisible, organic whole. First, a statement of universal significance: "All authority in heaven and on earth has been given to me." Second, a final commandment: "Go therefore and make disciples of all nations, baptizing them in the name of the Father and of the Son and of the Holy Spirit." Third, the promise which follows as a consequence of the commandment and vouchsafes it: "And lo, I am with you always." The conjunctions "therefore" and "and" reinforce this cohesion. The three themes are interdependent just as the three systems of our bodies—muscular, circulatory and nervous—are interdependent.

A

AUTHORITY IN THE UNIVERSE

The event of universal significance which seals Matthew's Gospel is that, after the crucifixion and resurrection, Christ is granted all authority over the whole universe (Matt 28:18). The teacher, the prophet, the Messiah is now declared to be "the Lord." This development changes the rhythm and the meaning of human history. The substance of what has happened is different from what it seems to be. True power is no longer in the hands of the emperor and of the Roman administrative machine. The progress of history does not depend upon the accumulated knowledge of the erudite and the wisdom of people on earth. Authority has been granted by the Almighty and Omnipotent Father, the God of love, to His Son, who is love incarnate in its utmost form, who accepted even the Cross. This truth constitutes the central axis of Christian faith. The real strength and influence of Christians depends upon the extent to which they live out and proclaim this reality.

The Church continues to proclaim the mystery of God as Trinity and the divine plan of salvation through Christ by the Holy Spirit. As "the mystical body of Christ," the Church radiates the glory of the living Lord to the whole universe. She lives throughout the ages with the intense eschatological hope that "the mystery of his [God's] will" is "set forth in Christ as a plan for the fullness of time to unite all things in him, things in heaven and on earth" (Eph 1:9–10).

As we proceed into the twenty-first century, with multitudes of studies and proclamations related to the critical subject of Christian unity and authentic Christian witness in today's world, it will be necessary to once again point out what is primary, essential: Our faith in Him to whom: "All authority in heaven and on earth has been given," and our continued faith that the Church is His body, "the fullness of him who fills all in all" (Eph 1:23).

B

JOURNEY TO ALL NATIONS

The commandment to "Go therefore and make disciples of all nations" (Matt. 28:19)—accentuated by the conjunction "therefore"—springs from the assurance of the Lord that, "All authority has been given to me." The first vision of universality is fixed by the risen Lord. However, this universal dimension is in no way linked to the current globalization of economic markets. The term globalization, which we speak of so often nowadays, brings with it the hidden danger that human beings will return to a law of the jungle, to a competitiveness that lacks moral sensibility and ethics. At a time when human beings are seeking to become "superhuman," they may, in fact, degenerate into subhumans. The purpose of the missionary commission of Christ's disciples "to all nations" is the universality of love which raises humanity to the God-Man (*theanthropos*), a "new creation." The purpose of the Eucharistic community, which the faithful in Christ constitute through the Holy Spirit, in all places, is the creation of a community of solidarity, a community of free human beings who love one another.

In the past many Europeans and Americans understood this last commandment of the Lord in geographical terms: Go unto the ends of Africa and Asia, where the Gospel has not yet been proclaimed. And yet it is obvious today that the most dangerous form of alienation—more dangerous still than religious ignorance—is the religious indifference which reigns in many traditionally Christian countries. Thus, in the twenty-first century the commandment of the risen Christ acquires a far broader dynamic: "Go therefore and make disciples of all nations" (Matt 28:19). Go to those nations which know little about Christ. Go also to the nations of Europe and America, some of whom have persecuted Christ in the twentieth century for decades. Go to those nations which, through arrogance or indifference, have pushed Christ to the margins and have replaced Him with their own "deities," such as money, sex or material well-being.

The work of the apostles of Christ has a dynamic that is defined by two components: the sacramental, "baptizing them," and the didactic, "teach them." The sacramental, as defined by the conscience of the early Church, acquires its perfect form in the Trinitarian formula: "In the name of the Father, and of the Son, and of the Holy Spirit." This sums up the inaccessible mystery of divinity and underlines that "learning" is completed by the power of God's grace. Whereas in the didactic, the emphasis is given not only to knowledge, but also to observance of all the commandments: "Teach them to observe all that I have commanded you" (Matt 28:20).

We are often tempted in our local churches, citing a variety of excuses, to put the most demanding of the commandments to one side; for example: the love of enemies, purity, humility, forgiveness, self-control, temperance, self-denial. However, Christian life is a single organic whole and the insistence on observing all the commandments does not constitute a kind of "moralizing" with which only conservatives can agree. It is actually the most fundamental of freedoms from every form of conventionality. In any case, the observance of the commandments is intimately linked to love of Christ and with "life in Christ." The Lord assures us that, "He who has my commandments and keeps them, he it is who loves me; and he who loves me will be loved by my Father, and I will love him and manifest myself to him" (John 14.21).

It is imperative that careful attention be given to reconnecting theological thought and daily life in agreement with the commandments of Christ. We must not lose ourselves *in abstract* theology which has no relation to Church life, or in a morality lacking in theological truth.

In this century of surprises which we have already begun, if we are to accomplish these things, it will be necessary to move into new areas; but also we must move away from the established order, systems of organization and ways of thinking. The commandment to "go" contains the implicit message that we must leave behind the place where we are and to which we are attached. Any journey to an unknown region holds hidden dangers. It is only natural then for the journey to "all the nations" to be characterized by unexpected hardships and adventures.

Our age has seen the accomplishment of a new distribution of technological knowledge, political power and wealth, but also new forms of poverty, destitution, injustice, and violence; which is not restricted, in fact, only to terrorism—linked in recent times to religious ideas—but include every form of violence. As Christians we are called to study together a whole host of problems, to look again at our duty and our potential to bring about Christian unity and to be a creative force in the world. [. . .]

It is sometimes proposed that the contribution of theology and the Church's activities should be limited exclusively to the so-called religious sphere. However, the Church's horizon includes the whole of humanity and the whole of creation. The characteristic term in the words of the Lord, with which we are occupied, is the word: "all" (πᾶς, πᾶσα, πάντα) "All authority has been given to me . . . All the nations . . . All that I have commanded you . . . All the days."

C

"ALL THE DAYS"

"And lo, I am with you." I, the Word, the *Logos*, the wisdom of the Father, the beginning and the end, the *Alpha* and the *Omega*— I am with you "all the days." Both on cloudless days when all is well, and on cloudy days when the mists of uncertainty surround you, and even on days of doubt and weakness when the storms rage; I am with you in times of hesitation when you lack courage; and will repeat to you as to Peter: "Oh man of little faith, why did you doubt?" (Matt 14:31). I am with you at the moment of unintentional betrayal to lead you back to repentance, and at times of witness or martyrdom which you suffer for love of me when the demonic powers of hatred and injustice attack you.

Awareness of the presence of the "Beloved"—He who is the fullness of love, constitutes the most essential element of the Christian experience. This awareness gives strength to us even in the most painful moments. It consoles and calms our existence when the destructive torrents overtake us and the "cords of Sheol" tightened about us (Ps 18:5). He strengthens and inspires us at times of creative endeavour. His presence fills us with long-lasting joy and calm light.

It is not a matter of some mental process, taking place in the noetic realm. It is the illumination of our whole existence by the radiating grace of the Holy Spirit. It is about a life "in Christ." The awareness and feeling of His presence can be experienced at times of prayer, of meditation on the Word of God, but primarily in times of worship. It is in the mysteries of the Divine Eucharist that we experience mystical union with the risen Lord. Progress in the spiritual life consists in continually deepening this personal relationship, but also by "continuing the liturgy after the Divine Liturgy" in every moment of our lives. The more we are aware of the presence of the risen Christ in our lives, the more each of our days will be filled with peace, with strength and with creativity.

What characterized the pioneers of the "Faith and Order" theological movement was an enthusiasm to struggle in order to overcome enmity and incomprehension accumulated from the past and which still divide the Christian churches and communities. There is no doubt that real steps forward have been made, and we give thanks for the excellent theologians who for these seventy-five years have contributed to these advances by the study of, not only what unities Christians, but also of what is holding them back from unity. Thus, they have facilitated realistic coexistence and acceptance of that which is "other," different. Events have shown that opposition to the dream of unity is strong and difficult to overcome. Those of us who today continue this work are also marked, among other things, with a wide variety of criticisms from those who are our so-called "own." What is important is that, no matter what happens, we continue our dialogue, reflecting together, meeting together, in faith, hope, and love. Of course, no one is ready to compromise matters of faith. However, in no way do we have the right to return to the closed fortresses of past centuries. We cannot ignore our responsibility towards the whole world, and the fervent prayer of Christ to His Father: "That they may all be one . . . that the world may believe that you have sent me" (John 17:21).

While preserving that which is most precious in our tradition, without simplifications or embellishments, we continue our efforts for *"rapprochement"* and common witness, "looking to Jesus the pioneer and perfecter of faith" (Heb 12:2). Let us continue to struggle "until the end of time" in whatever situation humanity finds itself, whatever its state of scientific or technological development, its discoveries or its achievements.

***

Let me conclude with a personal experience. It took place twelve years ago in August in Uganda. It was already dark when we arrived in Kampala, the capital, on our way back from a missionary camp in the centre of the country. In the complete darkness our old car violently hit an obstacle. The windshield broke into 1000 pieces and fell on me. Many of the pieces of glass fell into my eyes and I could no longer open them. In the abandoned African hospital where we went, our despair mounted. There were neither doctor, nor nurse, neither distilled water, nor even simply water. It seemed inevitable that I would lose my sight. I could see nothing. At this tragic moment a vital question, one with which I had begun my missionary service came to me: Is God enough for you? An inexplicable peace entered my soul. I felt the presence of He who promised His disciples: "I will be with you always." It was midnight when, finally, a young Ugandan optician appeared, Christopher Magibi, whom we had helped to study in Athens. By the light of a special ophthalmological lamp, he struggled to remove the glass that had gone into my eyes. He took out twenty-four pieces of glass. The next day we returned to Nairobi and then on to Europe for follow-up medical examinations and to start the healing process. My healing was accompanied by the radiating certainty: "I am with you always"—in all the days. While it seemed that this would end all my missionary endeavors, on the contrary, it gave birth to a new *diaconia*, a new service, with renewed faith, in an even more demanding mission field: Albania.

I'm sure that many people here today have had similar experiences at critical moments in their lives and perhaps my little story contributes to help them remember these times. The promises of the risen Christ are relived in the life of every generation in myriads of circumstances. It is not only on days of mist and storm that the presence of the risen Christ enlivens our soul with His mystical warmth, but even more so on the most astonishing days of our lives, the most creative ones, when the presence of the "Beloved" is felt the most. It is He who remains present on our journey like the sun that supports life on earth, day and night, summer and winter. We persevere then with hope in our efforts for unity and common Christian witness. We do not base this on our own capacities, knowledge or intelligence, but on the certainty that we are not alone in this endeavour, that we obey Christ's will. We continue on our way with total trust in Him to whom "All authority in heaven and on earth has been given," with the joyous certainty His promise has given us: "I am with you always, (all the days) to the end of time."

BIOGRAPHICAL SKETCH

ANASTASIOS YANNOULATOS, Archbishop of Tirana, Durrës and All Albania (1992 f.), has served as Professor of History of Religions at the National and Kapodistrian University of Athens (1972–1992) and today is Professor Emeritus of the same University and Honorary Member of the Academy of Athens.

He was born in Piraeus (November 4, 1929). He studied theology at the University of Athens, the history of religions, mission and ethnology at the Universities of Hamburg and Marburg in Germany, with a scholarship from the Alexander von Humboldt Foundation. He speaks Greek, English, French, and German; he reads Ancient Greek, Latin, Italian, Spanish, and Albanian; and he has worked with two African languages.

- Ordained to the Diaconate (August 7, 1960), to the Priesthood (May 24, 1964), and to the Episcopate as Bishop of Androussa (November 19, 1972), to be the General Director of the *"Apostoliki Diaconia* of the Church of Greece" (1972–1991).

- Studied and came to know the various religions—Hinduism, Buddhism, Taoism, Confucianism, Islam, African religions—in the countries where these flourish (India, Thailand, Sri Lanka, Korea, Japan, China, Kenya, Uganda, Tanzania, Nigeria, Mexico, Caribbean, and so forth.)

- He was awarded the Doctorate of the Theological School of the University of Athens (*summa cum laude*) (1970), has served as Dean of the same Faculty (1983–1986) and as corresponding member of the Academy of Athens (1993-2005). He has been awarded honorary doctorates of theology or of philosophy from eighteen Universities or University Schools or Departments. He is a member of many international scholarly societies.

Missionary Ministries

- As lay theologian (1954–1960), he worked as a preacher and catechist (Higher Catechetical School of St. Constantine of Omonoia); as a responsible leader for student circles, Bible study groups, seminars for young church leaders; as a leader in the youth and student camps of the Christian movement of "Zoe" (from which he resigned in 1963). As a presbyter, during his post-graduate studies in Germany (1965–1969), he served the Greek immigrants and students there.

- He played a pioneering role in rekindling interest for Orthodox Foreign Mission (from 1958). He served as General Secretary of the Executive Committee for Foreign Mission of "Syndesmos" (1958–1961), and as founder and president of the Inter-Orthodox Missionary Center *"Porefthendes"* (from 1961). He was a member of the International Committee for Missionary Studies of the WCC (1963–1969), the Secretary for Missionary Research and Relations with the Orthodox Churches in the WCC (Geneva 1969–1971), the Moderator of the Committee of World Mission and Evangelism (1984–1991) and of the Conference on World Mission and Evangelism in San Antonio, Texas (1989). He is a member of the German Society for Mission and of the International Society for Missionary Studies. He organized and directed the Center for Missionary Studies at the University of Athens (1971–1976) and the Inter-Orthodox Center of Athens for the Church of Greece (1971–1975). As General Director of the *Apostoliki Diaconia* he promoted various theological, educational, edifying and publishing programs of the Church; particularly, he developed the sector of Foreign Missions with support to the missionary regions of Africa, Korea, India, and with the organization of the Week of Foreign Mission.

- On the day after his ordination, he traveled to Eastern Africa in May, 1964. A serious attack of malaria caused him to return to Europe. He visited Africa repeatedly in 1967, 1968, 1974, and 1978, and during the following decade (1981–1990), as *Locum Tenens* (Acting Archbishop) of the Holy Metropolis of Eirenoupoleos (East Africa: Kenya, Uganda, Tanzania), he undertook the organization and development of the Orthodox Missions. There he founded and organized the Patriarchal School, Archbishop of Cyprus Makarios III, which he directed for ten years. He ordained sixty-two African priests (among them the first for Tanzania) and blessed forty-two Reader-Catechists from eight African tribes. At the same time he promoted the work of translation of the Divine Liturgy into four African languages; he labored for the stability of 150 Orthodox parishes and cells and for the construction of dozens of churches; he erected seven missionary stations; and directed the creation of schools and medical clinics.

- As Archbishop of Albania (1992 to the present), within tremendously difficult circumstances, he succeeded in resurrecting and reconstructing the Autocephalous Orthodox Church of Albania, which had been dissolved for twenty-three years (more than 400 parishes have been organized). He founded the Orthodox Theological Academy "Resurrection of Christ"; he educated and ordained 145 new clergy; he founded an orphanage, a residential facility for teenagers, three elementary schools and seventeen nursery schools; two residential Ecclesiastical Lyceums, one Technical Lyceum, two Institutes for professional training and Logos University, as well as fifty Youth Centers in various cities; and he led the effort for the translation and publication of liturgical and other books. He led the effort to build 150 new churches, the restoration of sixty ancient churches, and the repair of 160 damaged churches, as well as the erection of forty-five ecclesiastical centers (as a whole 450 buildings). In addition, he also promoted the work of building and repairing roads, aqueducts, bridges, clinics, hostels and schools. He developed the charitable work of the Church through the distribution of hundreds of tons of food, clothing, and medicines. He also promoted the publication of a newspaper, periodicals, and books. He organized a printing press, a candle factory, a woodworking shop, an iconography studio for the painting and the restoration of icons. Together with the work of revitalizing the Orthodox Church, he also developed innovative programs in the areas of health (such as the Annunciation Diagnostic Medical Center), in social welfare, in education, in agricultural developments, in culture and in ecology. At the same time, he struggled tirelessly to assist in relieving the many tensions in the Balkans. In 2000, after the proposal of thirty-three members of the Academy of Athens and many personalities of Albania, he has been nominated for the Nobel Peace Prize.

***

- His studies and articles have been translated into twelve foreign languages. (For his published writings see the section Publications of the Author.)

- His contributions to theology, to contemporary witness, to inter-Christian *rapprochement*, to the inter-Christian dialogue and to the peaceful coexistence of people have been recognized internationally. He has been repeatedly elected to distinguished positions of leadership in International Organizations. He has been Vice-President of the Conference of European Churches, (2003–2009). He has been honored with the medals and awards of many Orthodox Churches and various countries (24), including the Silver Medal of the Academy of Athens "as the inspiration and the pioneer of missionary theology and action" (1989), the Great Cross of the Order of Honor of the Greek Republic (1997), the Athenagoras Human Rights Award for 2001 (New York) and the Award for "distinguished activities for the unity of the Orthodox Nations" for 2005 (Moscow); the Great Cross of the Apostle Mark, of the Patriarchate of Alexandria and All Africa, (2009); and the Medal of *Gjergj Kastrioti Skënderbeu* by the President of Albania (2010) for his contribution to religious harmony and peaceful coexistence in Albania. He is President of the World Council of Churches (since 2006) and Honorary President of the World Conference of Religions for Peace (since 2006).

PUBLICATIONS OF THE AUTHOR

STUDIES IN HISTORY OF RELIGIONS

- *Τά πνεύματα μ'μπάντουα καί τά πλαίσια τῆς λατρείας των. Θρησκειολογική διερεύνησις πλευρῶν τῆς ἀφρικανικῆς θρησκείας. Διατριβή ἐπί διδακτορίᾳ,* ἐκδ. Πορευθέντες, Ἀθῆναι 1970, σελ. 294 +κγ΄+ Χ πίνακες.

- *«Κύριος τῆς Λαμπρότητος». Ὁ Θεός τῶν παρά τό ὄρος Κέννα φυλῶν.* Θρησκειολογική ἔρευνα, ἐκδ. Πορευθέντες, Ἀθῆναι 1971, σελ. 246. 2α ἔκδ. ἐπηυξημένη 1973, σελ. 272. 3η ἔκδ. 1983.

- *Ὁ ὄρθρος τῆς Ὀρθοδοξίας εἰς τήν Ἰαπωνίαν,* ἐκδ. Πορευθέντες, Ἀθῆναι 1971, σελ.70.

- *Various Christian Approaches to the Other Religions. A Historical Outline.* Porefthendes, Athens 1971, p. 134.

- *Μορφαί ἀφρικανικοῦ τελετουργικοῦ. Μύησις καί πνευματοληψία ἀνατολικῶς τοῦ «Ρουενζόρι».* Ἔρευνα θρησκειολογική, ἐκδ. Πορευθέντες, Ἀθῆναι 1972, σελ. 176. 2α ἔκδ. 1973, σελ.192. 3η ἔκδ. 1981.

- *Ρουχάν'γκα - Ὁ Δημιουργός. Συμβολή εἰς τήν ἔρευναν τῶν περί Θεοῦ καί ἀνθρώπου ἀφρικανικῶν δοξασιῶν,* ἐκδ. Πορευθέντες, Ἀθήνα 1975, σελ. 138. 2α ἔκδ. 1983.

- *Θέσεις τῶν χριστιανῶν ἔναντι τῶν ἄλλων θρησκειῶν* (Πανεπιστημιακές παραδόσεις), Ἀθήνα 1975, σελ.144.

- *Ὄψεις Ἰνδουϊσμοῦ – Βουδδισμοῦ* (Πανεπιστημιακές παραδόσεις), Ἀθήνα 1985, σελ. 176.

- *Ἰσλάμ. Θρησκειολογική ἐπισκόπησις,* ἐκδ. Πορευθέντες, Ἀθήνα 1975, σελ. 340. 14η ἔκδ. Ἀκρίτας, Ἀθήνα 2004. Νέα ἔκδοση (15η) ἐκσυγχρονισμένη, στή δημοτική, μέ πρόσθετο φωτογραφικό ὑλικό, Ἀθήνα 2006, σελ. 506.

Translations:

—Serbian: *Islam,* Kristianski Kulturni Tsentar, Belgrade 2005.

—Romanian: *Islam,* ed. Bizantina, Bucharest (to be published).

—English: *Islam*. St. Vladimir's Seminary Press (to be published).

• *Παγκοσμιότητα καί Ὀρθοδοξία*. Μελετήματα Ὀρθοδόξου προβληματισμοῦ, Ἀκρίτας, Ἀθήνα 2000, σελ. 286, 6η ἔκδ. 2006.

Translations:

—Serbian: *Globalizam i Pravoslavie*, Bogoslovskok Facultet, Belgrade 2002.

—English: *Facing the World. Orthodox Christian Essays on Global Concerns*, published jointly by St. Vladimir's Seminary Press: Crestwood, NY and WCC: Geneva, 2003.

—Romanian: *Ortodoxia si problemele lumii contemporane*, ed. Bizantina, Bucharest 2003.

—Albanian: *Globalizmi dhe Orthodhoksia*, Ngjallja, Tirana 2004.

—Bulgarian: *Pravoslaviete i Globalizatsiyata*, Fontatsiya, Demos, Sofia 2005.

• *Ἴχνη ἀπό τήν ἀναζήτηση τοῦ Ὑπερβατικοῦ. Συλλογή θρησκειολογικῶν μελετημάτων*, Ἀκρίτας, Ἀθήνα 2004, σελ. 496, 3η ἔκδ. 2006.

• *Θεός ἐφανερώθη ἐν σαρκί*, Μαΐστρος, Ἀθήνα 2006.

—Translation in Albanian: *Perëndia u shfaq në mish*, Ngjallja, Tirana 2006.

• *Μιά ἄλλη ἄποψη*, Κείμενα καί ἠχογραφήσεις (CD) ἀφηγήσεων, ὁμιλιῶν, στοχασμῶν, Bond-us music, Ἀθήνα 2007.

• *Νῦν πάντα πεπλήρωται φωτός*, Μαΐστρος, Ἀθήνα 2007.

—Translation in Albanian: *Tani te gjitha u mbushën me dritë*, Ngjallja, Tirana 2007.

• *Ἱεραποστολή στά ἴχνη τοῦ Χριστοῦ*, Ἀποστολική Διακονία, Ἀθήνα 2007, 2η ἔκδ. 2009, σ. 374.

• *Μοναχοί καί Ἱεραποστολή κατά τούς 4ο καί 9ο αἰῶνες*, Ἀκρίτας, Ἀθήνα 2008, σ. 98.

• *Ἕως ἐσχάτου τῆς γῆς*, Ἀποστολική Διακονία, Ἀθήνα 2009, σ. 388.

• *Στήν Ἀφρική*, Ἀποστολική Διακονία, Ἀθήνα 2009.

TEACHERS' MANUALS

• *Θεῖα μηνύματα* (συνεργασία μέ Ε. Βίττη), Ἀποστολική Διακονία τῆς Ἐκκλησίας τῆς Ἑλλάδος, Ἀθῆναι 1960, σελ. 346 + κ΄. Ζ΄ ἔκδ. 1978.

• *Πίστις καί ζωή*, Ἀποστολική Διακονία, Ἀθῆναι 1961, σελ. 300 + κβ΄. Ζ΄ ἔκδ. 1982.

- *Πνευματική πορεία*, Ἀποστολική Διακονία, Ἀθῆναι 1962, σελ. 348. Ζ΄ ἔκδ. 1981.

- *Mesazhe Hyjnore* (Albanian), Tirana 2009, p. 269.

OFFPRINTS

- *Εἰς τήν γραμμήν τῶν Πατέρων. Ἡ δυναμική κατανόησις τῆς παραδόσεως τῶν Τριῶν Ἱεραρχῶν.* Β΄ ἔκδ. Ἑτοιμασία, Ἀθῆναι 1971, σελ. 32. Α΄ δημοσ.: *Ἀκτῖνες* 24 (1961).

- *Τό θρησκευτικόν πρόβλημα εἰς τήν Ἀφρικήν.* Β΄ ἔκδ. Πορευθέντες, Ἀθῆναι 1971, σελ. 24. Α΄ δημοσ.: *Πορευθέντες* 3 (1961).

- *Κύριλλος καί Μεθόδιος – Δεῖκται Πορείας.* Ἀθῆναι 1966, σελ. 21. Ἀνάτυπον ἀπό *Ἐκκλησία* 53 (1966).

- *Τύποι ἱερέων ἀφρικανικῶν ἱεροβασιλείων,* Ἀθῆναι 1968, σελ. 28. Ἀνάτυπον ἀπό τόν τιμητικόν τόμον διά τόν Καθηγ. Β. Βέλλαν: *Πόνημα Εὔγνωμον,* Ἀθῆναι 1968.

- *Σκοπός καί κίνητρον τῆς Ἱεραποστολῆς (ἐξ ἐπόψεως θεολογικῆς).* Ἀθῆναι 1966, σελ. 21. Ἀνάτυπον ἀπό *Θεολογία* 37 (1966). 2α ἔκδ. 1971.

- *Monks and Mission in the Eastern Church during the Fourth Century,* Athens, 1966, p. 46. Reprinted from *Go Ye* 8 (1966). Republished: *International Review of Mission* 58 (1969), pp. 208–226.

- *Μοναχοί καί Ἱεραποστολή κατά τόν Δ΄ αἰῶνα εἰς τήν Ἀνατολήν,* Ἀθῆναι 1967, σελ. 47. Ἀνάτυπον ἀπό *Πορευθέντες* 8 (1966), 21 ἔκδ. 1969.

- *Ἀφετηριακαί σκέψεις διά τήν Ἐξωτερικήν Ἱεραποστολήν.* Ἀθῆναι 1968, σελ. 24. Ἀνάτυπον ἀπό *Πορευθέντες* 10 (1968), 2α ἔκδ. 1969. Δημοσιεύθηκε ἐπίσης στό περιοδ. *Ἐκκλησία* 55 (1968).

- *The Purpose and Motive of Mission* – From an Orthodox Point of View. Athens, 1968, p. 40. 1st publication: *International Review of Mission* 54 (1965), 2nd publication: *Go Ye* 9 (1967).

- *Initial Thoughts toward an Orthodox Foreign Mission,* Athens, 1969, p. 24. Reprinted from *Go Ye* 10 (1968).

- *Eine Kirche erwächt zur Mission,* Athens 1970, p. 8. Reprinted from *Jahrbuch Evangelischer Mission,* Hamburg 1970.

- *Ἀδιαφορία γιά τήν Ἱεραποστολή σημαίνει ἄρνησι τῆς Ὀρθοδοξίας,* Ἀποστολική Διακονία, Ἀθῆναι 1971. Γ΄ ἔκδ. 1973, σελ. 30.

- *Προοπτικαί καί θεολογικαί προϋποθέσεις τοῦ «Διορθοδόξου Κέντρου Ἀθηνῶν»,* Ἀθῆναι 1971, σελ. 16, Ἀνάτυπον ἀπό *Ἐκκλησία* 48 (1971).

- *The Inter-Orthodox Centre of Athens – Perspectives and Presuppositions,* Athens, 1973, p. 12.

- «Ἵνα ἵ κόσμος πιστεύσῃ», Ἀθήνα 1975, σελ. 10. Ἀνάτυπον ἀπό Ἐκκλησία 52 (1975).

- Λεωνίδας Ἰω. Φιλιππίδης. Ὁ ἐπιστήμων, ὁ ἄνθρωπος. Ἀθήνα 1976, σελ. 56. Ἀνάτυπον ἀπό τήν Ἐπιστημονικήν Ἐπετηρίδα τῆς Θεολογικῆς Σχολῆς τοῦ Πανεπιστημίου Ἀθηνῶν, τόμ ΚΑ΄.

- *Théologie, mission et pastorale.* Ἀθήνα 1979, p. 20. Reprinted from *Proche-Orient Chrétien* 29 (1979).

STUDIES AND ARTICLES IN REVIEWS AND COLLECTIVE WORKS

- "The Forgotten Commandment, Mt 28:19," *The World* 3 (1959), pp. 3–5.

- «Τό πρόβλημα τῆς προσωπικῆς ζωῆς», Ἀκτῖνες 23 (1960), σ. 361–366.

- «Ἡ ἱεραποστολική δρᾶσις τῶν Ἐκκλησιῶν τῆς Ἀνατολῆς εἰς Κεντρικήν καί Ἀνατολικήν Ἀσίαν», Πορευθέντες 3 (1961), τεῦχ. 10, σ. 26–31.

- "The Missionary Activities of the Churches of the East in Central and Eastern Asia," *Go Ye* 3 (1961), vol. 10, pp. 3–6.

- «Ἡ ἐπιστήμη δέν φθάνει», Σκαπάνη (Ἀπρ. 1961), σ. 22–23.

- «Ὁ οἰκουμενικός ἄνθρωπος», Σκαπάνη (Φεβρ. 1962), σ. 35–37.

- «Ἡ Ὀρθοδοξία εἰς τήν Κίναν», Πορευθέντες 4 (1962), τεῦχ. 14, σ. 26–30, τεῦχ. 15, σ. 36–39, τεῦχ. 16, σ. 52–55.

- «Ἡ Ὀρθοδοξία εἰς τήν Ἀλάσκαν», Πορευθέντες 5 (1963), τεῦχ. 17–18, σ. 14–22, τεῦχ. 19–20, σ. 44–47. Νέα ἐπεξεργασία, «Ἀλάσκα», Θρησκευτική καί Ἠθική Ἐγκυκλοπαιδεία, τόμ. 2 (1963), σ. 11–19.

- "Orthodoxy in Alaska," *Go Ye* 5 (1963), vol. 17–18, pp. 14–22, vol. 19–20, pp. 44–47. *Synopsis, Orthodoxy 1964.* A Pan-Orthodox Symposium, Athens, 1964, pp. 333–349, pp. 433–435.

- «Βυζάντιον, ἔργον Εὐαγγελισμοῦ», Θρησκευτική καί Ἠθική Ἐγκυκλοπαιδεία, τόμ. 4 (1964), σ. 19–59.

- «Διορθόδοξος Προσέγγισις», Ὀρθόδοξος Παρουσία 1 (1964), σ. 29–35.

- "Orthodoxy in the Land of the Rising Sun," *Orthodoxy 1964 – A Pan-Orthodox Symposium,* Athens, 1964, pp. 300–319, pp. 438–460.

- "Orthodoxy and Mission," *St. Vladimir's Theological Quarterly* 8 (1964), pp. 139–148.

- "Missions Orthodoxes", *Parole et Mission* 8 (1965), pp. 5–18.

- "Mission aus der Sicht eines Orthodoxen", *Neue Zeitschrift für Missionswissenschaft – Nouvelle Revue de science missionnaire* 26 (1970), pp. 241–252.

- "Réflexions d'un Orthodoxe sur la coopération inter-confessionnelle dans la Mission", *Oecuménisme en Mission, 40e semaine de Missiologie de Louvain*, Louvain, 1970, pp. 101–110.

- "Les Missions des Eglises d'Orient", *Encyclopaedia Universalis*, vol. 11 Paris, 1972, pp. 99–102.

- "Pour que le monde croie," *Contacts* 27 (1975), pp. 319–322.

- "Growing into Awareness," *Primal World Views: Christian Dialogue with Traditional Thought Forms*, ed. J. B. Taylor, Ibadan, Nigeria 1976, pp. 72–78. Republished, "Christian Awareness of Primal World-Views," *Mission trends* No 5, eds. G. Anderson, T. Stransky, New York – Toronto: Paulist Press, 1981, pp. 249–257.

- "Theology – Mission and Pastoral Care," *Procès-Verbaux du Deuxième Congrès de Théologie Orthodoxe à Athènes, 19-29 Août 1976*, Athènes, 1978, pp. 292–311. See also *The Greek Orthodox Theological Review* 22 (1977), pp. 157–180.

- "Mexico City 1963: Old wine into fresh wineskins," *International Review of Mission* 67 (1978), pp. 354–364.

- "A la redécouverte de l'ethos missionnaire de l'Eglise Orthodoxe". *Aspects de l'Orthodoxie*, Strasbourg 1978, pp. 78–96.

- «Θεολογία - Ἱεραποστολή καί Ποιμαντική». *Πρακτικά τοῦ Δευτέρου Συνεδρίου Ὀρθοδόξου Θεολογίας, Ἀθήνα 12-19 Αὐγούστου 1976*, Ἀθήνα 1980, σ. 291–309.

- "Discovering the Orthodox Missionary Ethos," *Martyria-Mission. The Witness of the Orthodox Churches*, ed. I. Bria, Geneva, 1980, pp. 20–29.

- "Relations between Man and Nature in the World Religions," *Bulletin – Secretariatus pro non Christianis*, 47 (1981), pp. 134–142. See also *Proceedings – World's Religionists Ethics Congress*, Tokyo 1983, pp. 149–159.

- "The Ascent of Human Nature," *International Review of Mission* 69 (1980), pp. 202–206. See also, *Your Kingdom Come. Mission Perspectives*, Geneva, 1981, pp. 237–242.

- «Ἕξι χριστιανικές θέσεις στό θέμα τῶν ἐκτρώσεων», Ἐκτρώσεις καί δημογραφικό πρόβλημα (Κέντρο Οἰκογενειακοῦ Προγραμματισμοῦ Μαιευτικῆς καί Γυναικολογικῆς Κλινικῆς Πανεπιστημίου Ἰωαννίνων), Ἰωάννινα 1982, σ. 59–65, 71, 75–79.

- "L'élévation de la nature humaine", *Que ton Règne Vinne! Perspectives missionnaires*, Geneva 1982, pp. 101–105.

- "Die Mystik in Byzanz", *Erbe und Auftrag* (Benediktinische Monatsschrift, Beuron, Germany) 59 (1983), pp. 437–449.

- "Worship – Service – Martyria." A paper for the Sixth Assembly of the WCC, *International Review of Mission* 72 (1983), pp. 635–639.

- «Ἐλθέτω ἡ βασιλεία σου, Ὀρθόδοξη μαρτυρία στή σύγχρονη οἰκουμένη», *Πάντα τά Ἔθνη* 2 (1983), τεῦχ. 7, σ. 4–5, τεῦχ. 8, σ. 4–6, τεῦχ. 9, σ. 4–6.

- «Ἰνδουϊστικές αἱρέσεις στόν ἑλλαδικό χῶρο», *Ἐκκλησία* 61 (1984), σ. 196–201.

- «Ἡ δοξολογική κατανόηση τῆς ζωῆς καί τῆς ἱεραποστολῆς», *Πάντα τά Ἔθνη* 5 (1986), τεῦχ. 17, σ. 20-27, τεῦχ. 18, σ. 4–7.

- "Les moines et la mission dans l'Eglise d'Orient au IVe siècle", περιοδ. *Paix* (Monastère orthodoxe Saint-Nicolas de la Dalmerie, F 34260), 1986, No. 47-48.

- «Ἀθήνα, πόλη συνεχοῦς θεολογικῆς καί πολιτιστική συμβολῆς». Εἰσήγηση στό ὁμώνυμο Συμπόσιο τῆς Θεολογικῆς Σχολῆς τοῦ Πανεπιστημίου Ἀθηνῶν. *Ἐθνικό καί Καποδιστριακό Πανεπιστήμιο Ἀθηνῶν - Ἐπίσημοι λόγοι*, τόμ. 28, Ἀθήνα 1988, σ. 363–369.

- "Remembering Some Basic Facts in Today's Mission," *International Review of Mission* 77 (1988), pp. 4–11.

- "Your will be done – Mission in Christ's way. A meditative introduction," *International Review of Mission* 77 (1988), pp. 173–178.

- "Emerging Perspectives on the Relationships of Christians to People of Other Faith – An Eastern Orthodox Contribution," *International Review of Mission* 77 (1988), pp. 332–346.

- «Βουδδισμός καί ἀγωγή», *Παιδαγωγική Ψυχολογική Ἐγκυκλοπαίδεια – Λεξικό.* Ἀθήνα, Ἑλληνικά Γράμματα, τόμ. 2 (1989), σ. 1025–1028.

- «Ὀρθόδοξη Ἱεραποστολή – Παρελθόν – Παρόν – Μέλλον». *Γενηθήτω τό θέλημά σου. Ἡ ἀποστολή τῆς Ὀρθοδοξίας σήμερα.* Ἐπιμ. Γ. Λαιμόπουλος, Νεάπολη – Θεσσαλονίκη 1989, σ. 69–95.

- "Orthodox Mission – Past, Present, Future," *Your Will be Done. Orthodoxy in Mission*, ed. G. Lemopoulos, Geneva: WCC, 1989, pp. 63–92.

- "Dein Wille geschehe – Mission in der Nachfolge Christi". *Dein Wille geschehe – Mission in der Nachfolge Jesu Christi. Welt-missionskonferenz in San Antonio, 1989*, Hrsg. J. Wietzke, Otto Lembeck, Frankfurt a.M., 1989, pp. 217–235. Also, *Jahrbuch 6. Des Evangelischen Missionswerkes in*

Südwestdeutschland. Mission bei uns gemeinsam mit den Partnern, Stuggart 1989, pp. 82–88.

- "Address by the Conference Moderator," *International Review of Mission* 78 (1989), pp. 316–328. Also, *The San Antonio Report, Your Will be Done. Mission in Christ's Way*, ed. Fr. R. Wilson, Geneva: WCC, 1990, pp. 100–114.

- «Γενηθήτω τό θέλημά Σου - Ἱεραποστολή στά ἴχνη τοῦ Χριστοῦ». Σάν Ἀντόνιο – Η.Π.Α., *Πάντα τά Ἔθνη* 9 (1990), τεῦχ. 33, σ. 3–7, τεῦχ. 34, σ. 35–38.

- «Ἰνδουϊσμός καί ἀγωγή», *Παιδαγωγική Ψυχολογική Ἐγκυκλοπαίδεια – Λεξικό*, τόμ. 4 (1990), σ. 2425–2429.

- «Παράδοση καί ὅραμα εἰρηνικῆς συνυπάρξεως τῶν θρησκευτικῶν κοινοτήτων στήν Ἀλβανία». Ὁμιλία κατά τήν ὑποδοχή ὡς ἀντεπιστέλλοντος μέλους τῆς Ἀκαδημίας Ἀθηνῶν, 14.12.1993, Ἀθήνα 1993. *Πρακτικά τῆς Ἀκαδημίας Ἀθηνῶν*, τόμ. 68 (1993), σ. 492–511. Βλ. καί *Ἐκκλησία* 71 (1994), σ. 231–234, σ. 279–282, σ. 329–330, σ. 360–363.

- «Μιά Ἐκκλησία σέ μακροχρόνιο πολύτροπο διωγμό». Ὁμιλία κατά τήν ἀναγόρευση εἰς ἐπίτιμο Διδάκτορα τοῦ Τμήματος Θεολογίας τοῦ Ἀριστοτελείου Πανεπιστημίου Θεσσαλονίκης, 13.12.1995, *Ἐπιστημονική Ἐπετηρίδα Θεολογικῆς Σχολῆς, Νέα Σειρά, Τμῆμα Θεολογίας, Ἀριστοτέλειο Πανεπιστήμιο Θεσσαλονίκης*, τόμ. 6, Θεσσαλονίκη 1996· ἀνάτυπο σελ. 28-48.

- «Ἄνθρωπος καί φύση στίς μεγάλες θρησκεῖες», *75 Χρόνια Γεωπονικό Πανεπιστήμιο Ἀθηνῶν, 1920–1995*, Ἰούνιος 1996, σελ. 93-105.

- "Byzantine and Contemporary Greek Orthodox Approaches to Islam," *Journal of Ecumenical Studies* 33:4, Fall 1996, pp. 512–527.

- "The Global Vision of Proclaiming the Gospel," *The Greek Orthodox Theological Review* 42, (1997) Nos. 3-4, pp. 401–417.

- "Address by the Conference Moderator on World Mission and Evangelism," San Antonio, 1989, *The Ecumenical Movement, An Anthology of Key-texts and Voices*, eds. M. Kinnamon and B. E. Cope, Geneva: WCC, 1997, pp. 388–392.

- "Turn to God Rejoice in Hope – *Anamnesis*." *Together on the Way*. Official Report of the 8th Assembly of the WCC, ed. Diane Kessler, Geneva: WCC, 1999, pp. 28–33.

- "Anamnesis", *Faisons route ensemble*. Rapport officiel de la Huitième Assemblée du Conseil oecuménique des Eglises, publié sous la direction de N. Lossky, Geneva: WCC, 1999, pp. 22–27.

- Ἐπίσης, "Anamnesis", *Ἐπιστημονική Ἐπετηρίδα Θεολογικῆς Σχολῆς*, Θεσσαλονίκη, Ἀριστοτέλειο Πανεπιστήμιο Θεσσαλονίκης, Τμῆμα Θεολογίας, Τιμητικό Ἀφιέρωμα στόν Ὁμότιμο Καθηγητή Ἀλέξανδρο Γουσίδη, τόμ. 9, 1999, σ. 13–18.

- «Οἱ θρησκεῖες δέν πρέπει νά ρίχνουν λάδι στή φωτιά τοῦ πολέμου», *Συνέντευξη στόν Γρ. Καλοκαιρινό, Καθημερινή*, 11.4.1999. "Religion mustn't add fuel to the fire of conflict". Interview Gr. Kalokairinos, *Herald Tribune*, 13.4.1999.

- "May Peace and Justice Once More Reign in the Balkans," *For the Peace from Above: An Orthodox Resource Book on World Peace and Nationalism*, ed. *Syndesmos* The World Fellowship of Orthodox Youth, Byalistok, Poland 1999, pp. 160–163. It was also published in French, in SOP 240 (June 1999), and in the newspaper *Zeri i Popullit*, Tirana, May, 1999.

- "Orthodoxe Mission. Vergangenheit, Gegenwart, Zukunft", *Die Orthodoxe Kirche*. Eine Stand-Ortbestimmung an der Jahrtausend-wende. Festshrift für Anastasios Kalis, herausgegeben von Eumenius von Lefka, Athanasios Basdekis und Nikolaos Thon, Frankfurt am Main, Lembek, 1999, pp. 93–121.

- «Ἡ Ὀρθοδοξία ἐνώπιον τῆς τρίτης χιλιετίας», *Ὁ Θησαυρός τῆς Ὀρθοδοξίας 2000. Ἱστορία, μνημεῖα, τέχνη*, Β΄ τόμος, Ἐκδοτική Ἀθηνῶν, Ἀθήνα 2000, σ. 12–21.

- «Ἐκκλησία τῆς Ἀλβανίας. Ἱστορική-πνευματική παράδοση», *Ὁ Θησαυρός τῆς Ὀρθοδοξίας 2000. Ἱστορία, μνημεῖα, τέχνη*, Β΄ τόμος, Ἐκδοτική Ἀθηνῶν, Ἀθήνα 2000, σ. 486–506.

- "Orthodoxy Faces the Third Millenium," *The Splendour of Orthodoxy 2000 years. History, Monuments, Arts*. Vol. II, *Patriarchates and Autocephalous Churches*, Ekdotike Athinon, Athens, 2000, pp. 12–21.

- "The Church of Albania. History and Spiritual Tradition," *The Splendour of Orthodoxy 2000 years. History, Monuments, Arts*. Vol. II *Patriarchates and Autocephalous Churches*, Ekdotike Athinon, Athens 2000, pp. 486–506.

- «Ἀνάμνηση», *Σύναξη* 73, (Ἰανουάριος-Μάρτιος 2000), σ. 5–10.

- «Ἡ Ὀρθοδοξία πρό τῆς ραγδαίας ἐξελίξεως τῶν θετικῶν ἐπιστημῶν – Διαπιστώσεις καί προτάσεις», *Διεθνές Ἐπιστημονικό Συνέδριο: Ἐπιστῆμες, τεχνολογίες αἰχμῆς καί Ὀρθοδοξία*, 4-8.10.2000, Ἱερά Σύνοδος τῆς Ἐκκλησίας τῆς Ἑλλάδος, Ἀθήνα 2002, σ. 33–43. Καί *Ἐφημέριος*, ἔτος 49, τεῦχ. 11, Νοέμβριος 2000.

- «Τρία κρίσιμα διαχρονικά θέματα», *Ἐλευθεροτυπία*, 19.11.2001.

• «Νά μήν μπλέκουμε θρησκεία μέ τρομοκρατία», Συνέντευξη στόν Στ. Τζίμα, *Καθημερινή*, 14.10.2001.

• «Ἡ συμβολή στήν ὑπερνίκηση τῆς βίας: Ἄμεσο ἐνδιαφέρον καί χρέος τῶν Ἐκκλησιῶν». *Πειραϊκή Ἐκκλησία*, τεῦχ. 122, Δεκέμβριος 2001, σ. 45–50.

• "Responsabilité apostolique et dimension universelle de l'Eglise", SOP 263 (Decembre 2001), pp. 23–27.

• "Problems and Prospects of Inter-religious Dialogue", *Ζῶ δέ οὐκέτι ἐγώ, ζῇ δέ ἐν ἐμοί Χριστός*, Ἀφιέρωμα στόν Ἀρχιεπίσκοπο Δημήτριο, Ἐπιμέλ. Σ. Δαμασκηνός, Φ. Δωρῆς, Β. Κύρκος, Ἰ. Μουτσούλας, Γ. Μπαμπινιώτης, Κ. Μπέης, Θ. Πελεγκρίνης, Α.Ν. Σάκκουλας, Ἀθήνα 2002, σ. 1–8.

• «Ἡ ἠθική στίς ἐπιχειρήσεις. Ἡ ἐταιρική εὐθύνη καί ἡ κοινωνική ἀλληλεγγύη», *Οἰκονομικός Ταχυδρόμος*, 9 Νοεμβρίου 2002, σ. 18–20.

• «Ἡ διαχρονική μετοχή τῆς χριστιανικῆς πίστεως στήν οἰκοδόμηση τῆς Εὐρώπης» *Ἐκκλησία*, 70 (2003), σ. 351–356.

• «Orthodoxe Mission», Leitfaden *Ecumenische Missionstheologie*, hrsg. Chr. Tahlin-Sander, An. Schultze, D. Werner, H. Wrogemann, Chr. Kaiser, Güttersloch, 2003, pp. 113–129.

• "The Spirit of Love," *The Adriatic Sea. A Sea at Risk, a Unity of Purpose*, eds. N. Ascherson and An. Marshall, Athens, *Religion Science and the Environment*, 2003, pp. 89–91.

• «Καί ἰδού ἐγώ μεθ᾽ ὑμῶν εἰμι πάσας τάς ἡμέρας ἕως τῆς συντελείας τοῦ αἰῶνος» (Ματθ. 28:20), *Σύναξις Εὐχαριστίας. Χαριστήρια εἰς τιμήν τοῦ γέροντος Αἰμιλιανοῦ*, Ἰνδικτος, Ἀθήνα 2003, σ. 111–118.

• "Confessing Christ Today," *The Bonds of Unity, Syndesmos: fifty years of work for Orthodox youth and unity*, ed. H. Bos, Athens: Syndesmos, 2003, p. 177-190.

• "The Apostolic Responsibility and Worldwide Dimension of Orthodoxy. Keynote Address at the Syndesmos Festival", St Morin, France, 30.8.2001. *Bonds of Unity*, ed. H. Bos, Syndesmos, Athens 2003, pp. 199–208.

• "Developing Shared Values and Common Citizenship in a Secular and Pluralistic Society: How Religious Communities Can Contribute," *Facilitating Freedom of Religion or Belief: A Desk Book*, eds. T. Lindholm, W. Colterham, Jr., and Bahia G. Tachsib Leek, Netherlands, Kluwer Law International, G. Reuben Clark Law School, Brigham Young University, Provo, Utah, 2004.

• «Ἡ ἀναζήτηση τῶν πανανθρωπίνων ἀξιῶν. Ἡ ἄποψη τῶν θρησκειῶν», *Universal Values*, International Symposium Proceedings, eds. L.G.

Christophorou and G. Contopoulos, Academy of Athens, May 26–28, 2004, pp. 279–293.

- «Οἱ θρησκεῖες καί ἡ φτώχεια τοῦ κόσμου», *Σύναξη* 94 (2005), σ. 41–52.

- «Εὐρωπαϊκή συνύπαρξη Χριστιανῶν – Μουσουλμάνων», *Ἡμερησία*, 30.12.04–2.1.05.

- «Πρός μιά σταθερή εἰρηνική συμβίωση στά Βαλκάνια», *Ἐκδηλώσεις τιμῆς πρός τόν Μακαριώτατο Ἀρχιεπίσκοπο Τιράνων, Δυρραχίου καί πάσης Ἀλβανίας κ. Ἀναστάσιο, Βόλος 31 Μαΐου 2005, Λάρισα 1 Ἰουνίου 2005, Πανεπιστήμιο Θεσσαλίας*, σ. 33–39.

- «Ἀναζητώντας τέσσερις μεγάλες ἀξίες ζωῆς», ἔνθ. ἀν., *Πανεπιστήμιο Θεσσαλίας*, σ. 69–75.

- «Ἡ οἰκογένεια, κύτταρο τῆς κοινωνίας πού ἐμπνύει ἡ χριστιανική πίστη», *Καθημερινή*, 24 Δεκ. 2006, σ. 24.

- «Ἡ θρησκευτική συνείδηση καλεῖται νά ἀντισταθεῖ», *Ἐλεύθερος Τύπος*, 30 Δεκ. 2006, σ. 21.

- «Ὁ τριπλός θρίαμβος», *Καθημερινή*, 7-8 Ἀπρ. 2007. σ. 8.

- "La manifestation de la gloire de Dieu à tous les hommes", *Chemins de la Christologie orthodoxe*, ed. A. Argyriou, Desclée, Paris 2005, σ. 23–36.

- "God, in your grace transform the world," *A festa da vida*. Documents and Reports from the WCC 9th Assembly in Porto Alegre, *The Ecumenical Review* 58 (January/April 2006) No. 1-2, pp. 6–15.

- "Transform le monde, Dieu, dans ta grâce", SOP 307 (April 2006), pp. 19–26.

- «Ἡ μεταμόρφωση τοῦ κόσμου», *Ἀνάπλασις*, ἀρ. φ. 423, Μάιος-Ἰούνιος 2006, σ. 67–70.

- "Rediscovering Our Apostolic Identity in the 21st Century," *XVII General Assembly Report of the World Fellowship of Orthodox Youth – Syndesmos 14-22 July 2003, Durrës, Albania*, Athens, 2006, pp. 37–51.

- «Χριστιανικές ἀρχές τῆς εἰρηνικῆς συνυπάρξεως». *Ἀντίδωρον τῷ Μητροπολίτῃ Μεσσηνίας Χρυσοστόμῳ Θέμελῃ, Καλαμάτα 2006. τόμ. 1ος*, σ. 179–187.

- «Οἱ Χριστιανοί στήν πολυθρησκευτική Ἑνωμένη Εὐρώπη», *Προοπτικές τῆς Εὐρώπης. Πρακτικά ἑλληνογερμανικοῦ συμποσίου. Ἐπιμ. W. Schultheiss, Εὐ. Χρυσός, Ἵδρυμα τῆς Βουλῆς τῶν Ἑλλήνων, Ἀθήνα 2007*, σ. 97–109.

- "Christen in einem multi-religiesen geeinten Europa", *Europa Perspektiven*, Beitrage eines Deutsch-griechischen Symposiums, verl. Ev. Chrysos und W. Schultheiss, Athens 2007, pp. 91–104.

- «Πολυθρησκευτική Εὐρώπη καί Ὀρθοδοξία», *Ἀναστάσιος Ἀρχιεπίσκοπος Τιράνων, Δυρραχίου καί πάσης Ἀλβανίας, Ἐπίτιμος Διδάκτωρ τοῦ Τμήματος Ἱστορίας*, 20 Μαρτ. 2007, Ἰόνιο Πανεπιστήμιο, Κέρκυρα 2007, σ. 27–42.

- «Ξενιτειά», *Καθημερινή*, 23 Δεκ. 2007, σ. 29.

- "La lumière du Christ et l'Europe", SOP 324 (Jan. 2008), pp. 97–109.

- «Πάσχα 2008 - ᾿Ελπίδα καί δύναμη», *Καθημερινή*, 26-27 Ἀπρ. 2008, σ. 21.

- «Ἡ Ὀρθόδοξος Αὐτοκέφαλος Ἐκκλησία τῆς Ἀλβανίας Σήμερα» (2008), *Ἱστορία τῆς Ὀρθοδοξίας*, ἐκδ. Road, Ἀθήνα 2008.

- Πρόλογοι σέ διάφορα βιβλία: Ἀπόστολος (1979), Θ. Λειτουργία τοῦ Ἁγίου ᾿Ιωάννου τοῦ Χρυσοστόμου (1980), Παλαιά Διαθήκη (1981), Καινή Διαθήκη (1981) στίς σειρές: «᾿Επί τάς πηγάς»(1973), «Λογική Λατρεία» (1980 ἐξ.). *WCC: Your Will be Done—Orthodoxy and Mission* (1989). *Orthodox Editions* (Nairobi-Athens): Θ. Λειτουργία στίς ἀφρικανικές γλῶσσες: Κισουαχίλι (1985), Κικούγιου (1986), Λουγκάντα (1987). Καινή Διαθήκη (1993). ᾿Επίσης πρόλογοι σέ 7 λειτουργικά καί θεολογικά βιβλία στά Ἀλβανικά (1992–2003). Καί στό βιβλίο τοῦ Κ. Clemens, *The Churches in Europe as Witnesses to Healing*, Geneva 2003.

PERIODICALS - JOURNALS

- Founder and editor of the bilingual missionary quarterly *Porefthendes–Go Ye* (1960–1970), of the quarterly review *Panta ta Ethne* (All the Nations) (1981–1992), in Greek. And in Albanian: the monthly journal *Ngjallja* (Resurrection) (since 1992) and the quarterly review *Kërkim* (Research) (since 2009).

From the 230 essays and articles some have also been translated into Russian, Swedish, Finnish, Serbian, Romanian, Bulgarian, Spanish and Albanian.

INDEX